MOODY'S
BIBLE CHARACTERS
COME ALIVE

With Many Dramatic Episodes

D. L. Moody

Edited by John W. Reed

D1417888

Baker Books

A Division of Baker Book House Co
Grand Rapids, Michigan 49516

© 1997 by John W. Reed

Published by Baker Books
a division of Baker Book House Company
P.O. Box 6287, Grand Rapids, MI 49516-6287

Printed in the United States of America

Library of Congress Cataloging-in-Publication Data

Moody, Dwight Lyman, 1837–1899.
   [Bible characters come alive]
   Moody's Bible characters come alive : with many dramatic episodes / D. L. Moody ; John W. Reed, editor.
      p.   cm.
   Includes bibliographical references.
   ISBN 0-8010-9036-9 (paper)
   1. Bible—Biography. I. Reed, John (John W.), 1927–   . II. Title.
BS571.M66   1997
220.9'2—dc21   97-11671
[B]

For information about academic books, resources for Christian leaders, and all new releases available from Baker Book House, visit our web site:
http://www.bakerbooks.com

Moody's
Bible Characters
Come Alive

Also edited by John W. Reed
1100 Illustrations from the Writings of D. L. Moody

By John W. Reed, Frank Minirth, and Paul Meier
Beating the Clock: A Guide to Maturing Successfully

By John W. Reed and Reg Grant
The Power Sermon: Countdown to Quality Messages for Maximum Impact
Telling Stories to Touch the Heart

Contents

Introduction

It has been my privilege over the past three years to become intimately acquainted with the writings of D. L. Moody. When Paul Engle, Professional Books Editor at Baker Book House, encouraged me to work on a new edition of *D. L. Moody's Illustrations,* I scanned into my computer a great number of Moody's sermons. As I did the tedious work of cutting and pasting, I began to notice phrases repeatedly appearing as Moody spoke on Bible characters. A brief excerpt from his sermon "The Thief on the Cross" serves as an example: "I can imagine the thought flashing into his soul that Jesus can't be a man like himself. I can imagine him saying to himself, 'I wouldn't ask for mercy on my enemies.' I seem to hear this thief talking to himself in this way. . . ."

Having preached on Bible characters for years, I am amazed at the insight Moody had into the life experiences of the women and men of the Bible. His sermon on the prodigal son brings tears to my eyes every time I read it, and I have read it many times in the preparation of this volume. Listen to his words and see Moody's passionate imagery in your mind: "I see the young man's father as he comes running to meet his long departed son, as if the spirit of youth has come upon him. See his long white hair floating in the wind as he leaps over the highway; the spirit of youth has come back to him. The servants look at him and wonder what has come over him. It is the only time God is represented as running, and that is to meet a poor returning prodigal soul."

Moody's insight on the prodigal's elder brother caught me in the middle of an "elder brother" thought and brought me under conviction of God's Holy Spirit. His touching description of the healed demoniac of Gadara's return to the home he had violently shattered will remain with me as long as I have sensibility.

I have tried to collect here all of Moody's comments on Bible characters whether brief or extended. To make them accessible I have added subtitles and scripture references. It is a pleasure for me to imagine that D. L. Moody's vibrant applicational style will enflame the minds and hearts of this current generation.

I wish to express my deepest gratitude to Vada Garner, formerly a reference librarian at Dallas Seminary and now on the library staff of Criswell College, for finding sources from the libraries of the English-speaking world. I am grateful to the Interlibrary Loan personnel from all those libraries for their cooperation. Thanks is due also to my granddaughter Jana Beam for her faithful labor in cleaning up the scanned text and assisting in the editing.

1 Abel

Genesis 4

Abel was the first man who went to heaven, and he went by way of blood. So we find it in all the worship of God from the earliest times. In the story of Abel and Cain we are told, "In process of time it came to pass, that Cain brought of the fruit of the ground an offering unto the LORD. And Abel, he also brought of the firstlings of his flock and of the fat thereof. And the LORD had respect unto Abel and to his offering: but unto Cain and to his offering he had not respect. And Cain was very wroth, and his countenance fell" (Gen. 4:3–5).

Cain brought a bloodless sacrifice—he brought of the fruit of the ground—and Abel brought a bleeding lamb. In the morning of grace God had marked a way for men to come to him, and that way was the way that Abel took. Cain came to God with a sacrifice of his own, in his own way. Cain, perhaps, reasoned that he did not see why the products of the earth—why the fruit—should not be as acceptable to God as a bleeding lamb. He did not like the idea of a bleeding lamb, and so he brought his fruit.

We do not know how the differences developed between those two boys. Both must have been brought up in the same way; both came from the same parents. Yet in the offerings presented there was a difference between them. One made the right choice. The other made the wrong choice. It is always right to come to God through the blood.

2 Abraham

Abraham's Call to Canaan

Abraham started to go to the land of Canaan. In the eleventh chapter of Genesis we are told that when he had gotten about halfway he stopped at Haran; and it seems that he stayed there about five years (Gen. 11:31).

Halfway at Haran

That is just the way with a great many people. They try to leave their sins and go into the Promised Land of abundant life by faith. They make a start, and get about halfway, and there they stop. Oh how many people there are who are dwelling at Haran instead of pushing on to Canaan.

I believe that there are a great many Christians who are what might be called Haran Christians. They only half obey. They are not out-and-out for God. How did God get Abraham out of Haran? His father died. It was affliction that drove Abraham out of Haran. A great many of us bring afflictions on ourselves because we are not out-and-out for the Lord. We do not obey him fully. God had plans he wanted to work out through Abraham, and he couldn't work them out as long as Abraham was there at Haran. Affliction came; Abraham left Haran and started for the Promised Land.

A great many people are afraid of the will of God. Yet I believe that one of the sweetest lessons we can learn in the school of Christ is the surrender of our wills to God, letting him plan for us and rule our lives. If I know my own mind, if an angel should come from the throne of God and tell me that I could have my will done the rest of my days on earth and that everything I wished should be carried out, or that I might refer it back to God and let God's will be done in me and through me, I think in an instant I would say, "Let the will of God be done."

I can't look into the future. I don't know what is going to happen tomorrow; in fact, I don't know what may happen before night. So I can't choose for myself as well as God can choose for me. It is my wisest choice to surrender my will to God's will.

Moving Past Haran

How did God get Abraham out of Haran? If you will turn to Genesis 11:32, you will find out. "And the days of Terah [Abraham's father], were two hundred and five years: and Terah died in Haran." That is just the way God has to do with a great many other people besides Abraham. They are settled in the wrong place. They are doing the wrong work. They are not pushing on to the land the Lord has said he will give them for an inheritance. In order to start them on the way to Canaan, God is obliged to send them some affliction. The very thing we think is the greatest calamity is just what God uses to awaken us and send us forward on the way of our duty.

In Genesis 12:1–4 we read, "Now the LORD had said unto Abram, Get thee out of thy country, and from thy kindred, and from thy father's house, unto a land that I will show thee." Now notice the promise, "And I will make of thee a great nation, and I will bless thee, and make thy name great; and thou shalt be a blessing: and I will bless them that bless thee, and curse him that curseth thee: and in thee shall all families of the earth be blessed. So Abram departed, as the LORD had spoken unto him; and Lot went with him: and Abram was seventy and five years old when he departed out of Haran."

I have been thinking this morning about this city of Chicago as it has been for the past sixteen years. We were getting rich and looking for great things, and the Civil War came on. That woke up the church a good deal, but after it was over they settled down at Haran again. Then came the Chicago fire; and I said to myself, "Surely this will bring the church out of Haran"—but it didn't. We were crying unto God for awhile, but presently the city was as much given up to money making as ever. It kept on getting worse and worse; and then along came the financial panic, and it isn't over yet.

There are a great many men and women out of work in these hard times, and people say, "What is to become of these gamblers and rum sellers who come to Christ and give up their old ways of life?" Some of them say, "If I could only see how to live, I would forsake my sins and turn to God."

Some of these fallen women say, "Just give us a place where we can get our living first, and then we will come to Christ." I wouldn't turn my hand over to get a thousand of them that way; they would all go back again. Let them first get out of Haran; out of Babylon; out of Sodom; let them seek first the kingdom of God, and his righteousness, and then all other things will be added unto them (Matt. 6:33).

Why, my friends, it doesn't take any faith at all if we can see how the thing is coming out. You must be willing to leave everything to God and follow him where you can't see. That is the meaning of faith. Trust God to deliver you, soul and body. But God will not have a person whom he can't test, or one that will not walk by faith.

There was a young man here some years ago whom I was trying to lead to Christ. He was out of work, and I had found a situation for him, though I didn't let him know it, for he was saying to me, "Just let me get a place to work, and then I'll attend to religion."

"No," said I, "that is the wrong place to begin. Seek the kingdom of God first, and get the work afterward." And I held him to it, and didn't let him know I had a place for him till after he had given his heart to Christ.

Entering Canaan

Abraham found Canaan full of kings and cities, and he didn't know how he was ever to get possession of the land; but he took it by faith (Gen. 12:4–9). He was seventy-five years old when he got there, and God kept him there twenty-five years more before he gave him the promised son. Yet he staggered not through unbelief. He believed the promise of God, who had told him he would make his seed as the stars of heaven for multitude, and as the sand which is on the seashore. Stars stand for heavenly people—sands for earthly people; so the promise included both this world and the next.

What could he do but believe, a solitary man, in that land? Not only was his faith tested by finding the land preoccupied by other strong and hostile nations, but he had not been there a great while before a great famine came upon him.

Abraham Looks to Egypt

No doubt a great conflict was going on in his breast, and he said to himself, "What does this mean? Here I am, thirteen hundred miles away from my own land, and surrounded by a warlike people. And not only that, but a famine has come. I must get out of this country to get food for my family."

Now, I don't believe that God sent Abraham down to Egypt. I think that God was only testing him, that he might in his darkness and in his trouble be drawn nearer to God. I believe that many times trouble and sorrow are permitted to come to us that we may see the face of God, and be shut up to trust in him alone. But Abraham went down into Egypt, and there he got into trouble by denying that beautiful Sarah was his wife (Gen. 12:10–20). He feared that the Pharaoh would kill him to obtain Sarah as his own wife.

That is the blackest spot on Abraham's character. But when we get into the Egypt of spiritual disobedience we will always be getting into trouble.

Abraham became rich; but we don't hear of any altar—in fact, we hear of no altar at Haran, and we hear of no altar in Egypt. When he came up with Lot out of Egypt, they had great possessions, and they increased in wealth, and their herds had multiplied, until there was a strife among their herdsmen.

Abraham and Lot Separate

Now it is in chapter thirteen that Abraham's character shines out again. He might have said that he had a right to the best of everything, because he was the older, and because Lot would probably not have been worth anything if it had not been for Abraham's help. But instead of standing up for his rights to choose the best of the land, he surrenders it, and tells his nephew to choose: "If thou wilt take the left hand, then I will go to the right; or if thou depart to the right hand, then I will go to the left" (Gen. 13:9).

Lot Chooses Sodom

Here is where Lot made his mistake. If there was a man under the sun that needed Abraham's counsel, and Abraham's prayers, and Abraham's influence, and to have been surrounded by the friends of Abraham, it was Lot. He was just one of those weak characters that needed bolstering. But his covetous eye looked upon the well-watered plains of the valley of the Jordan that reached out toward Sodom, and he chose them (Gen. 13:11–13). He was influenced by what he saw. He walked by sight, instead of by faith. I think that is where a great many Christian people make their mistake, walking by sight, instead of by faith (2 Cor. 5:7).

If he had stopped to think, Lot might have known that it would be disastrous to him and his family to go anywhere near Sodom. Abraham and Lot must both have known about the wickedness of those cities on the plains, and although they were rich and there was chance of making money, it was better for Lot to keep his family out of that wicked city. But his eyes fell upon the well-watered plains, and he pitched his tent toward Sodom and separated from Abraham.

Abraham at Hebron

Now, notice that after Abraham had let Lot have his choice, and Lot had gone off to the plains, for the first time God had Abraham alone. His father had died at Haran, and he had left his brother there. Now, after his nephew had left him, he moved down to Hebron, and there built an altar. "Hebron" means communion.

Here it is that God came to him and said,

> "Look from the place where thou art northward, and southward, and east-ward, and westward: for all the land which thou seest, to thee will I give it, and to thy seed for ever. And I will make thy seed as the dust of the earth: so that if a man can number the dust of the earth, then shall thy seed also be numbered. Arise, walk through the land in the length of it and in the breadth of it; for I will give it unto thee."
>
> Then Abram removed his tent, and came and dwelt in the plain of Mamre, which is in Hebron, and built there an altar unto the LORD.

Genesis 13:14–18

Abraham's Spiritual Vision

It is astonishing how far you can see in that country. God took Moses up on Pisgah and showed him the Promised Land. In Palestine, a few years ago, I stood in that place. I found I could look over and see the Mediter-ranean. I could look into the valley of the Jordan and see the Dead Sea. And on the plains of Sharon I could look up to Mount Lebanon, and up at Mount Hermon, away beyond Nazareth. You can see with the naked eye almost the length and breadth of that country.

So when God said to Abraham that he might look to the north, and that as far as he could see he could have the land; and when he told Abraham to look to the south, with its well-watered plains that Lot coveted, and to the east and the west, from the sea to the Euphrates, then God gave his friend Abraham a clear title, no conditions whatever, saying, "I will give it all to you."

Lot chose all he could get, but it was not much. Abraham let God choose for him, and was given all the land. Lot had no security for his choice, and soon lost all. Abraham's right was maintained undisputed by God the giver.

Do you know that the children of Israel never had faith enough to take possession of all that land as far as the Euphrates? If they had, probably Nebuchadnezzar would never have come and taken them captive. But that was God's offer; he said to Abraham, "Unto your seed I will give it forever, all the way to the valley of the Euphrates." From that time on God enlarged Abraham's tents. He enriched his promises and gave him much more than he had promised down there in the valley of the Euphrates when he first called him out. It is very interesting to see how God kept adding to the promise for the benefit of his friend Abraham.

Lot's Selfish Vision

Let us go back a moment to Lot, and see what Lot gained by making that choice. I believe that you can find five thousand Lots to one Abraham today. People are constantly walking by sight, lured by the temptations of men and of the world. Men are very anxious to get their sons into lucrative positions, although it may be disastrous to their character; it may ruin them morally and religiously, and in every other way. The glitter of this world seems to attract them.

Someone has said that Abraham was a far-sighted man, and Lot was a short-sighted man; his eye fell on the land right around him. There is the one thing that we are quite sure of—he was so short-sighted that his possessions soon left him. And you will find that these people who are constantly building for time are disappointed.

Lot in Sodom

I have no doubt that the men of Sodom said that Lot was a much shrewder man than his uncle Abraham, and that if he lived twenty-five years he would be the richer of the two, and that by coming into Sodom he could sell his cattle and sheep and goats and whatever else he had for large sums, and could get a good deal better market than Abram could back there on the plains of Mamre.

For awhile Lot did make money very fast, and became a successful man. If you had gone into Sodom a little while before destruction came, you would have found that Lot owned some of the best corner lots in town, and that Mrs. Lot moved in what they called the bon ton society or "upper ten." And you would have found that she was at the theater two or three nights in the week. If they had had progressive euchre, she would have played as well as anybody; and her daughters would have danced as well as any other Sodomites.

We find Lot sitting in the gates, he was getting on amazingly well. He might have been one of the principal men in the city: Judge Lot, or the Honorable Lot of Sodom. If there had been a Congress in those days, they would have run him for a seat. They might even have elected him mayor. He was getting on amazingly well and becoming wonderfully prosperous.

Lot Taken Captive

But by and by there comes a war. If you go into Sodom, you must take Sodom's judgment when it comes, for it is bound to come. The battle

turned against those five cities of the plain and they took Lot and his wife
and all that they had (Gen. 14:1–12). One man escaped and ran off to
Hebron and told Abraham what had taken place. Abraham took his servants—three hundred and eighteen of them—and went after these victorious kings, and soon he returned with all the booty and all the prisoners.

Abraham and Melchizedek

On Abraham's way back with the spoils one of the strangest scenes of
history occurs. Whom should he meet but Melchizedek, who brought out
bread and wine; and the priestly king blessed the father of the faithful
(Gen. 14:18–20). After the old king of peace had blest him, Abraham met
the king of Sodom, who said, "Give me the persons, and take the goods
to thyself." But Abraham replied, "I will not take from a thread even to a
shoelatchet, and that I will not take any thing that is thine, lest thou
shouldest say, I have made Abram rich" (Gen. 14:21, 23).

There is another surrender. There was a temptation to get rich at the
hands of the king of Sodom. But the king of Salem had blessed him, and
this world did not tempt him. It tempted Lot, and no doubt Lot thought
Abraham made a great mistake when he refused to take this wealth; but
Abraham would not touch a thing. He spurned it and turned from it. He
had the world under his feet; he was living for another world. He would
not be enriched from such a source.

Every one of us is met by the prince of this world and the Prince of Peace.
The one tempts us with wealth, pleasure, and ambition, but our Prince and
Priest is ready to succor and strengthen us in the hour of temptation.

Lot's Salvation

A friend of mine told me some years ago that his wife was very fond of
painting, but that for a long time he could not see any beauty in her paint-
ings; they all looked like daubs to him. One day his eyes troubled him and
he went to see an oculist. The man looked in amazement at my friend and
said, "You have what we call a short eye and a long eye, and that makes
everything a blur."

The oculist gave him some glasses that just fitted him, and then he
could see clearly. Then, he said, he understood why his wife was so carried away with art, and he built an art gallery and filled it with beautiful
things, because everything looked so beautiful after he had his eyes
straightened out.

Now there are lots of people that have a long eye and a short eye, and they make miserable work of their Christian life. They keep one eye on the eternal city and the other eye on the well-watered plains of Sodom. That was the way it was with Lot: he had a short eye and a long eye. It would be pretty hard work to believe that Lot was saved if it were not for the New Testament. But there we read that Lot's righteous soul was "vexed" (2 Peter 2:7)—so he had a righteous soul, but he had a stormy time. He didn't have peace and joy and victory like Abraham.

Abraham's Self-Surrender

After Abraham had given up the wealth of Sodom that was offered him, then God came and enlarged his borders again—enlarged the promise. God said, "I am thy shield, and thy exceeding great reward" (Gen. 15:1).

God promised to protect him. Abraham might have thought that these kings he had defeated might get other kings and other armies to come, and he might have thought of himself as a solitary man, with only three hundred and eighteen men, so that he might have feared lest he be swept from the face of the earth. But the Lord came and said, "Abraham, fear not."

That is the first time those oft repeated words "fear not" occur in the Bible. "Fear not, for I will be your shield and your reward."

I would rather have that promise than all the armies of earth and all the navies of the world to protect me—to have the God of heaven for my Protector. God was teaching Abraham that he was to be his Friend and his Shield, if he would surrender himself wholly to God's keeping and trust in his goodness. That is what we need—to surrender ourselves up to God fully and wholly.

In Colorado the superintendent of some works told me of a miner who was promoted, came to the superintendent, and said, "There is a man that has seven children, and I have only three, and he is having a hard struggle. Don't promote me, but promote him."

I know of nothing that speaks louder for Christ and Christianity than to see a man or woman giving up what they call their right for others, and "in honor preferring one another" (Rom. 12:10). Abraham was constantly surrendering his own selfish interests and trusting God.

Abraham's Fame

What was the result? Of all the men that ever lived Abraham is the most renowned. He never did anything the world would call great. The largest army he ever mustered was three hundred and eighteen men. How Alexander would have sneered at such an army as that. How Caesar would have looked down on such an army! How Napoleon would have curled his lip as he thought of Abraham with an army of three hundred and eighteen!

We are not told that Abraham was a great astronomer. We are not told that he was a great scientist. We are not told that he was a great statesman, or anything the world calls great. But there was one thing he could do—he could live an unselfish life, and in honor could waive his rights, and in that way he became the friend of God. In that way he has become immortal.

There is no name in history as well-known as the name of Abraham. Even Christ is not more widely known, for the Mohammedans, the Persians, and the Egyptians make a great deal of Abraham. His name has been favorably known for centuries and centuries in Damascus.

God promised him that great men, warriors, kings, and emperors should spring from his loins. Was there ever a nation that has turned out such men? Think of Moses, Joseph, Joshua, Caleb, Samuel, David, Solomon, and Elisha. Think of Elijah, Daniel, Isaiah, and all the other wonderful Bible characters that have sprung from this man!

Then think of Peter, James, John, Paul, and John the Baptist, a mighty army. Remember Jesus, their redeemer and ours! No man can number the multitude of wonderful men that have sprung from this one man called out of the land of the Chaldeans, unknown and probably an idolater when God called him. Yet how literally God has fulfilled his promise that through him he would bless all the nations of the earth. All because Abraham surrendered himself fully and wholly to let God bless him.

Abraham Is Tested

Abraham became an old man, and the Lord put his faith to one last trial (Gen. 22:1–14). The Lord said, "Take now thy son, thine only son Isaac, whom thou lovest, and get thee into the land of Moriah; and offer him there for a burnt offering upon one of the mountains which I will tell thee of" (Gen. 22:2).

That must have been a terrible time for Abraham. Probably he lay awake most of the night, thinking of this strange command of God; but I am sure he didn't tell his wife anything about it for fear she would try to make him disobey. God had given him a son in his old age, and now it seemed as if he were going to take him away again. But then Abraham knew that God was wiser than he, and if he took away his son he was just as able to raise him up from the grave.

So he does not delay, but rises up early in the morning, saddles his donkey, takes with him two young men, Isaac his son, and some wood for a burnt offering, and starts on his journey.

His wife wants to know where he is going. He tells her he is going away to a mountain to offer up sacrifice to God, but he doesn't tell her that he is going to offer up Isaac as that sacrifice.

As Abraham goes on, he looks at his boy and says to himself, "It is a strange commandment that God has given. I love this boy dearly. I do not understand it, but I do know it is all right, for the Judge of all the earth makes no mistakes." An order from the Judge of heaven is enough for Abraham.

The first night comes, their little camp is made, and Isaac is asleep. But the old man does not sleep. He looks into the face of his sleeping boy, and sadly says to himself, "I will have no boy soon. I shall never see him on this earth again. But I must obey God."

I can see Abraham marching on the next day, and you might have seen him drying his tears as he glanced upon that only son and thought upon what he had been called upon to do. The second night comes; tomorrow is the day for the sacrifice. What a night that must have been to Abraham! Hear him say within his soul, "Tomorrow I must take the life of that boy—my only son, dearer to me than anything on earth—dearer to me than my life."

I can see them going along together—the old man and his son. They are very silent, and Isaac imagines there is something weighing heavy on his father's mind. They travel all that day, and lie down to sleep at night, but I fancy Abraham doesn't sleep much. He thinks of his son who was given him in his old age, and of the strange journey he is making to offer up this sacrifice. We don't hear that he prayed to the Lord to spare Isaac. Probably he left that all with the Lord.

On the third day Abraham lifts up his eyes and sees the place afar off, and when they come near, he says to the servants, "Stay here with the donkey; and I and the lad will go yonder and worship, and come again to you." So Abraham takes the wood and puts it on the back of his son.

He takes the fire and the knife, and along with his boy prepares to ascend Mount Moriah, from which could be seen the spot where, a few hundred years later, the Son of man was offered up.

The young man doesn't know what to make of it. Here are all the preparations for a burnt-offering except for the offering itself. "Where is the lamb?" asks Isaac.

Abraham answers, "My son, God will provide himself a lamb."

So they come together to the top of the mountain, and the old man, with trembling hands, builds an altar, and takes the wood, and puts it in order on the top of it.

When everything is ready, he says to his son, "Isaac, sit down here a little while. I want to talk with you." So they sit down together, and the old man, his voice trembling with emotion, tells his son how the Lord called him out of Ur of the Chaldees a great many years ago, when he was a heathen and an idolater, and promised to make him the father of a great nation. He explains that God has been in communion with him for fifty years and what God has done for him.

He reminds Isaac also about his own life—how the Lord has sent his angels to him, and how they promised that he should have a son in his old age. "And now, Isaac, it seems strange—I cannot understand it—but three nights ago the Lord stood by me, and told me to bring you to the top of this mountain and offer you up as a burnt offering. I don't know why God wants me to do this. But there is nothing else to do but to obey. You must suffer, and I must sacrifice you. It is a great deal harder for me, Isaac, than it will be for you. So let us both go down on our knees and pray to him."

After they have sent up a petition to God, Abraham lays Isaac on the altar and kisses him for the last time. The young man is entirely overwhelmed, but he doesn't make any resistance—doesn't run away. He just gives himself up to God according to the word of his father, and takes his place on the top of the wood that has been placed upon the altar, just as he has seen the sacrifice laid to be offered to the Lord.

And now the old man takes the knife, raises it high in the air, and, looking up with one heartbroken cry to God, he is about to plunge it into the heart of his son when he hears a voice. "Abraham! Abraham! Lay not thine hand upon the lad," says the Lord, "for now I know that thou fearest God, seeing thou hast not withheld thy son, thine only son, from me" (Gen. 22:12).

Now, my friends, notice: whenever God has been calling me to higher service, there has always been a conflict with my will. I have fought against it, but God's will has been done instead of mine. When I came to Jesus Christ, I had a terrible battle to surrender my will and to take God's will. When I gave up business, I had another battle for three months; I fought against it. It was a terrible battle. But oh, how many times I have thanked God that I gave up my will and took God's will.

Then there was another time when God was calling me into higher service, to go out and preach the gospel all over the land instead of staying in Chicago. I fought against it for months; but the best thing I ever did was when I surrendered my will, and let the will of God be done in me.

Abraham's Blessing

Because Abraham obeyed God and held back not even his only child, God enlarged his promises once again, "And the angel of the Lord called unto Abraham out of heaven the second time, and said, By myself have I sworn, saith the LORD, for because thou hast done this thing, and hast not withheld thy son, thine only son: that in blessing I will bless thee, and in multiplying I will multiply thy seed as the stars of the heaven, and as the sand which is upon the sea shore; and thy seed shall possess the gate of his enemies; and in thy seed shall all the nations of the earth be blessed; because thou hast obeyed my voice" (Gen. 22:15–18).

O my friends, God was a great deal more tender with Abraham than he was with himself. When his own Son was dying upon a cross on that very same mountain he didn't send a victim to take his place, but left him there to die, the just for the unjust, that he might redeem us and bring us back to God. There was no voice heard on Calvary to save the Son of Man. Yet God showed mercy to the son of Abraham.

You fathers and mothers, just picture how you would suffer if you had to sacrifice your only son. And think what it must have caused God to give up his only Son. We are told that Abraham was glad. This manifestation of Abraham's faith so pleased God that he showed him the grace of heaven and lifted the curtain of time to let him look down into the future to see the Son of God offered, bearing the sins of the world.

What about your faith, my friend? Abraham is called the father of the faithful (Rom. 4:16). Are you a child of Abraham? Do you believe in God so much that you are willing to obey no matter what it may cost you?

3 Adam

Salvation a Present Experience

I wish to choose as my text Luke 19:10, "For the Son of Man is come to seek and to save that which was lost." I want to ask the audience to ask themselves this question, "Am I saved, or am I lost?" For certainly you must be either saved or lost. Now I am not asking you if you belong to some church, or if you read your Bible, or if you pray, but are you saved? It strikes me that it is a question that ought to interest everyone, and everyone here ought to be able to answer the question.

Present salvation is the only salvation worth having. The idea that you may be saved at some future time is not worth having, because we may be disciplined; we may be taken away with a stroke; we may be ushered into eternity before tomorrow morning, and what we need is present salvation, and to be able to say, "I am saved."

There are some people who say that it is presumptuous for a man to say that he is saved. It is great presumption for a man not to say that, if he has reason to believe that he is saved. Job says, "I know that my Redeemer liveth" (Job 19:25). John says, "We know that we have passed from death unto life, because we love the brethren" (1 John 3:14). Peter says, "Christ, . . . according to his abundant mercy hath begotten us again to . . . an inheritance incorruptible, and undefiled, and that fadeth not away, reserved in heaven for you, who are kept by the power of God through faith unto salvation ready to be revealed in the last time" (1 Peter 1:3–5). There is a salutary touch about that. Paul says, "For we know that if our earthly house of this tabernacle were dissolved, we have a building of God, an house not made with hands, eternal in the heavens" (2 Cor. 5:1).

It is the privilege of every child of God to know present salvation. Every man and woman that is not saved should be aware of their condition. God will teach you tonight, if you are willing to confess that you are lost, if you will let him be your teacher. Let us not deceive ourselves. Just ask yourselves the question, "Am I saved or am I lost?" It is the lost ones that I want to speak to tonight, because it was the lost ones that Christ came to save. He came to call sinners, not the righteous. He came to seek and to save that which was lost (Luke 19:10). He came for no other purpose—only to save sinners.

Need for Salvation

I met a person not long ago who said, "I am lost. I have committed so many sins that God doesn't love me. God doesn't care for me anymore."

Now I may be speaking to some tonight that think they are so far from God that God hasn't any love for them, that he doesn't care for them. Now let me say that instead of proving that you aren't lost, you need to confess that you're a sinner. Christ came to save the ungodly. Then confess yourself to be ungodly. If I want to buy a piece of land, I can't get too good a title for the land. The best title you can have to salvation is to find out that you are lost.

Adam and God's Love

It was Adam's fall that brought out God's love. God never told Adam when he put him in Eden that he loved him. It was after he was lost that God said that. It was that very thing that brought out the love of God (John 3:16).

There was an Englishman in Chicago the winter before the great fire who was much impressed with the sudden growth of the city. He went back to Manchester, England, where he told the people about the city only forty years old, with all its fine buildings, its colleges, its churches. It was, he thought, a most wonderful city. But no one seemed to take any interest in Chicago.

"But," he says, "one day the news came flashing over the wires that Chicago was on fire. The moment the people heard about the Chicago fire, they became suddenly interested in Chicago. Then every man that I had tried to tell about Chicago became suddenly interested, and they couldn't hear too much." The news came flashing over the wires that half of the city was burnt. "Well," he said, "there were men here that couldn't help but weep."

At last the news came that one hundred thousand people were burned out of their houses and were in danger of starvation, unless immediate help was sent. Then these men came forward and gave their thousands. It was the calamity of Chicago that brought out the love and pity of those men.

4 Ahab

1 Kings 16:29–34; 21:1–29

There is a familiar saying, "Every man has his price." Ahab had his, and he sold himself for a garden (1 Kings 21). Judas sold himself for thirty pieces of silver, and Esau for a mess of pottage. Ahab sold himself just to please a fallen woman. We might go on citing the men who have sold themselves. It is easy for us to condemn these men, but let us see if there are not men and women doing the same thing today.

How many are selling themselves tonight for nothing of real value! It is easy enough to condemn Judas, Herod, and Ahab, but in doing this do we not condemn ourselves?

We thought that slavery was hard. We thought it hard that those poor black people should be put upon the block in the market and sold to the highest bidder; but what do you think of those men who sell themselves today to evil? Ahab sold himself to evil, and what did he get?

The prophet Elijah was the best friend that Ahab had, but Ahab did not think so; he thought that Elijah was his enemy. Ahab was a religious man—that is, he thought he was. He had eight hundred and fifty prophets (1 Kings 18:19). "And what king has more? What king does more for religion than I?" So he would have said.

There is a difference between religion and having Christ. There are a great many people that have religion, but have no Christ in it—that have not a spark of Christianity.

Ahab and Jezebel

Ahab was very religious, but he began wrong. His marriage was his first wrong step. He did not care about the law of God. He wanted to strengthen his kingdom by marrying a foreign princess (1 Kings 16:31).

I can imagine the people said, "We have outgrown the laws of Moses. We don't want your God; we have something better. Here are the nations all around us worshipping Baal, and we will worship Baal."

Ahab's wife, Jezebel, wanted the patriarchs and the prophets put to death, and they were put to death (1 Kings 18:4). Obadiah had a few, but wherever they were found they were put to death. I suppose they said of Elijah, "That man belongs to the old Puritanical school. He was bigoted and narrow. The idea of only worshipping one God!"

Ahab and Elijah

Ahab was willing to turn away from the God of Elijah, but he did not like to have Elijah reprove him, and thus the prophet was his enemy. Many a man who has a good, praying mother thinks that mother is his enemy.

Ahab thought the God of Elijah was not going to carry out his warning. I will leave it to you if the man who warns you of danger is not the best friend you have. If I saw a man about to walk over a precipice and he was blind and I did not warn him, would not the blood of that man be required at my hands? Would not I be guilty morally?

Jezebel hated Elijah, and she disliked him for his warnings (1 Kings 19:2). Suppose I am going home at night—at midnight—and I see a building on fire and I pass along and say not a word about it, and the occupants are all asleep and I go right home and go to bed, and in the morning I find that fifteen people in that house were burned up—how you would condemn me! And if in preaching the gospel I do not warn you about your danger—about your sins and God's punishment—what will you say to me when I meet you at the eternal throne?

I don't want you to think that I am trying to please the people by preaching that the just and unjust will fare alike. You may be successful for a time. Ahab had two grand and glorious victories upon the battle field, and he was a very popular man for awhile (1 Kings 20:1–21).

Ahab and Naboth

Ahab built a palace of ivory, and when his beautiful palace was finished, he found there was a poor man who had a garden near it. Ahab wanted the garden. He came to Naboth, the poor man, and wanted him to sell his garden. But Naboth said, "I can't do that. It is against the law of my people."

Then Ahab said to him, "I will give you a better place than this, and I will give you a better vineyard than this."

But Naboth was firm, and would not agree to sell his garden.

Many men would have liked to sell to the king. Such a man would have said, "We know it is against the law, but Naboth is foolish not to sell to the king."

Naboth said, "God forbid that I should sell."

Ahab returned to his palace, where he pouted like a child. Jezebel noticed him, and began to speak with him. She asked, "What is the matter?"

Ahab answered like a peevish child, "I want Naboth's garden."

And she asked him, "Why don't you take it?"

Ahab explained the complication. Again she asked, "Are you not king of Israel?"

"Yes"

"Well! Then why don't you just take it? But don't worry, I will get it for you, and it won't cost you anything. I will arrange it."

Then Jezebel sent that infamous letter to the truculent elders. Those elders were just as bad as Jezebel. They knew that Naboth served the God of heaven. The instructions of the letter were followed. The two witnesses said they saw Naboth despise God and the king, and so he was taken out and stoned to death. I can see him kneeling there and the crowds taking up the stones and hurling them at him (1 Kings 21:1–16).

Ahab Condemned

When Ahab went down to take possession of that vineyard there was a message that had come from the throne of heaven (1 Kings 21:17–29). God had been watching him. He notices all of us, and there is not a hellish act that has been, or is going to be, committed but God knows about it.

Elijah stood before Ahab as he went down to that garden, and Ahab got out of his chariot and met him. He knew that Elijah knew everything, and he did not like to be reproved. Ill-gotten gains do not bring peace. If you get anything at the cost of the truth or honor, it will be peace lost for time, and perhaps for eternity.

As he walked through that garden, Ahab looked up and said, "Why, isn't that Elijah?" He knew it was, and he knew what it meant.

Elijah walked up to him and asked, "Have you killed and taken possession?"

Ahab thought, "I wonder how he found that out. He knows all about me."

And then Elijah said, "In the place where the dogs licked the blood of Naboth they shall lick thy blood."

Then Ahab asked the prophet, "Mine enemy, have you found me out?"

Elijah answered, "Yes. Because you have sold yourself to evil, you must be found out."

A few years before, Ahab had laughed at Elijah, but he now remembered that everything Elijah's God had predicted had been done. He could not get these words out of his mind, "In the place where the dogs licked the blood of Naboth they shall lick thy blood."

Sometimes just one act that we can do in a minute will cost us years of trouble and pain. Little did Ahab think that it was going to cost him his kingdom and cause his whole family to be swept from the face of the earth when he gave the promise to Jezebel to write that letter.

Ahab lived three years after Elijah met him in that garden, and how many times do you suppose those awful words of Elijah came back to him? Jezebel tried to help him, but she couldn't. He wanted to improve the garden, and no doubt he did improve it; but whenever he walked there the words came to him which Elijah had spoken.

Then the time came for the judgment against Ahab to be carried out, and it was done just as Elijah predicted (1 Kings 22:1–40). God will keep his word.

5 Andrew

What makes the Dead Sea dead? It is all the time receiving, never giving out anything. Why is it that many Christians are cold? Because they are all the time receiving, never giving out anything. You go every Sunday and hear good sermons, and think that is enough. You are all the time receiving these grand truths but never give them out. When you hear it, go and scatter the sacred truth abroad.

Instead of having one minister to preach to a thousand people, this thousand ought to take a sermon and spread it till it reaches those that never go to church or chapel. Instead of having a few, we ought to have thousands using the precious talents that God has given them.

Andrew got the reputation of bringing people to Christ. He went about it in the right way. I imagine that when Christ wanted these mighty deeds done, he went out and hunted up Andrew.

Andrew inquired of the people, "Have you seen anything of Peter?"

And when he found Peter he brought him to Christ (John 1:40–42). Little did Andrew know of the importance of the day when he brought Peter to Christ.

Little did he think that on that day he did the greatest act of his life. What joy must have filled his heart when he saw three thousand brought under the influence of the Spirit by that holy titan. Oh, you can't tell what results will follow if you just improve the talent God has given you by bringing one Simon Peter to Christ.

We read that when the Greeks came and wanted to see Jesus, Andrew met them and brought them all to Christ (John 12:21–22). Andrew had a reputation of bringing sinners to God. That is a good reputation. I would rather have that reputation than any other. Oh, the joy there is in bringing people to Christ! This is what we can do if we will. If God has only given us half a talent, let us make good use of that.

6 Barabbas

Matthew 27:16–26; Mark 15:7–15; Luke 23:18

I have often thought what a night Barabbas must have spent just before the day when Christ was crucified. As the sun goes down, he says to himself, "Tomorrow—only tomorrow—and I must die on the cross! They will hang me up before a crowd of people. They will drive nails through my hands and feet. They will break my legs with bars of iron; and in that awful torture I shall die, and go up to the judgment with all my crimes upon me."

Perhaps they let his mother come to see him once more before dark. He may have had a wife and children, and they may have come to see him for the last time.

He couldn't sleep at all that night. He could hear somebody hammering in the prison yard and knew they must be making the cross. He would start up every now and then, thinking he heard the footsteps of the officers coming for him. At last the light of the morning looks in through the bars of his prison.

"Today—this very day—they will open that door and lead me away to be crucified!"

Soon he hears them coming. No mistake this time. They are unbarring the iron door. He hears them turning the key in the rusty lock. The door swings open. There are the soldiers. Good-by to life and hope! Death, horrible death, now—and after death, what will there be then?

The officer of the guard speaks to him, "Barabbas, you are free!"

He hears the strange words, but they make no impression on him. He is so nearly dead with fear and horror that the good news doesn't reach him. He hears it, but thinks it is a foolish fancy, or that he is asleep and dreaming.

He stands gazing a moment at the soldiers, and then he comes to himself and cries, "Don't laugh at me. Don't make sport of me! Take me away and crucify me; but don't tear my soul to pieces!"

Again the officer speaks, "Barabbas, you are free! Here, the door is open; go out, go home!"

Now he begins to take in the truth; but it is so wonderful a thing to get out of the clutches of the Roman law that he is afraid to believe the good news. And so he begins to doubt and asks how it can be. They tell him that Pilate promised the Jews the release of one prisoner that day and that the Jews have chosen him instead of one Jesus of Nazareth, who was condemned to be crucified.

Now the poor man begins to weep. This breaks his heart. He knows this Jesus. He was in the crowd picking pockets when Jesus fed the five thousand hungry people.

"What! That just man to die, and I, a thief, a highwayman, a murderer, go free!" In the midst of his joy his heart breaks at the thought of being saved at such a cost.

Sinner, that is the gospel. Christ died for you, "the just for the unjust" (1 Peter 3:18). Come out of your prisons. Throw away the chains of sin. You were justly condemned, but Jesus died to save you. Let your heart break in penitence. Weep tears of love and joy.

I never knew a person who accepted these glad tidings who was ever disappointed. Now, God does not offer us good tidings, and when we come to look, find it bad news. Very often we hear in the world something which we think is good news, but after a little while we find out that it is very bad. It is not so with the gospel. It is the best news a person can ever hear.

1

Bartimaeus

Mark 10:46–52; Luke 18:35–43

Bartimaeus Learns of Christ

In the eighteenth chapter of Luke we have a story. As Christ was coming into Jericho, there was a poor blind man sitting by the wayside begging people to give him a farthing, and crying out, "Have mercy on a poor blind man!"

I don't know how long he had been blind, but he was poor enough, and miserable enough. He had come to be a beggar, and I suppose he had a pretty hard time of it.

One morning one of his neighbors comes along and says, "Good morning, Bartimaeus. I have good news for you."

"What is it?" says the beggar.

"There is a man of Israel who can give you sight."

"Oh, no!" says the blind beggar. "That can't be. There is no chance for me. I haven't got eyeballs even. I was born blind, and there is no chance of my ever receiving my sight. I shall never see. In fact, I never saw the mother who gave me birth. I never saw the wife of my bosom. I never saw my own children. I never saw in this world. I have never seen the light of heaven, but I expect to see in the world to come."

"Let me tell you," says the neighbor, "I have just come down from Jerusalem, where I saw that carpenter, Jesus of Nazareth, who had opened the eyes of a man that was born blind, and I never saw a man with better sight. He doesn't even have to use glasses."

Then hope rises for the first time in this poor man's heart, and he says, "Tell me how the man got his sight."

"Oh," says the other, "Jesus first spat on the ground and made clay and put it on his eyes, and then he told him to wash his eyes in the pool of Siloam, and he would receive his sight. Sure enough, he came back with two good eyes. More than that, Bartimaeus, he doesn't charge anything; you have no fee to pay! You just tell him what you want, and you get it without money and without price. It doesn't require a politician's signature or any kind of influence. You just call upon Jesus yourself. And if he ever comes this way, don't let him go back without your going to see him."

And Bartimaeus said, "I will try it. There is no harm in trying it."

And so it is, my Christian friends, with Christ today. Ask him what you want, and you have God's own word that you shall receive it.

Did you ever see a man that went to God and asked him properly for a good thing that he didn't get it? Ask the Lord always, and he is ready to give. And I can imagine the joy with which Bartimaeus received these glad tidings.

Bartimaeus Meets Christ

In what a forlorn and desperate condition had Bartimaeus been! You can see him being led out by one of his children along the streets from day to day, or by a faithful dog, to ask alms from his fellows as they passed by him.

He would say, "Give a poor blind beggar a farthing. I have been blind these many years. I am destitute. Help me."

He is in his accustomed place. He hears the footsteps of a crowd approaching, and he asks, "What does it mean? Who is that coming?" And they say, "It is Jesus of Nazareth who is passing by."

I can imagine the thrill that pervades the poor man. Here is Jesus of whom he has heard. Here is his great chance, his golden opportunity. This is his time, and he cries out with a loud voice, "Jesus, thou Son of David, have mercy on me."

Some of those who went before—perhaps Peter was one of them—rebuked him, thinking the Master was going up to Jerusalem to be crowned king, and didn't want to be distracted. They never knew the Son of God when he was here. He would hush every harp in heaven to hear a sinner pray; no music would delight him so much.

But the blind man still lifted up his voice, and cried louder, "Thou Son of David, have mercy on me!"

The prayer reached the ears of the Son of God, as prayer always will. When Jesus heard the blind beggar, he commanded him to be brought. So they ran to him, and said, "Be of good comfort; rise, he calleth thee."

When Jesus saw Bartimaeus, he said, "What wilt thou that I shall do unto thee?"

"Lord, that I may receive my sight."

"Receive thy sight."

Immediately his eyes were opened. He could see! What a moment in his life. Now the beggar follows with the crowd, glorifying God. I can imagine he sang as sweetly as my friend Mr. Sankey; no one sang sweeter than he when he shouted, "Hosanna to the Son of David!"

I can imagine when he gets into the city he says to himself, "I will go down and see Mrs. Bartimaeus and the children."

After all these years of blindness what a joy it must have been to be able to see his wife and children for the first time!

8

Blind Man

John 9

In John 8 Christ had been telling the people that he was the light of the world, and that if any man would follow him he should not walk in darkness, but should have the light of life. After making a statement of that kind, Christ often gave an evidence of the truth of what he said by performing some miracle. If he had said he was the light of the world, he would show them in what way he was the light of the world. John 9 gives the account of the healing of a man born blind.

The Blind Man's Confession of Christ

There were two extraordinary men living in the city of Jerusalem when Christ was on earth. One of them has come down through history nameless—we do not know who he was; the name of the other is Nicodemus. One was not only a beggar, but blind from his birth; the other was one of the rich men of Jerusalem. Yet in the Gospel of John, there is more space given to this blind beggar than to any other character. The reason so much has been recorded of this man is because he took his stand for Jesus Christ.

This blind man was not afraid to confess Christ when it was very dangerous to do so. Christ had given him his sight, and he had given Christ his heart. This man was born blind. But what I want to call your attention to is his confession (John 9:8–9). They were having a controversy over him, and some people said, "This is the very man who was born blind, whose eyes the Prophet of Nazareth has opened."

Others said, "This is not the same man at all, only somebody who looks like him."

But he said, "I am he."

Now if he had been like a good many people he would have said to himself, "There is a great storm brewing. The chief men of the city are divided about this man. Some of them think he is a prophet, and some say he is an impostor, so I guess I had better keep still. I have got my sight in any case. I think I'll go home and keep out of this excitement."

But he didn't talk that way at all. He said right out, "I am he."

In the first place, with his heart he had believed unto righteousness, and now with his mouth he makes confession unto salvation (Rom. 10:10). He was not going to hold his peace. His eyes had been opened, and he now began to tell his experience.

Experience! That is what makes our Friday noon testimony meetings so interesting. Ah, my friends, the world can't get over the facts of experience. All the unbelievers in the world can't get over such a fact as the conversion of Saul.

One of the greatest hindrances to the progress of the gospel today is that the narration of the experience of the church is not encouraged. There are a great many men and women who come into the church, and we never hear anything of their experiences, or of the Lord's dealings with them. If we could, it would be a great help to others. It would stimulate faith and encourage the more feeble of the flock.

The apostle Paul's experience has been recorded three times. I have no doubt that he told it everywhere he went; how God had met him; how God had opened his eyes and his heart; and how God had blessed him. Depend upon it, experience has its place; the great mistake that is made now is in the other extreme. In some places and at some periods there has been too much of it—it has been all experience; and now we have let the pendulum swing too far the other way. I think it is not only right, but exceedingly useful, that we should give our experience. This man bore testimony to what the Lord had done for him.

Someone once wrote an article against the work of a certain revivalist, and one of his friends said to him, "What are you going to do about it? That is a strong argument against you."

"I shall do nothing at all," was his reply. "Let the work speak for itself."

The Blind Man's Unique Experience

Notice now that this man at once obeyed the Master, who had anointed his eyes with clay—enough to spoil his sight if it had been good—and then told him to go and wash. The man might have made a great many objections. But no, he goes right away and does just as he is bid, and when he has done it he gets his sight (John 9:6–7).

Somebody might say, "Why couldn't Christ have saved him all that trouble, and have spoken the word, and opened his eyes on the spot?" Well, he could have done so. He did in another place. But, my friends, God never repeats himself. He never made two men just alike, or converted two men just alike. That is where a great many people blunder, looking for God to give them somebody else's experience.

Suppose Bartimaeus had gone from Jericho and had met the other blind beggar at the gate of the city of Jerusalem, and asked him how it was he got his sight; suppose they began to compare notes—one telling his experience, and the other telling his. Imagine the first saying, "I don't believe you've got your sight, because you didn't get it in the same way that I got mine."

Would the different ways the Lord Jesus had in healing them make their cases the less true? Yet there are some people who talk just that way now. Because God does not deal with some exactly as he does with others, people think that God is not dealing with them at all. No two persons were ever converted exactly alike, so far as my experience goes. Each one must have an experience of his own. Let the Lord give sight in his own way.

There are thousands of people who keep away from Christ because they are looking for the experience of some dear friend or relative. They should not judge their conversion by the experiences of others. They have heard someone tell how he was converted twenty years ago, and they expect to be converted in the same way.

People should never count upon having an experience precisely similar to that of someone else of whom they have heard or read. They must go right to the Lord himself, and do what he tells them to do. If he says, "Go to the pool of Siloam and wash," then they must go. If he says, "Come just as you are," and promises to give sight, then they must come, and let him do his own work in his own way, just as this blind man did.

It was a peculiar way by which to give a man sight; but it was the Lord's way; and the man's sight was given him. We might think it was strange to make the blind man fill his eyes with clay. True, he was now doubly blind; for if he had been able to see before, the clay would have deprived him of his sight. But the Lord wanted to show the people that they were not only spiritually blind by nature, but that they had also allowed themselves to be blinded by the clay of this world, which had been spread over their eyes. But God's ways are not our ways. If he is going to work, we must let him act as he pleases.

Shall we dictate to the Almighty? Shall the clay say to the potter, "Why hast thou made me thus?" (Jer. 18:6; Rom. 9:21). Who art thou, O man, that repliest against God? Let God work in his own way; and when the Holy Ghost comes, let him mark out a way for himself. We must be willing to submit, and to do what the Lord tells us, without any questioning whatever.

The Blind Man's Testimony

In John 9:12 the blind man's neighbors ask, "Where is he?"

"I don't know," answers the man. You see he doesn't try to tell more than he knows. So, young converts, don't you try to tell more than you know. Don't get puffed up with conceit and spiritual pride over what the Lord has done for you.

Again, they ask him how he got his sight, and he tells his experience over again (John 9:15). Don't be afraid to tell your experience so long as God blesses anybody by it.

He told a straightforward story, just what the Lord had done for him. That is all. A witness ought to tell what he knows, not what he does not know. He didn't try to make a long speech. It is not the most flippant and fluent witness who has the most influence with a jury.

Here are the three degrees of this man's progress. First, he confesses himself a saved man. Second, he tells what Christ has done for him; and, third, having gotten done talking about himself, he begins to talk about the Master, and to preach him as a prophet. So with you. Get done talking about yourselves as quickly as you can, and begin to talk about Christ.

The Blind Man's Spiritual Insight

"And it was the sabbath day when Jesus made the clay, and opened his eyes. Then again the Pharisees also asked him how he had received his sight. He said unto them, He put clay upon mine eyes, and I washed, and do see. Therefore said some of the Pharisees, This man is not of God, because he keepeth not the sabbath day. Others said, How can a man that is a sinner do such miracles? And there was a division among them" (John 9:14–16).

Then they say unto the blind man again, "What sayest thou of him, that he hath opened thine eyes?" (John 9:17).

What an opportunity he had for evading their questions! He might have said, "Why, I have never seen him. When he met me I was blind; I could not see him. When I came back, I could not find him. I have not formed any opinion yet." He might have put them off in that way; but he said, "He is a prophet."

There were no infidels or philosophers there who could persuade him out of that. And there were not men enough in Jerusalem to make him believe that his eyes were not opened. Did he not know that for over twenty years he had been feeling his way around Jerusalem; that he had been led by children and friends; and that during all those years he had not seen the sun in its glory, or any of the beauties of nature? Did he not know that he had been feeling his way through life up to that very day?

And do we not know that we have been born of God, and that we have had the eyes of our souls opened? Do we not know that old things have passed away and all things have become new, and that the eternal light has dawned upon our souls? Do we not know the chains that once bound us have snapped asunder, the darkness is gone, and the light has come? Have we not liberty where we once had bondage? Do we not know it? If so, then let's not hold our peace.

Let's testify for the Son of God, and say, as the blind man did in Jerusalem, "One thing I know, that whereas I was blind, now I see" (John 9:25). I have a new power. I have a new light. I have a new love. I have a new nature. I have something that reaches out toward God. By the eye of faith I can see yonder heaven. I can see Christ standing at the right hand of God. By and by, when my journey is over, I am going to hear that voice saying, "Come hither," when I shall sit down in the kingdom of God.

If you can get young Christians to talk, not about themselves, but about Christ, their testimony will have power. Many converts talk altogether about their own experience—"I . . . I . . . I . . . I." But this blind man got away to the Master, and said, "He is a prophet." He believed, and he told them what he believed.

The Blind Man's Parents

> But the Jews did not believe concerning him, that he had been blind, and received his sight, until they called the parents of him that had received his sight. And they asked them, saying, Is this your son, who ye say was born blind? How then doth he now see? His parents answered them, and said, We know that this is our son, and that he was born blind; but by what means he now seeth, we know not: or who hath opened his eyes, we know not: he is of age; ask him: he shall speak for himself. These words spake his parents, because they feared the Jews; for the Jews had agreed already that if any man did confess that he was Christ, he should be put out of the synagogue. Therefore said his parents, He is of age; ask him.
>
> John 9:18–23

I have always had great contempt for those parents. They had a noble son, and their lack of moral courage then and there to confess what the Lord Jesus Christ had done for their son makes them unworthy of him. They say, "We do not know how he got it," which looks as if they did not believe their own son. "He is of age; ask him."

It is sorrowfully true today that we have hundreds and thousands of people who are professed disciples of Jesus Christ, but when the time comes that they ought to take their stand, and give a clear testimony for him, they testify against him. You can always tell those who are really converted to God. The new man always takes his stand for God; and the old man takes his stand against him. These parents had an opportunity to confess the Lord Jesus Christ, and to do great things for him; but they neglected their golden opportunity.

If they had but stood up with their noble son, and said, "This is our son. We have tried all the physicians, and used all the means in our power, and were unable to do anything for him; but now, out of gratitude, we confess that he received his sight from the prophet of Galilee, Jesus of Nazareth," they might have led many to believe on him. But, instead of that, they said, "We know that this is our son, and that he was born blind: but by what means he now seeth, we know not."

Do you know why they did not want to tell how he got his sight? Simply because it would cost them too much. They represent those Christians who don't want to serve Christ if it is going to cost them anything. They don't want to have to give up society, position, or worldly pleasures. They don't want to come out. This is what keeps hundreds and thousands from becoming Christians.

It was a terrible thing to be put out of the synagogue. In these days, if a man is put out of the Presbyterian Church they may take him into the Methodist Church, and when the Methodists turn him out he can go and join the Episcopalians; but they didn't have any Presbyterians, Methodists, Episcopalians, Congregationalists, and Baptists in those days. There was only one Jewish "church", and it was a terrible thing to be put out of that. So his parents compromised the matter by turning it all over to their son. "He is of age; ask him."

The Blind Man's Witness

"Then said they to him again, What did he do to thee? How opened he thine eyes? But he answered them, I have told you already, and ye did not hear: wherefore would ye hear it again? Will ye also be his disciples?" (John 9:26–27).

This was a most extraordinary man. Here was a young convert in Jerusalem not a day old, trying to make converts of these Pharisees—men who had been fighting Christ for nearly three years! He asked them if they would also become his disciples. He was ready to tell his experience to all who were willing to hear it. If he had covered it up at the first, and had not come out at once, he would not have had the privilege of testifying in that way, neither would he have been a winner of souls. This man was going to be a fine soul-winner.

I venture to say he became one of the best workers in Jerusalem. I have no doubt he stood well to the front on the day of Pentecost, when Peter preached, and when the spiritually wounded were around him; he went to work and told how the Lord had blessed him, and how he would bless them. He was a worker, not an idler, and he kept his lips open.

It is a very sad thing that so many of God's children are silent about the Gospel; yet it is true. Parents would think it a great calamity to have their children born dumb; they would mourn over it, and weep; and well they might. But did you ever think of the many dumb children God has? The churches are full of them. They never speak for Christ. They can talk about politics, art, and science. They can speak well enough and fast enough about the fashions of the day; but they have no voice for the Son of God.

Dear friend, if he is your Savior, confess him. Every follower of Jesus should bear testimony for him. How many opportunities each one has in society and in business to speak a word for Jesus Christ! How many opportunities occur daily wherein every Christian might be "instant in season and out of season" in pleading for Jesus! In so doing we receive blessing for ourselves, and also become a means of blessing to others.

This man wanted to make converts of those Pharisees, who only a little while before had their hands full of stones, ready to put the Son of God to death and even now had murder in their hearts. They reviled him, saying, "Thou art his disciple; but we are Moses' disciples. We know that God spake unto Moses: as for this fellow, we know not from whence he is" (John 9:28–29).

Why, it is unreasonable! If Jesus Christ were a man only, how could he give that man sight? Let philosophers, skeptics, and infidels answer the question. Neither had he to wear glasses. He received good sight, not short sight or weak sight, but as good sight as any man in Jerusalem, and perhaps a little better. They could all look at him and see for themselves. His testimony was beyond dispute.

The Blind Man Cast Out of the Synagogue

After his splendid confession of the divinity and power of Christ, the Pharisees answered, "Thou wast altogether born in sins, and dost thou teach us?" And they cast him out (John 9:34). They could not meet his argument, and so they cast him out. So it is now, if we give a clear testimony for Christ, the world will cast us out. It is a good thing to give our testimony so clearly for Christ that the world dislikes it. It is a good thing when such testimony for Christ causes the world to cast us out.

Let's see what happened when they cast him out. "Jesus heard," that is the next thing. No sooner did they cast him out than Jesus heard of it. No man was ever cast out by the world for the sake of Jesus Christ but he heard of it; indeed, he will be the first one to hear of it. "Jesus heard that they had cast him out; and when he found him, he said unto him, Dost thou believe on the Son of God? He answered and said, Who is he, Lord, that I might believe on him? And Jesus said unto him, Thou hast both seen him, and it is he that talketh with thee. And he said, Lord, I believe! And he worshipped him" (John 9:35–38).

That was a good place for any man to be—at the feet of Jesus. We shall meet this man by and by in the kingdom of God. His testimony has been ringing down through the ages these last nineteen hundred years. It has been talked about wherever the Word of God has been known. It was a wonderful day's work that man did for the Son of God. Doubtless there will be many in eternity who will thank God for his confession of Christ.

By thus showing his gratitude in coming out and confessing Christ, he has left a record that has stirred the church of God ever since. He is one of the characters that always stirs one up, imparting new life and fire, new boldness and courage when one reads about him.

This is what we need today as much as ever—to stand up for the Son of God. Let the Pharisees rage against us; let the world go on mocking, and sneering, and scoffing. We will stand up courageously for the Son of God. If they cast us out, they will cast us right into his own bosom. He will take us to his own loving arms. It is a blessed thing to live so godly in Christ Jesus that the world will not want you—that they will cast you out.

He was full of faith. I like to have some young converts round me. They are so full of faith, they believe in all sorts of things which other people think are almost impossible. Their faith leaps over all mountains.

Oh, may God help us to confess the Lord Jesus Christ, who has opened our blind eyes and made us to see his face and to read the mystery of his word, and who has opened up to the eyes of our faith the glories of eternal life!

9 Caleb

Numbers 13

Caleb and Joshua are great favorites of mine. They have a ring about them. They were not all the time looking for hindrances and obstacles in their way. They got their eyes set on God.

The Spies Sent Out

You remember how those men were sent forward to spy out the land of Canaan. They had been sent out for forty days to go over that land. They went from the wilderness of Zin to Rehob, and thence unto Hebron. And when they reached the brook of Eshcol they secured "a branch with one cluster of grapes, and bare it between two upon a staff; and they brought of the pomegranates and of the figs" (Num. 13:23).

They were gone forty days, and the twelve men brought back what Congress would call a majority and a minority report (Num. 13:26–33). The men reported that they had gone unto the land to which they were sent, and that surely, it flowed with milk and honey. And so God's word was true. They found milk and honey. And they brought along those wonderful grapes.

But ten of them were full of unbelief. They further reported that they saw giants there—the sons of Anak, which come of the giants. The Hittites, Jebusites, Amalekites, and Amorites dwelt there. They were all there, and also those great giants, in whose sight they were as grasshoppers. It was a great war city, and they asked themselves if they looked as though they were able to war with such giants. They said, "We are not able."

They undoubtedly brought back maps and charts, and said, "There is the region. It would be monstrous for us to attempt to take it. There are massive iron gates and a great wall, and we are not able to take it. We are defenseless people without any weapons. We will not be able to overcome those people."

The Failure of the People

I can imagine one man said, "Why, I looked up at those giants, and I seemed as a little grasshopper, and I felt as small as a grasshopper. We cannot hope to cope with those giants. It is a good land, but we will not be able to go up and possess it."

Then they began to murmur. It does not take a very great while to get unbelievers to murmuring. But Caleb tried to encourage them. He says to them, "Let us go up at once, and possess it; for we are well able to overcome it" (Num. 13:30).

Joshua joined in with Caleb, and they proved two with the faith. To be sure, they were in the minority; but if the Lord is with us we are able to prove a powerful majority over the enemy. They determined to take it, and encouraged the people to take possession of Canaan. The people took up stones, and would have stoned them to death. But "the glory of the Lord appeared in the tabernacle of the congregation before all the children of Israel" (Num. 14:10).

And about three million people wandered in the wilderness for forty years, until all the men laid themselves down in the desert grave and were kept out of the Promised Land—all on account of their unbelief (Num. 14:11–38). And I believe today that four-fifths of the church is wandering around in the wilderness, far away from the cross of Calvary and the Promised Land. We are able to have victory with God with us.

Ten men were looking at all those obstacles that this new land presented to them, while these two men—Caleb and Joshua—looked up yonder. And they saw God's face and remembered the waste in Egypt, the crossing of the Red Sea, the destruction which was brought upon the Philistines, and the water from the flint rock; and they believed that God was able—as he most certainly was—to give them that land he had promised.

Centurion at Capernaum

Matthew 8:5–13; Luke 7:1–10

I want to call your attention to the centurion at Capernaum. He is one of those nameless characters that shines very brightly upon the stage of history. For some reason the Holy Ghost hasn't given us his name. There are quite a number of nameless characters that have shone very brightly in this world in the Scripture.

A good many of us would like to know who that woman at the well was; she is one of those characters we would like to meet when we get to heaven. We would like to know the name of that woman whom he met way up on the coast of Tyre; that blind beggar that had courage to speak out his convictions and stand boldly for Christ; that little maid that told Naaman, or the wife of Naaman, about the prophet Elisha and set two kingdoms into commotion.

And here is another character, this centurion, who shines very brightly, a light in the dark places. I tell you, the brightest and purest pearls come from the darkest caverns of the ocean. And here is a pure gem, a diamond shining in that little town. Such a man is this centurion, not only in Capernaum but in the Roman army.

Now, if there was a class of people that the Jews despised, it was the Gentiles, and the one Gentile nation they detested the most was the Romans. Yet this man had so lived in Capernaum that he had won their favor and esteem; he had commanded the respect, not only of his own soldiers, but of those Jews that would naturally have hated him.

He went to Christ and wanted Christ to heal his servant because he loved the nation. They thought because he had built them a synagogue that he was one of the grandest of men, and it looks as if God left all his work to go and heal this centurion because he was worthy. Perhaps they said, "The very synagogue I occupied last Sabbath was built by this centurion. Now, come, because he is worthy."

Integrity and Responsibility

Now, if you will just follow the whole scene you will find that Christ wanted to teach another lesson. I remember being in Scotland a few years ago, and on my way to the church a friend said, "I hope you will not bear very hard on whisky. The steeple on the church where you are going to preach was built by a distiller, and it would hurt his feelings if you should say anything about whisky."

That was not the way to keep me from saying anything about it, you know. I had to give my opinion about steeples that were built with whisky money. There are a good many who have an idea that distilling is all right if they will only give their money to the church. That will cover a multitude of evil and make it all right.

These Jews thought this centurion was all right because he had built them a synagogue. Now, a man may build a synagogue and still be a black-hearted villain. But not so with this centurion; I don't think it was because he had built a synagogue that his name shines so bright in history. I will tell you what I think. He wanted Christ to come and heal his servant, and I suppose that servant was a slave.

A different set of people we have now! Most of us, if we have a servant and he gets sick, we just get him home as quickly as possible, or to some hospital. Perhaps we get a free bed if we can. We get him off our hands because we don't want to be bothered with a sick servant. We have paid them their wages, and we think that is the end of our responsibility. Not so with the centurion. It wasn't his son, nor his daughter, nor his wife, nor mother. It wasn't some member of his family, not anyone that was bound to him by the tie of nature, but a servant, and he was very dear to him.

Lifting the Fallen

Ah, my dear friends, there is a lesson. I don't believe this nation has ever seen a better day to show our friendship toward those who are down. The gulf has been becoming deeper and darker for twenty years, and now we have a good opportunity to bridge the gulf. Let the millionaires look very carefully now after the men who have been piling up their wealth for them. Follow the footsteps of this centurion, and see what will come out of it. He won the esteem of every servant he had. Do you tell me that if that servant was very dear to him, the centurion was not dear to the servant?

I was in California some time ago, and quite a number tried to tell me that the Chinese person hadn't a soul, and that a Chinese person wasn't capable of loving. I said, "It is utterly false. Every person has a soul! There is not a son or daughter of Adam on earth that isn't capable of loving." Before I left California they told me of a man who got a Chinese person just as he came to this country, and took him into his family and treated him kindly, and by and by the Chinese person became his body servant. At last misfortune overtook his master. He died and left his widow without any means of support.

The poor Chinese person had worked hard and long, day and night, to get back to China. Every company that brings a Chinese person to this country has to sign a contract that they will bring him back dead or alive. Sometimes they scrape the flesh off the bones and send them back to be buried in their own country. This man had been working and toiling hard to get money to go back, but when he found that his master had left his mistress without money, he took the thousand dollars and insisted upon her taking it. And yet they say a Chinese person cannot love!

My dear friends, you cannot expect anything better from the world, but when you find those who profess to be Christians, what is going to become of the cause of Jesus in the world? I wonder if you are looking after those who serve you. Are any of them unfortunate just now? Are they in need? Your soup houses may be all right, but I wouldn't like to have a servant of mine go to a soup house. Would you? I wouldn't like to have a man who is toiling for me degrade himself by going to a house to beg for soup.

My friend Professor Drummond went off into the heart of Africa, and when he returned he told me he believed the Africans, as a nation, were not capable of loving; he believed they understood a knock over the head better than kindness. I believe that is utterly false, and I believe if we walk on that line, we are never going to reach this world.

I have great admiration for that centurion who thought a good deal of his servant, and I tell you that kind of thing will kill out anarchy, kill out nihilism, sweep them from the face of the earth. No, it is one thing to come out here and say "amen," and another thing to carry it out in your home. You just want to watch that you don't get into the place of some Pharisee. You treat men as they should be treated, and see if you don't win their esteem and respect.

The Gospel and Bread

As I said before, now is our day. The workingmen are seeing hard times, and if there was ever a time for the church of God to show kindness, it is at present, for they are far from the church today. They have been taught to believe that the church doesn't care for them. The great mass of the workingmen of this country have been alienated from the church of God.

Now is the time to look well after your servants, your clerks, and those whom you employ, and see if you can't help them now when they are down. A little act of kindness will go a great deal farther than the sermons just now. We need good employers just now to go and pick up those men who have been slain, as it were, by this financial panic that is sweeping over the land.

Did the world ever see such a day? Take up your morning paper. Men are starving for the want of work. Starving? May God deliver us. It would be a good thing for us to get on our backs so that we can just look up to heaven. A man said to me the other night when I was talking on this subject, "Your old gospel won't put bread into the mouths of the people."

My friends, don't you believe it. That is just what it will do. You want to remove the cause of this trouble and I believe the gospel of the Son of God is the only thing that will do it. If men will stop drinking whisky, it will buy bread for their children, won't it? If they will stop their gambling, don't you think it will put some money into bread and the family will have something to eat? If they will stop this cursed adultery, don't you think the wives and children will be looked after?

This man may have been a leper. How many of your servants have a disease a thousand times worse than the leprosy? A kind act may turn them into the kingdom of God, and it would be a grand day if we could see a revival of righteousness going over this land as it did in 1857. Then there was a sweep of salvation that went across the continent and brought five hundred thousand into the church of God.

And so out of this financial crash that is upon us, and out of this great panic, let every businessman and every woman that has employees look well now and see if you cannot win them. Don't send them off to any charitable institution, but just take care of them yourselves. Don't go and blow a trumpet and say that you have done so much for your people; but do it kindly and quietly.

I don't suppose this centurion ever thought of what he had done for his servants. He wanted his servant healed, and so he sent these men, these Jews, for Christ to heal them. There is a double staff. That man was full of faith and full of humility. If you want to be successful in working for God, that is just the thing. It isn't often that the two meet in one man. Did you know it? But this man had exalted thoughts of God and very low thoughts of himself.

Now, I want to call your attention to a fact. If you find a man that has very high thoughts of himself he will have very low thoughts of God. I met a man in the inquiry room the other night who thought he was the very best man in town, and he thought God was the most insignificant being that there ever was. This centurion was little in his own sight; he was insignificant. He was a centurion in the Roman army, but this man never thought of himself. He thought that the Jews were better than he, so he sent them to get Christ to come and heal the servant.

Thank God for humility and faith! His faith was as bold as a lion, his humility as meek as a dove, as meek as a lamb, and he had power. And he shines on and on, and has been shining for nineteen hundred years. He is going to shine on forevermore. Why? Because he wasn't low and mean and selfish.

Now, I have heard all kinds of men and women praised, but there is one character that you never hear praised. Can you think of the man or woman who is never praised? Do you know who it is? It is a supremely selfish man or woman. Take A. T. Stewart, for instance. Did you ever hear of anyone praising him? One of his clerks got sick and couldn't come to the store for two, or three, or ten weeks; his wages were cut right off; he wasn't responsible.

Who is my brother? "Am I my brother's keeper?" He didn't feel any responsibility for any man that helped him make his great fortune. Why, I was in New York when he was dying, and there was a sort of a jubilee all over the city! They were glad the old miser was going. They were telling stories right there in his marble palace. His wife might have mourned, but if she did she was about the only mourner he had. What a glorious opportunity he had to become immortal and live forever!

I pity these men that hold on with a tight grip to everything they have. I heard of a man once that was always telling his servant that he was going to do a great thing for him, "I am going to remember you in my will." His servant named Sam got his expectations up very high. When the man came to die it was found that all he had willed Sam was to be buried in the family lot. That was the big thing, you know. Sam said he wished he had given him ten dollars and let the lot go.

If you want to show kindness to people, show it to them while you are living. I heard a man say that he didn't want people to throw bouquets to him after he was dead and say, "There, smell them." Now this is the time for action. This man acted. He was going to try to save the life of that servant. That is what we want to do. I have gotten so tired and sick of this splitting hairs over theology and men talking about higher criticism. Man, let us go out and get these fallen men up. Lift them up toward God and heaven. We want a practical kind of Christianity.

I was in England some time ago and they had a great corps of bishops and the highest ecclesiastical men having a discussion which lasted for days to see whether they should wear a black or white gown. Man, throw aside your gown and give them the gospel. That is what they need. This man's servant was dying and he went to work to save him.

The Gospel for Employees

You have employees that are dying without God and without hope. Don't think because they work for you eight or ten hours a day that your responsibility ends there. I believe God will hold you responsible. You businessmen can reach those people who are employed by you a good deal better than the ministers.

We are living in altogether different days from what our fathers did. Those old days have gone now. We treat our employees just about as we do a sewing machine. If they do their work, well all right; but if they don't we kick them out. They may go to ruin, become defaulters, and bring a stain upon the whole family, and you think it is nothing to you. It is a good deal to you. That centurion looked after his servants. Look after your people. See that they don't work seven days in the week. Don't make a man do what you don't want to do yourself.

I would like to have you take this centurion into your heart and see if you are like him. Perhaps you have built a synagogue. You may stand well abroad, but how do you stand at home? Do you stand well there? This man stood well with his servants; he stood well abroad, just because he was a real true man, although he was a Gentile and a Roman.

11 Christ

Christ's Birthplace

You will find the following text in Luke 2:7: "And laid him in a manger, because there was no room for them in the inn." For four thousand years the world had been looking for Christ. Prophets had been prophesying, and the mothers of Israel had been praying and hoping that they might be the mother of that child, and now that he has arrived, we find that he is laid in a borrowed cradle.

He might have come with all the grandeur and glory of the upper world. He might have been ushered into the world with ten thousand angels; yea, legions upon legions of angels might have come to herald his advent. He might have been born in a palace or a castle. He might have been born upon a throne if he had chosen to, but he became poor for your sake and mine. He passed by mansions and thrones and dominions, and went down into a manger.

Not only was his cradle borrowed, but almost everything that he had was borrowed. It was a borrowed beast he rode into Jerusalem on; it was a borrowed grave they laid him in.

When the Prince of Wales came to this country, what a welcome he received. There wasn't anything too good for him. When the Prince of Russia came to this country, I saw as he was escorted up Broadway, and cheer upon cheer went up all the way. New York felt honored that they had such a guest. The Prince of Wales during the past few months has been in India, and what a reception he has been receiving there!

When the Prince of heaven came down, what kind of a reception did he meet with? There were no hallelujahs from the people. He found that there was no room in Bethlehem for him. When he arrived, not only the king, but all Jerusalem, was troubled. When the wise men told Herod he was King of the Jews, and that they had seen his star in the East (Matt. 2:2–9), not only the king upon the throne, but all Jerusalem, was in trouble. Every man that had been looking for him seemed to be troubled, and the whole city was excited.

The king commanded all infants under a certain age to be slain. No sooner did news come that he is born than the sword was unsheathed, and followed him, you may say, all the way through his life to Calvary.

And has the world grown better? Is not this world about like that little town in Bethlehem—there is no room for him? What nation wants him today? Does this nation want him? Suppose you should put it to a popular vote. I don't believe there is a town in the whole republic that would vote for him. Does England want him? England and the United States are perhaps the most Christianized countries on the globe, but I don't believe there is a town in England or in this country that would vote for him.

In fact, I might say, does the church of God want him? We have got the forms, and we are satisfied with them, but we deny the power. I am ashamed to say that there are many of our churches that really wouldn't want him. There would be a different state of things in the church of God today if Christ should come. A great many church members do not want him; they say, "My life is not right to welcome him."

There are very few families in the whole city of New York that would make room for him. They would make room for the greatest drunkard in New York rather than make room for him. Don't think the world is better if it doesn't make room for him. If he should go to Washington, do you think they would make room for him there? If a man should get up in Congress and say, "Thus saith the Lord," they would hoot him out. If Christ should go there, they would say, "He is too good, he is too honest, we don't want him, we don't want honest men."

When it comes to receiving the real, personal God, the world doesn't want him, the nations of the earth don't want him. Does France want him? Does Italy want him? Oh, my friends, there is no room for Christ, yet it would be a glorious day if there was room for him. I believe the millennium would soon be here.

When Christ went to Decapolis, he found a man there filled with devils, and he cast out those devils, and the men of Decapolis came out and begged him to go out of their coasts.

Take what you call the fashionable society of New York. Is he wanted there? They will talk about this church and that church; they will talk about Dr. So-and-So, and the Rev. So-and-So, and talk about the Bible in schools, but when it comes to a real, personal Christ, and you ask them, "Do you want Christ in your heart?" they say, "Oh, sir, that is out of taste."

I pity the man or woman that talks in that way. Is he wanted in commerce? Is he wanted on Wall Street? If he were, men would have to keep their books differently. Commercial men don't want him.

You may ask the question, "Well, where is he wanted; who wants him? Where is there room for the Son of God? Who will make room for him?"

I wonder if there is anyone here that ever had that feeling for five minutes. I think I have had that feeling for a day. There are some who wonder how people can commit suicide. It's no wonder to me. When men feel that there is no room for them, that no one wants them, when they feel that they are a burden to their friends, and a burden to themselves, why it drives them mad.

I remember one day when I felt as if no one wanted me. I felt as if there was no room for me. For about twenty-four hours I had that awful feeling that no one wanted me. It seems to me as if that must have been the feeling of Christ. His neighbors didn't want him. Those Nazarenes didn't want him; they would have taken him to the brow of the hill and dashed him to the bottom. They would have torn him limb from limb, if they could. He went down into Capernaum, and they didn't want him there. Jerusalem didn't want him. There was no room.

To me, there is one of the most touching verses in the Bible in the closing part of the seventh chapter of John. I believe it is the only place where Christ was left alone, "Every man went unto his own house. Jesus went unto the mount of Olives" (John 7:53–8:1). I have often thought I would like to have met him upon that mount. He was on the mount alone. There was no home for him in Jerusalem. He was looked upon as a blasphemer; some thought he was possessed of devils, and so he was left alone.

You could have seen him under an olive tree, alone, and I imagine that night you could have heard him crying to God for his own. And perhaps it was on that memorable occasion, or a similar occasion, when he said, "The foxes have holes, and the birds of the air have nests; but the Son of man hath not where to lay his head" (Matt. 8:20; Luke 9:58).

Jesus Found Room at Bethany

Thanks be to God there was a place. I have often thought of that little home at Bethany. It says that Martha received him into her house. It was the best thing that Martha ever did; and do you think she ever regretted it? Little did she know that her loved brother was soon going to die (John 11:1–44) when she made room for Jesus. Ah, it was the best thing that Martha and Mary ever did when they received the village carpenter, the despised Nazarene, into their home. He used to have to walk down to the city two miles to Bethany, but there he always found room.

Make Room for Jesus

Think of the blessing that came on that home because they made room for Jesus. Mothers, if you will make room for him, you will entertain the best guest, the best stranger you ever entertained. You need Jesus, and will be wise to make room for him. If you make room for him here in your hearts, he will make room for you up there. He says in John 14:1–2, "Let not your heart be troubled: ye believe in God, believe also in me. In my Father's house are many mansions: if it were not so I would have told you. I go to prepare a place for you."

Instead of his disciples comforting Christ, there is Christ giving to comfort them. And now, while he is up yonder preparing a place for us, shall we not make room for him down here? If the nations won't make room for him, if the church won't make room for him, if the families won't make room for him, thanks be to God, we can make room for him in our hearts.

He says you are the temples of the Holy Ghost. "Know ye not that your body is the temple of the Holy Ghost?" (1 Cor. 6:19). Will you make room for him this afternoon, young lady? Is there room for self? Is there room for the world? Is there room for pride? Is there room for jealousy? Is there room for everyone and everything else but the Son of God? Will you turn him away, or will you today make room for him?

Isn't it the very best thing you can do to make room for Christ? When he made this world, he made room for us, plenty of it. He made room for himself in our hearts, but a usurper has come. My friends, won't you let the Son of God into your hearts, and won't you let him dwell with you? The only room the world found for him was on the cross of Calvary.

Now, suppose he were to come here tonight. Were he to come into this hall, and go through this assembly, would he not find room in your hearts and mine, or will your heart be full like that full inn in Bethlehem? Will you this afternoon, just while I am speaking, say, "Lord Jesus, I make room for you in my heart"?

Mother, ought not gratitude for him who has made a place for your loved ones in heaven lead you to make room for him? Won't you say, "Here is plenty of love, won't you come and dwell in my heart?" Just the very minute you receive him, he will come. Am I speaking this afternoon to some poor fallen woman? Let me say to you, he received just such, and today he will come into your heart if you will just make room for him.

How many are there today that never have thanked the Lord Jesus for the blessings he has showered upon them! And, my friend, don't let this day pass without saying, "Jesus, there shall be room in my heart for thee hereafter," and then by and by he will receive you up yonder. If you will make room for him here in your heart, you may be sure he will make room for you in one of his Father's mansions.

Oh, this day and this hour, my friends, make room for Christ! Dear friends, don't you want him? Today, won't you make room for him? Won't you just bow your heads, and, when you pray, pray that every soul that wants Christ may come to him now.

Christ Works as a Carpenter

On hearing the news of the death of the king, Joseph brings Jesus back to Nazareth. There he remained for thirty years.

I once read of the founder of the Russian Empire going down to a Dutch seaport as a stranger and in disguise, that he might learn how to build ships and return home and impart this knowledge to his own subjects. People have wondered at that. But this is a far greater wonder, that the Prince of Glory should come down here and learn the carpenter's trade. He was not only the son of a carpenter, but he was a carpenter himself. His father was a carpenter, and he was a carpenter too, for we read that they brought it up against him that he was a carpenter (Matt. 13:55; Mark 6:3).

We read that when he was come into his own country, he taught them in their synagogue, insomuch that they were astonished, and said: "Whence hath this man this wisdom and these mighty works? Is not this the carpenter's son?" (Mark 6:1–6).

Right here is one lesson that we ought to learn, and that is, when Christ was here he was an industrious man. I have often said on this platform that I have never known a lazy man to be converted. If one ever was converted, he soon gave up his laziness. I tell you that laziness does not belong to Christ's kingdom. I do not believe a man would have a lazy hair on his head if he was converted to the Lord Jesus Christ. If a man has really been born of the Spirit of Christ, he is not lazy. He wants to find something to do, and no kind of manual labor is degrading. It is honorable.

If our Master, who is the Prince of Peace and the King of Glory, could leave heaven and come down here and work as a village carpenter, let us not think that manual labor is beneath our notice. Let us be willing to go out and work. If we cannot find what we want, let us do what we can. If we can earn only twenty-five cents a day, let us earn that rather than do nothing. We not only need something to occupy our hands, but also our minds.

Christ Feeds the Multitude

The people replied, "Moses gave our fathers manna to eat in the desert." "No," says Christ, "Moses gave you not that bread from heaven;

but my Father giveth you the true bread from heaven. . . . Verily, verily I say unto you, he that believeth on me hath everlasting life. I am that bread of life. Your fathers did eat manna in the wilderness, and are dead. This is the bread which cometh down from heaven, that a man may eat therof, and not die. I am the living bread which came down from heaven: if any man eat of this bread, he shall live for ever: and the bread that I will give is my flesh, which I will give for the life of the world" (John 6:32, 47–51).

I can see Jesus as he takes the bread and blesses it, and gives it to the disciples to give to the multitude. Here is Andrew with a piece of the loaf in his hand, beginning to distribute it among the crowd. I seem to see him breaking off a small piece for the first man, for fear the bread won't hold out, but when he sees that the loaf isn't any smaller for what he has broken off he goes to the next man and gives him a larger piece. Still there is no loss of bread. Then he gives the third a good generous portion, and when he finds that the bread doesn't grow any smaller he goes on breaking off great pieces, giving to everyone as much as he likes. (Matt. 15:36; Luke 9:16; John 6:11).

If we will use what we have, Christ will see that more opportunities will follow.

Christ's Transfiguration

When Peter wanted to put Christ on a level with Moses and Elijah, then it was that God the Father took them away after the transfiguration (Matt. 17:1–8; Mark 9:2–10). Jesus Christ has no peers; there is no one to be compared to him. He excels against the lawgiver and all the prophets. His name is above every other name under heaven. If you want power with God, just get as far from the world as you can and as close to Jesus as you can. Get near to Christ and you will never want to go back to the world. People may call you narrow, but God uses a narrow man and a narrow woman.

All our work that is separate from Christ will be just hay, wood, stubble, and chaff; it will be burned up when God comes to test our works. What we need is to be out of sight ourselves, so that when people see us they won't think of us, but of Christ. We must decrease, but he must increase.

Mr. Spurgeon draws a very vivid picture of the transfiguration. He says: "When the cloud came and received Moses and Elijah out of sight, and they were taken back into the other world, what would have been the result if Jesus Christ had gone, too? What a dark night it would have been if our Lord and Master had been caught up with Moses and Elijah, and no

Christ had died for our sins. Oh, how Jesus Christ lit up this world! But suppose that Christ had gone up to heaven on the other side of Calvary, and had never finished his work."

Suppose that God in his love for his Son had said, "I can't let those men spit upon you and smite you. I will take you back to my bosom." What darkness would have settled down on this world! But Moses disappeared, and Elijah disappeared, and Christ only was left, for Christ is all. The law and the prophets were honored and fulfilled in him. My dear friends, the longer I live the more I am convinced that what this world needs is Jesus Christ. If we preach him more, live him more, and love him more, and let him be constantly held up to this lost world, we shall accomplish something out of our lives.

Christ's Character

The Pharisees

We call witnesses to the person and work of Jesus Christ. First we call the Pharisees. We know how they hated him. Come, Pharisees, tell us what you have against the Son of God. "This man receiveth sinners" (Luke 15:2). What an argument to bring against him! Why, it is the very thing that makes us love him. He receives sinners. If he had not, what would have become of us?

Have you nothing more to bring against him than this? "He saved others; himself he cannot save" (Matt. 27:42; Mark 15:31). And so he did save others, but he could not save himself and save us too. So he laid down his own life for yours and mine. Yes, Pharisees, you have told the truth for once in your lives!

Caiaphas

Now, let us call upon Caiaphas. Let him stand up here in his flowing robes. "Caiaphas, you were chief priest when Christ was tried. You were president of the Sanhedrin. You were in the council-chamber when they found him guilty. You yourself condemned him. Tell us: what did the witnesses say? On what grounds did you judge him?"

"He hath spoken blasphemy," says Caiaphas. "He said, 'Hereafter shall ye see the Son of Man sitting on the right hand of power, and coming in the clouds of heaven' (Matt. 26:42; Mark 14:62). When I heard that, I found him guilty of blasphemy. I rent my mantle, and condemned him to death."

Yes, all that they had against him was that he was the Son of God; and they slew him for the promise of his coming for his bride.

Pilate

Now, let us summon Pilate. Let him enter the witness box. "Pilate, this man was brought before you. You examined him. You talked with him face to face. What think ye of Christ?" Pilate says, "He said he was the King of the Jews, but I find no fault in him." Such is the testimony of the man who examined him! And, as he stands there, the center of a Jewish mob, there comes along a man, elbowing his way in haste. He rushes up to Pilate and gives him a message. He tears it open; his face turns pale as he reads—"Have thou nothing to do with that just man: for I have suffered many things this day in a dream because of him" (Matt. 27:19). It is from Pilate's wife—her testimony to Christ.

Judas

And now, look—in comes Judas. He ought to make a good witness. "Come, tell us, Judas, what do you think of Christ. You knew the Master well. You sold him for thirty pieces of silver. You betrayed him with a kiss. You saw him perform those miracles. You were with him in Jerusalem. What think ye of him?" I can see him as he comes into the presence of the chief priests. I can hear the money ring as he dashes it upon the table—"I have betrayed innocent blood" (Matt. 27:4).

The Centurion at the Cross

Let us ask the centurion, who was present at the execution. "Centurion, you had charge of the executioners. You saw that the order for his death was carried out. You saw him die. You heard him speak upon the cross. Tell us, what do you think of Christ?" Hark! Look at him; he is smiting his breast as he cries, "Truly, this was the Son of God" (Matt. 27:54; Mark 15:39).

The Thief on the Cross

I will go to the thief upon the cross and ask what he thought of Christ. At first he railed upon him and reviled him. But then he thought better of it. "This man hath done nothing amiss," he says (Luke 23:41).

The Devils

I might go further. I might summon the very devils themselves and ask them for their testimony. Have they anything to say of him? Why, the very devils called him the Son of God (Luke 8:28)! In Mark we have the unclean spirit crying, "Jesus, thou Son of the most High God" (Mark 5:7).

Christ's Death

At last Jesus cried, with a loud voice, "It is finished" (John 19:30). Perhaps not many on earth heard it, or cared about it when they did hear it; but I can imagine there were not many in heaven who did not hear it. If they have bells in heaven how they must have rung out that day: "It is finished! It is finished!" The Son of God had died that poor sinful man might have life eternal. I can imagine the angels walking through the streets of heaven crying, "It is finished!" The mansions of that world ringing with the glad tidings, "It is finished!" It was the shout of victory. All you have to do now is look and be saved.

You have seen the waves of the sea come dashing up against a rocky shore. They come up and beat against the rock, and, breaking into pieces, go back to gather fresh strength, and again they come up and beat against the rock only to be again broken into pieces. And so it would seem as if the dark waves of hell had gathered all their strength together and had come beating up against the bosom of the Son of God; but he drives them all back again with that shout of a conqueror: "It is finished." And with that shout he snapped the fetters of sin and broke the power of Satan.

12 Cleopas

Luke 24:13–35

"And, behold, two of them went that same day to a village called Emmaus, which was from Jerusalem about threescore furlongs" (Luke 24:13). In the account of the two disciples going to Emmaus you will notice that they were very sorrowful. They ought to have been the happiest mortals on earth. It was the dawn of a new dispensation; it was the first day, you might say, of a new world. Here we have the first sermon that was preached after the resurrection, and it was preached by the Lord himself.

The Risen Christ Appears

He found these two disciples very sorrowful; their hopes had all died. They were going back to their home seven or eight miles away. There was great danger, they thought, in Jerusalem. The head of their company had been crucified, and there was a storm rising against his disciples. Over and over again he had told them, before he left them, that on the third day he would rise from the dead.

This was the third day, and instead of having faith to believe that he had risen, when the report came from the very foremost of the disciples those that stood nearest to Christ and loved him perhaps the most—they were so full of unbelief that they doubted the word of the disciples that had brought the message. They are going back into the country with their hearts crushed, bleeding, broken, and very sad.

There has always been a great discussion as to who the two were. One we know—Cleopas—who was the uncle of Christ. Some have thought that Luke himself was the other, and different ones have been selected as the second. Now, I am inclined to think that instead of being two men these two were a man and his wife. I think it would be interesting to realize that a woman was one of the disciples that went to Emmaus.

59

In John 19:25 we read: "Now there stood by the cross of Jesus his mother, and his mother's sister, Mary the wife of Cleopas, and Mary Magdalene."

We know, then, that Mary, Cleopas's wife, was there at the cross, and it wasn't likely that her husband would go off into the country seven or eight miles away when there was so bitter a feeling in the city, and leave his wife in peril. It doesn't say that these were two men, they were two disciples—and if it was Cleopas and his wife they were uncle and aunt of Jesus Christ.

Christ Comforts with Scripture

As they went and were sad, Christ came along and walked with them. Someone has said that we don't sufficiently realize that if any two of us make Jesus the subject of our conversation he himself will be of our company. Where two or three are gathered together in his name he is in the midst.

People have often wondered how it could be that Cleopas, one of his disciples, should not have known him. That is not so strange. You remember that Jehovah appeared to Abraham as a way-faring man; to Jacob as a wrestler; to Joshua as a soldier with a drawn sword; so that he may have appeared to these disciples in a way that they should not know him until he had gone from them. They were so taken up with their sorrow that they had forgotten all the sweet promises he had left of what he would do after his resurrection. That seemed to be hidden from them.

When Christ drew near, he said unto them, "What manner of communications are these that ye have one to another, as ye walk, and are sad?" (Luke 24:17). Then he began to unfold to them the Scriptures. Now, do you know, if they had gone to the Scriptures in the time of their trouble, as they ought to have done, they would have lost sight of their trouble? He took them right to the Word of God, where they could get comfort.

There are four things I want to call to your attention: (1) Their minds were opened that they should understand the Scriptures. (2) He caused their hearts to burn within them. When God opens up the mind, and we receive the Word, then the heart begins to burn; and there isn't anything that will cause the heart to burn with joy and gladness like the Word of the living God. (3) He opened their eyes, so that they should know him. (4) He revealed himself unto them.

This man and his wife are going back from Jerusalem to their home in Emmaus. On the way a stranger joins them and begins to talk with them. As they draw near the town the day is far spent, and the evening is coming on. When they get to their home the stranger has made his company so precious, and his words so sweet, that they ask him to spend the night. And that is another proof to me that it was a man and wife, because "they constrained him" (Luke 24:29). A man and wife could constrain a person to stay over night, but two mere friends would hardly do so. It would be just like a man and wife to say, "Come in, we wish you would. We have plenty of room." So they all went in together.

I can imagine this woman preparing the evening meal, and as the two men sit there talking together, every once in a while the woman stops and listens. She can't help it. Oh, those words were so sweet! I wish every word the Son of God uttered on that occasion had been put on record. What an experience it must have been to hear Christ tell the meaning of the sacrifice of Isaac, and the brazen serpent and the ceremonies of the great day of atonement; to hear him expound the fifty-third of Isaiah, and the twenty-second Psalm, and the other passages in Moses and the prophets concerning himself! What an unfolding of Scripture, and how their hearts were thrilled as they learned those blessed truths!

Some people say that we have outgrown the Old Testament, that the New Testament is all we need. But Christ used it; it was all he had. He set his seal upon it. It is recorded that he made quotations from at least twenty-two of the thirty-nine books. He referred to them constantly and said that they must be fulfilled. Saphir has said that the gospel narrative is like a high tableland, but we cannot be spared the ascent from Genesis to Malachi. The one theme of the Old Testament is the Messiah, and until you realize that, you have not found the key to its treasures.

Christ Reveals Himself

At last the evening meal is prepared, and they sit down and begin. I can just imagine Cleopas turning to the stranger and saying, "Will you ask the blessing?"

Then Christ raised those pierced and wounded hands and perhaps that is the way he revealed himself to them. They saw the prints in the palms of his hands, the wounds that had been made at Calvary. And he is gone. Someone has said that now, as at Emmaus, Jesus loves to make himself known in the breaking of the bread.

I do not believe they touched a morsel of supper their hearts were so full, but they said, "We must go back to Jerusalem and take the news."

They went back much more quickly than they came out, their hearts leaping within them for joy. They found the disciples and brought the glad tidings, "He is risen! We have seen him, and he has talked to us."

To their dying day how they must have told over and over how they saw him on that journey! Oh, that Christ might come, and cause our hearts to burn within us. Let us pray that he may open our eyes and our understanding, and that he may just give us a fresh vision of himself!

13 Cornelius

Acts 10:1–11:18

We plan one meeting a week in Farwell Hall, at which the way of life shall be explained. A good many people come to the noon meeting who cannot come to the Tabernacle, and we want to show them how to come to Christ. I will call your attention this morning to the conversion of Cornelius, and try to point out the way in which you, like him, may become a Christian.

Peter before the Jerusalem Council

Peter was brought before the brethren at Jerusalem to give an account of himself for preaching the gospel to the Gentiles (Acts 11:1–21). Christ had told his disciples to go into all the world and preach the gospel to every creature, but the idea never seemed to get into their heads. I don't know that we should ever have had the gospel at all if it hadn't been for the persecutions which drove the apostles out of Jerusalem.

Peter belongs to the exclusive brethren, and when he is told to go and preach the gospel to Cornelius he must have a sheet let down from heaven three times in order to show him that what God has cleansed he must not call common or unclean, and to show him that it is his duty to preach to Gentiles as well as Jews.

In the fourteenth verse of Acts 11, Peter is telling them how he happened to go. He says he was sent for by Cornelius to tell him "words" whereby he and all his house should be saved.

Now just look at that. Cornelius wasn't to be saved by his feelings, nor his efforts, nor his alms; he was to be saved by words—the words of Peter preaching Jesus Christ to him. By such words not only Cornelius and all his house, but all sinners everywhere, are to be brought into the kingdom of God.

Cornelius Believes the Gospel

Let us take a look at Cornelius. If we had such a man here among us we should find him a regular attendant at church, and one who said his prayers every day. He was a devout man, and feared God with all his house. He was a benevolent man also. He gave much alms to the people. I don't doubt he would give away a great many Thanksgiving turkeys. And what is more, the Bible says he "prayed to God always" (Acts 10:2).

Now, a great many people would say, "Such a man as that doesn't need converting; he is good enough already." But the Lord didn't seem to think so, for we find him getting up a meeting—about the only meeting he ever did get up—in order to have Cornelius converted.

He tells him to send men to Joppa and call for one Simon, whose surname is Peter. This Gentile is commanded to send after a Jew to preach the gospel to him—just the kind of a man he didn't like; and so you will often find that God sends his message of grace and mercy to people by the very last means they would have chosen.

In Acts 10:6 we find that the Lord knew the house, and the street, and the name of the man with whom his servant Peter was lodged: "He lodgeth with one Simon a tanner, whose house is by the sea side." God always knows all about his own people. So Cornelius sends his bodyguard thirty miles away to Joppa, and when they tell Peter their errand he goes away with them to preach the gospel to this Gentile.

In the last part of this chapter we have the substance of Peter's sermon on this occasion. Now, what was it that he preached to Cornelius? He didn't preach science, literature, or a great long mess of theology, but he preached unto him Jesus Christ, whom he declared to be "Lord of all." He believed in the deity of Christ, you see. That was the substance of Peter's preaching always—Jesus Christ and him crucified. That was pretty much all he knew how to preach. If you had taken that away from him, you would have taken all his stock in trade.

He preached a short sermon and came right to the point, "Whosoever believeth in him shall receive remission of sins" (Acts 10:43); and when he got to this point in the discourse we are told that "the Holy Ghost fell on all them which heard the word" (Acts 10:44). Now, I suppose there might have been some people there who did not hear; perhaps they were looking around, paying attention to other things besides the "words" that Peter was preaching. And, if there were any such, the Holy Ghost didn't fall on them, but only on those who heard the word.

My friends, you who hear the word of God today, accept it as Cornelius did, with all your house, and the Holy Ghost will fall on you as it did on them. Now, that is plain enough, and that is just the way to be saved. May the Holy Ghost fall upon us now and seal us to the day of redemption!

14 Daniel

I want to talk to you about the prophet Daniel. His name signifies, "God with him"; not the public with him, not his fellowmen with him, but God with him. Therefore, he had to report himself to God and hold himself responsible to God.

Daniel Taken Captive

In the third year of King Jehoiakim, Nebuchadnezzar came up against Jerusalem and took ten thousand of its chief men to carry them captive to Babylon (Dan. 1:1–2). I am glad that these chief men who stirred up the war were the ones who fell into Nebuchadnezzar's hands. Unlike too many of the ringleaders in wars, they got the punishment on their own heads.

We don't know how old Daniel was when we first hear of him, probably about seventeen. King Nebuchadnezzar had given orders to take some of the best and brightest of the Hebrew captives, and bring them up among his wise men; they were to be taught in the learning of the Chaldeans, and to be fed with meat and wine from the king's table. Among these young men were Daniel and his three friends (Dan. 1:6), who had, doubtless, been converted under the preaching of Jeremiah, the weeping prophet.

I suppose a good many people mocked at Jeremiah when he lifted up his voice against their sins, and laughed at his tears, and said of him, as a good many say of us, that he was getting up a false excitement. But these four young men listened to his preaching and had the courage to come out on the Lord's side.

And right here is the secret of this man's success. The Scripture tells us that this man, Daniel, knew God. There are a great many professing Christians who never get on intimate terms with God, and so they never amount to much; but Daniel knew and trusted the God of Abraham, Isaac, and Jacob even from his youth.

Daniel Reveals Purpose of Heart

Now, no young man ever comes to the city without having great temptation cross his path as he enters it. And just at this turning point in his life, as in Daniel's, must be the secret of his success. This was the secret of young Daniel's success: He took his stand with God right upon his entering the gate of Babylon. He cried to God to keep him steadfast, and he had need to cry hard.

There was a law of his God that no man should eat meat offered to idols, and now here comes a commandment from the king that these young men should be fed upon meat from his table, which Daniel knew had been sacrificed in idol worship. "But Daniel purposed in his heart that he would not defile himself with the portion of the king's meat, nor with the wine which he drank" (Dan. 1:8).

If he had been like some of our Chicago Christians he would have said, "Well, it can't be helped. I don't like to defile myself this way. The law of God forbids it, and if I were only home in Jerusalem I never would do it in the world. But really I don't see how I am going to help it. We are nothing but slaves in Babylon, and if the king should hear of our disobedience he would take our heads off in no time—and we can't be expected to run such a risk as that."

Then I suppose some of our modern professors of religion would have advised Daniel after this fashion, "Young man, I understand you are thinking about refusing the king's meat and wine; don't you do it. There is no use in your setting aside this meat and wine; it is only a kind of pharisaism. The moment you take this stand, you say, in effect, you think you are better than other people. When you are in Rome, do as the Romans do. When you are in Jerusalem you must keep the commandments. But nobody could possibly think of your keeping them down here in Babylon."

Now there is no doubt but the devil told Daniel just that same thing. He wanted him to do in Babylon as the people of Babylon did; but Daniel had courage to stand up to the law of his God and say, "No!" Consequences! Never mind the consequences; there wasn't any such word in his dictionary. When it came to a question of obeying the law of his God, he was going to obey, and let God take care of the consequences. Just hear what is said in this eighth verse of the first chapter of this book: "Daniel purposed in his heart."

Now, the trouble with a great many people is, that when they purpose to do right they only purpose in their heads, and that doesn't amount to much. If you are going to be a Christian, you must purpose to serve God way down in your hearts. "With the heart man believeth unto righteousness" (Rom. 10:10). So the young Israelite determined that he would not eat the king's meat, nor drink the king's wine, because it was against the law of his God. Instead he got the eunuch to bring him and his friends pulse and water (Dan. 1:9–14).

Now just look at the reason Daniel and his friends gave to the king's servant. They didn't try to dodge the question at all; they said right out at once, "We cannot do this, because the law of our God forbids it."

I am afraid some of you, if you had been in their places, would have tried to hide behind some excuse. You would have said you weren't feeling well, or that meat and wine didn't agree with you. Not so with Daniel. He tells that heathen why he can't eat the king's meat and drink the king's wine. I have no doubt the man respected him for it. But the servant said it wouldn't do at all—"If you don't eat, the king will find it out; he will see you sometime looking lean and thin, and will ask what the matter is; and when he finds out that I have brought you something else, I shall lose my head, and you will lose yours."

"Just try us for ten days," said Daniel. "Give us vegetables to eat, and water to drink, and see how we get along on it." So the servant tried them on the pulse and water, and when they came before the king the eunuch's fears were all gone, for the faces of Daniel and his friends were fairer and fatter than any of the others (Dan. 1:15).

Some people think wine makes them look better, and that they cannot get along without it. Just look at their red noses and bloated faces. It is God's truth, and Daniel tested it, that cold water, with a clear conscience, is a good deal more healthy than wine. Some people say they cannot get along without stimulants; but I tell you, all the stimulant a person needs is the word and the grace of God.

There was a soldier down in Tennessee when I was in the army, a great, strong, hearty fellow, who was a teetotaler. He did not drink any alcoholic beverages. One day, when the army was on a long march, somebody offered him a drink of whisky.

"I am a teetotaler," was his reply.

"Never mind that, you are in the army now; besides, you need some stimulant to help you on this long march."

The man took out a pocket Bible and held it up before the face of his tempter, and said, "That is all the stimulant I want."

Just so with Daniel; he took God's side in this question and held to God's terms, and God made him strong and healthy and gave him favor with those who saw his honesty. Above all, God gave him peace in his own soul.

Nebuchadnezzar's Dream

The next thing we hear of Daniel is when the king has had a dream, and all the wise men are called to interpret it (Daniel 2). And now I seem to see an officer coming in, laying his hand on Daniel's shoulder, and arresting him in the king's name. "What is the matter?" asks Daniel.

"I am very sorry," says the officer, "but the king had a dream last night, and when he woke up he could not remember it. So he called all his wise men together and asked them to tell him his dream and then to interpret it for him. When no one of them could do it the king was angry and commanded that all the wise men be put to death. You belong to that group, so you will have to die with the rest of them."

"It seems to me the king is rather hasty," says Daniel. "Just let him give us a little time, and I will show him his dream, and the interpretation also."

The Dream Revealed to Daniel

That night Daniel and his three friends had a little prayer meeting together. Perhaps they read the story of Joseph, and how the dreams of old Pharaoh were revealed to him, and how he came to be a great man in Egypt afterward. They knew that all secret things were known to God, and they asked him to reveal this one. Then they went to bed and slept soundly.

I don't think many of you would have gone to sleep with such danger as that hanging over your heads. But Daniel slept, and in his sleep the king's dream was revealed to him (Dan. 2:19). Next morning there was a great stir all about the palace. It had gotten out that a young Hebrew captive was going to tell the king his dream and save the lives of all the wise men in Babylon, and everybody was anxious to know about it.

I can see the young man brought into the presence of the mighty monarch. He stands there without the slightest fear, because his God in whom he trusts has made him master of the situation. There must have been joy among those wise men when they found out that this youth was able to reveal the king's dream and save their lives for them.

The king looks at him, and says, "Young man, can you tell me my dream and the interpretation of it?"

"My God can tell it," answers Daniel; and then he begins, "O king, whilst thou didst lie with thy head on thy pillow thou didst dream, and in thy dream thou sawest a great image—"

"That's it!" says Nebuchadnezzar, his face lighting all at once. "That's it. I remember it now."

"Yes, sir," says Daniel, "my God revealed it to me last night in a dream." You see, my friends, he doesn't take any credit to himself, but gives all the glory to God (Dan. 2:30).

The Dream Interpreted by Daniel

Then Daniel, in a deathlike stillness, unfolded all the interpretation and told the king that the golden head of the great image represented his own government (Dan. 2:31–38). I suppose Babylon was the biggest city ever in the world. It was sixty miles around. Some writers put the walls from sixty-five to eighty-five feet high and twenty-five feet wide. Four chariots could drive abreast on top of them. A street fifteen miles long divided the grand city, and hanging gardens in acres made the public parks. It was like Chicago—so flat that they had to resort to artificial mounds; and, again like Chicago, the products of vast regions flowed right into and through it.

This great kingdom, Daniel told the king, was his own; but he said a destroying kingdom should come, and afterward a third and fourth kingdom, when, at the last, the God of heaven should set up his kingdom (Dan. 2:38–44). Daniel lived to see the first kingdom overthrown, when the Medes and Persians came in, and centuries after came Alexander, and then the Romans.

I believe in the literal fulfillment, so far, of Daniel's God-given words and in the sure fulfillment of the final prophecy of the "stone cut out of the mountains without hands" that by and by shall grind the kingdoms of this world into dust, and bring in the kingdom of peace. Then will be the millennium, and Christ will sway his scepter.

I imagine some of you would have tried to soften that interpretation a little. It was a pretty hard thing for Daniel to stand up there before that great monarch and tell him that his kingdom was to be like the dust of the summer threshing floor. But the king was greatly pleased with Daniel, and made a great man of him; and for his sake put his three friends also into office. You see when Daniel got into a good place he didn't forget his friends. God had blessed them signally in the time of danger, and what was, perhaps, a harder thing, he gave them grace in the time of prosperity to keep them true to him. Their faith and their fortunes seemed to wax strong together.

Nebuchadnezzar's Golden Image

Not long afterward—maybe it was the dream that put it into his head— Nebuchadnezzar made a great image of gold, and set it up in the plain of

Dura, near to the city. It was about ninety feet high, and about nine feet wide. I rather think the king intended that image to represent himself. He was going to have a universal religion, and he was going to be head of it; so he gave orders to all the nobility and the officers of his kingdom to come to the dedication of this golden image (Dan. 3:1–2).

I don't know where Daniel was at this time; perhaps he was in some other part of the country on business. I am sure he was not at the dedication, or we should have been likely to hear of him. However, his friends, Shadrach, Meshach, and Abednego, were there, along with the rest of the counselors and satraps, high secretaries and princes of the people. Their enemies were there, too, watching for the chance to get them out of the way. A faithful servant of God is sure to have enemies.

It was a great day when the image was unveiled. I seem to see it flashing in the sunlight, the vast throng of worshipers standing around it, and the king at the head of a splendid procession of his lords and ladies coming across the plain with banners flying and music playing. Really it must have been a trying time for these three men, who were so much out of fashion as not to bow down to the great idol when everybody else was doing it.

Then a herald cried out, "To you it is commanded, O people, nations, and languages, that at what time ye hear the sound of the cornet, flute, harp, sackbut, psaltery, dulcimer, and all kinds of music, ye fall down and worship the golden image that Nebuchadnezzar the king hath set up: and whoso falleth not down and worshipeth shall the same hour be cast into the midst of a burning fiery furnace" (Dan. 3:4–5).

Shadrach, Meshach, and Abednego Refuse to Bow

These three men heard the commandment, but there was another commandment which they had not forgotten: "Thou shalt have no other gods before me" (Exod. 20:3). The king said, "Bow down." God said, "No." It didn't take them a minute to decide which to obey.

Now I suppose some people would have said, "You might just bow down a little. You needn't worship, you know, just bend your knee a little. That won't do any harm. You needn't say any prayer to the idol." Not a bit of it; these men were not going to compromise their consciences, and their enemies knew it very well. They utterly refused to bend their knees to the god of gold.

Ah! How many people are there in this city who cry, "Give me gold, give me money, and I will do anything." Perhaps those people think that men in Nebuchadnezzar's time ought not to have bowed down to the golden idol, but they themselves are worshipping a golden idol every day. Money is their god.

Now the hour has arrived, everything is ready. The king makes a sign with his hand, and the cornets, the sackbuts, and all the other instruments give a great blast, and the whole multitude fall down on their faces before the great image which Nebuchadnezzar has set up.

No, not all. There are three pairs of stiff knees in that kingdom. Their enemies had taken care to put them into the front rank, where they could watch them, and find occasion to accuse them to the king. I seem to see those fellows looking out of the corners of their eyes, when, by the king's commandment, they should have been worshipping the idol. And I can hear them saying to themselves, "Aha! We have caught you now."

Then they go straightway and tell the king (Dan. 3:8–12). "Oh, king, live forever! Do you know that there are three men in your country who will not bow down to you?

"No," says the king, "who are they?"

"Oh, they are some of those Hebrew captives; they don't bow down with the rest of us, and we thought you would like to know it."

"Bring them to me," says the king, in a great rage. "I will see whether these fellows are going to disobey my orders like that." It is quite likely he would have ordered their heads to have been taken off at once if he had not remembered that they were particular friends of Daniel. And now they stand face to face with the great king.

"What is this I hear of you?" asks Nebuchadnezzar. "It is said you disobey my orders, and won't bow down and worship my golden image. Now I'll try you once more; then, if you don't bow down, into the furnace you go."

We don't know who the speaker was on that occasion; perhaps it was Shadrach. He stands there with his two friends, looking calmly at the king, and thinking of the fiery furnace without the slightest fear, and this is what he says: "We are not careful to answer thee in this matter. Our God whom we serve is able to deliver us from the burning fiery furnace, and will deliver us out of thine hand, O king. But if not, be it known unto thee, O king, that we will not serve thy gods, nor worship the golden image which thou hast set up" (Dan. 3:16–18).

The Three Men Thrown into the Furnace

"Who is this God of yours that is able to deliver you out of my hand?" says the king, screaming with rage. "Go and heat that furnace seven times hotter than ever, and thrust these fellows into it. Be quick. I will not have any such rebels in my kingdom."

So some of the king's servants hurry away to the furnace to stir up the fire. Others seize Shadrach, Meshach, and Abednego, and take them away. When the furnace doors are opened the fire is so hot that it burns the king's servants to death, but it does not harm the three men who are cast headlong into it. Then the king goes to look into the furnace, and what is his astonishment as he sees four men instead of three, walking in the midst of the fire, as safely as if in the midst of his garden (Dan. 3:19–25).

"Did I not tell you to cast in three men, and lo! I see four walking about in the fire, and the form of the fourth is like the Son of God!" Yes, Jesus walked there with them. The Lord himself was with his three faithful servants. The great Shepherd looked down from heaven, and saw those three sheep of his flock about to be cast into the fire, and he made haste and came down himself to see that they suffered no harm. Ah! Jesus is always with his people. You can never do any real harm to a man who is one of God's obedient children. The fire only burned off the devil's bands, but didn't singe a hair of their heads.

Doesn't Christ say that the hairs of our heads are all numbered? Now, who of you ever heard of a mother who loved her little child well enough to count the hairs on its curly head? But the Lord loves his children so well that he counts their hairs—every one. My friends, let us remember that it is safe always to do what God wants us to do. If our way to heaven lies through fire and water, it is all the same, it is all right; that is the proper way for us to go.

Then the king came to the mouth of the furnace and called those servants of the most high God to come forth. Nobody could take them out of such a fire, but they came out of their own accord. Then Nebuchadnezzar spake and said, "Blessed be the God of Shadrach, Meshach, and Abednego, who hath sent his angel, and delivered his servants that trusted in him, and have changed the king's word, and yielded their bodies, that they might not serve nor worship any god, except their own God. Therefore I make a decree, That every people, nation, and language, which speak any thing amiss against the God of Shadrach, Meshach, and Abednego, shall be cut in pieces, and their houses shall be made a dunghill: because there is no other god that can deliver after this sort" (Dan. 3:28–29).

And then we find the king promoting these men, so that instead of being burned to death for their disobedience they came to be more honorable than ever (Dan. 3:30). Ah, my friends, what we want is Christians with some backbone, men and women who stand up for the right, and never mind what the world may say. If we only had a few such Christians in Chicago as Shadrach, Meshach, and Abednego, I believe there would be ten thousand conversions in the next twenty-four hours.

Nebuchadnezzar's Second Dream

The next thing we hear is that the king has had another dream (Dan. 4:4–5). He seems to have been a great man for dreams. This time he saw a great tree which "reached unto heaven, and the sight thereof to the end of all the earth . . . and, behold, a watcher and a holy one came down from heaven; he cried aloud, and said thus, Hew down the tree, and cut off his branches, shake off his leaves, and scatter his fruit: let the beasts get away from under it, and the fowls from his branches: Nevertheless, leave the stump of his roots in the earth. . . . Let his heart be changed from man's, and let a beast's heart be given unto him; and let seven times pass over him . . . to the intent that the living may know that the most High ruleth in the kingdom of men, and giveth it to whomsoever he will" (Dan. 4:11–17).

For a time Daniel stands motionless. Does his heart fail him? The record simply says that for one hour he was astonished. The ready words doubtless rush to his lips, but he dislikes to let them out. He does not want to tell how the king's kingdom and mind are going to depart from him, and he is to wander forth to eat grass like a beast.

The king, too, hesitates; a dark foreboding for a time gets the better of curiosity. But soon he nerves himself to hear the worst, and speaks very kindly, "Do not be afraid to tell me, O Daniel! Let not the dream or its interpretation trouble thee."

At last Daniel speaks (Dan. 4:22–27), "Oh king, thou art the man. God has exalted thee over every king and over all the world, but thou shalt be brought low. Thou shalt be driven out from men, and shalt eat grass among the beasts of the field; but thy kingdom—as the great watcher spared the stump of the tree—shall afterward return to thee. Wherefore, Oh king, break off thy sins by righteousness and thine iniquities by showing mercy to the poor, if it may be a lengthening of thy tranquillity."

Nebuchadnezzar's Pride

And straightway the king repented in sackcloth and ashes, and God stayed the doom (Dan. 4:28). But twelve months from that time we see Nebuchadnezzar walking in his palace and boasting, "Is not this great Babylon that I have built by the might of my power, and for the honour of my majesty?" (Dan. 4:30).

And behold, while he yet spake a voice came from heaven, saying, "Thy kingdom hath departed." And undoubtedly God then touched his reason, and straightway he ran madly through the gates to eat grass. But at last the Lord had mercy on him. His counselors and princes gathered about him again and brought him back to his palace. And the king's heart was softened. I think he became truly converted to God, and from this time we don't hear him saying any more, "Is not this great Babylon that I have built?" Instead we hear him blessing the Most High, and praising and honoring the God whose dominion is everlasting, and whose kingdom is from generation to generation.

Nebuchadnezzar's Proclamation

And now the king makes one more proclamation, different from all the others (Dan. 4:34–37). Up to this time he has been telling other people what to do; now he begins to speak of his own duty, and he says, "I, Nebuchadnezzar, will do this, and do that. I praise and extol and honor the King of heaven, all of whose works are truth." He has found out his own duty. His heart is softened, and although we do not hear anything more of him, I have no doubt that Daniel and he used to walk the streets of Babylon arm in arm, and talk over their experiences together.

And when the king died I feel quite sure that he went safely to heaven, to be welcomed by the God of Daniel. Through the long eternity King Nebuchadnezzar will rejoice that that young man, Daniel, when he came down to Babylon, did not follow the fashion of that wicked capital, but took his stand for God, though it might have cost him his life.

Daniel and Belshazzar

The next thing we hear of Babylon is that the grandson of Nebuchadnezzar, a wild young prince called Belshazzar, has come to the throne. Of this prince we have only one glimpse. The feast scene (Daniel 5) is the first and last we have of him, and it is enough. It was a great feast, and fully a thousand of his lords sat down together. In those days feasts sometimes lasted six months. How long this one lasted we don't know. The king caroused with his princes and satraps and all the mighty men of Babylon, drinking, rioting, and praying to gods of silver and gold and brass and stubble—just what we are doing today, if we bow the knee to the gods of this world.

They come together in a great banquet chamber, and they drink and carouse all night long. They do not care that the armies of Cyrus are besieging the city. They trust in Babylon's high walls and its gates of brass, and feel themselves perfectly safe. At last, when the head of the young king has been quite turned with wine, he orders the golden vessels which his grandfather had taken from God's temple at Jerusalem to be brought into the banquet hall that they may drink from them in honor of the gods of Babylon. So, they drink wine from them—drink toasts to idols and harlots. And, undoubtedly, as they are drinking they scoff at the God of Israel.

God's Handwriting Appears on the Wall

I think if you will read the word of God carefully, you will find that judgment always comes suddenly and unexpectedly. I see these revelers swearing and rioting when, suddenly, the king turns pale and trembles from head to foot. Above the golden candlesticks, on a bare space on the wall, he sees the writing of the God of Zion. He distinctly sees the terrible fingers. Drunk as he is, the miserable king is frightened.

Belshazzar sends for the wise men of Babylon to come in and read that writing. He offers that the man that can read the writing shall be clothed in fine linen, and in purple. He shall have a golden chain around his neck, and shall be made the third ruler in the realm. Those wise men tried to read it, but they were not acquainted with God's handwriting. That is the reason these skeptics and infidels don't understand the Bible. They don't know God's handwriting. With all the wisdom of the Chaldeans, they could not make out that handwriting. They failed, utterly failed.

The king and all his lords were astonished. They never had seen it on that fashion before. It was a strange handwriting. The queen comes in, and she tells the monarch that there is a man in his kingdom who has not been heard of for fifteen years; where he has been we are not told. But she tells Belshazzar that when Nebuchadnezzar reigned, and the wise men failed to tell him his dream and the interpretation, there was a man by the name of Daniel that could tell the king his dream and the interpretation.

She said to Belshazzar, "Send for the prophet Daniel and he will read the handwriting on the wall."

Daniel is sent for, and the king says to him, "If you read that handwriting and tell me what it means, I will give you great gifts, and I will make you the third ruler in the realm."

When Daniel looks up there, you can imagine how silence reigns through that audience. Every eye is upon him. The king looks at him, and Daniel says, "Let your gifts be to others but I will read to you the handwriting."

He knew his God's handwriting. It was very familiar to him, and without any difficulty he can read the words. "MENE, MENE, TEKEL, UPHARSIN."

"What does it mean?" cries the king.

God's Handwriting Is Interpreted by Daniel

Now I have no doubt that a good many king's attendants, if they had seen such writing upon the wall of the king's palace, would have softened the meaning of it a little, and not have given it in its full strength, for fear of offending the king. But that is not Daniel's fashion at all. He reads it just as God writes it. "MENE; God hath numbered thy kingdom, and finished it.

TEKEL; Thou art weighed in the balances, and art found wanting. PERES; Thy kingdom is divided, and given to the Medes and Persians" (Dan. 5:25–28).

Ah, you poor miserable King Belshazzar! Even now the soldiers of Cyrus have turned away the waters of the Euphrates, and are coming into your city along the empty banks. The soldiers are battering away at the door of your palace, and before morning your blood shall be spilled upon the stones, along with the wine which you have been drinking out of the vessels from God's holy temple at Jerusalem. You are weighed in God's balance and found wanting.

We All Shall Be Weighed

But it is not my object tonight to talk about that king that reigned twenty-five hundred years ago. I don't want to take you back that far. I want to get down to this city if I can. I want to get into this audience tonight, and I want to ask every man and woman in this assembly, if you should be summoned into eternity at this hour, or at the midnight hour, would it be said, "Thou art weighed in the balances and art found wanting?"

My friends, suppose God should begin to weigh some of you today. Suppose you were to step into the balances now, don't you think you would be found wanting? Get into God's scale, take along with you your education, and your wealth, and your dignity, and your fine clothes, and everything you have that is splendid, and let the Lord put the Ten Commandments against you, and up you will go like feathers—"weighed in the balances, and found wanting." Only they who have Christ in their souls can stand the test of God's weighing. Dare you step into the balances today?

Daniel and Darius

After a while Darius the Mede comes to the throne of Babylon. He must have met Daniel somewhere in his travels, for no sooner does he set up the kingdom than he puts Daniel into a place of great power. He chooses a hundred and twenty princes, whom he places over the kingdom. Over these princes he appoints three presidents, and he makes Daniel the president of the presidents, so that he really is the first man in the kingdom after the king.

The Plot against Daniel

Daniel's business is to "see that the king suffer no damage"; that is, he is to keep watch of the accounts, to see that nobody cheats the king. This must

have been a very difficult place, and Daniel must have had his hands full.
He had to watch those hundred and twenty rascals who were all the while
trying to steal something off the revenue, and to go over their accounts again
and again, so as to be certain that they were correct to a penny.

It was not long before Daniel became very unpopular with the princes.
I seem to hear them talking among themselves in this way, "There is that
miserable old Jew, Daniel. If we only had him out of the way we could
make no end of money. We would very speedily be rich. We could have
our country houses and our city houses, and our fine horses and chariots, and live in the very highest style off the revenue of this kingdom; but
that old fellow watches us as narrowly as a cat watches a mouse. We can't
cheat him, even in a shilling."

"Why," says another, "I never saw such a man in all my life. I gave in an
account the other day that was only a few dollars short; and didn't he
send it back to me, and make me pay the difference? I wish he were back
in Jerusalem, where he came from."

However, the king trusted Daniel; and he was such a thoroughly good
and honest man that they could find no way to revenge themselves upon
him. But at last they struck on one weak point, as they called it—he would
worship no one but the God of Israel. The law of his God was his only
assailable side.

The conspirators reasoned in their plotting, "We shall not find any
occasion against this Daniel, unless we find it against him concerning the
law of his God." What an honor! Nothing wrong with him, even in the eyes
of these bad men, except that he was too faithful to his God! How many
of you are likely to be complained of on that account?

Finally, they hit upon a plan which they thought might possibly succeed. One night when they were closeted together in secret, one of the
princes said to the rest, "I think I have got a plan that will work. You know
King Darius is very popular, and he is very proud of it. The people praise
him a great deal, and he likes it. Now suppose we ask him to establish a
royal decree, that whosoever shall ask a petition of any god or man for
thirty days, save of the king, he shall be cast into the den of lions. That
will be putting the king in the place of the gods, and he is more likely to
be flattered by that than by anything I can think of. Then, if once we can
get that old Hebrew into the lion's den, we shall make a good deal more
money than we have been able to do with him watching us all the time."

This notion seemed to please the princes very well. They drew up the
document immediately. It would not do to let Daniel hear of it before the
king should sign it, and so they appointed a committee to take the decree
down to the palace the very first thing in the morning. There were some
lawyers among these hundred and twenty princes. I seem to see them
drawing up the proclamation with great care according to law, making it

firm and binding, laughing to themselves, and saying: "The laws of the Medes and Persians change not. If once we can get Darius to stamp this document with his signet ring, Daniel is done for, sure enough."

So the committee goes down to the palace the next morning to obtain the king's signature. They begin by flattering him. If a man wants another to do a mean thing he always begins by appealing to his vanity. "O king, we have been thinking how popular you are in your kingdom, and what you might do to make yourself even more famous than you are. And we have come to the conclusion that, if you would publish a decree that nobody in the kingdom, for thirty days, should pray to any other god except yourself, it would turn the hearts of all the people toward you even more than now. We should then have a universal religion, and the king would be at the head of it."

Darius felt flattered by this proposition. He turned it over in his mind, and presently said, "That seems sensible."

"All right," said the princes. "We thought you would like it; and in order that there might not be any delay, we have the document here already drawn up. Now if you will please stamp this with your signet ring, we shall have it published right away."

The king takes the document, reads it over, and stamps his seal upon it; and the committee goes away, laughing and saying, "Ha, ha! Old Hebrew, we will have you in the den of lions before night."

Daniel in the Lion's Den

The princes lost no time in publishing the new decree of the king. I can imagine someone of Daniel's friends, who had seen the document, going up to his office in great haste to give him warning that there was some trouble brewing. "Have you heard the news, Daniel? Those hundred and twenty princes have gone and gotten Darius to publish a decree that nobody shall pray to any other god except to the king for thirty days. That is a conspiracy against you. Now I want to give you a little advice; and that is, to get out of this town in a hurry."

But Daniel says, "I can't leave my responsibility. I suspect these hundred and twenty princes will cheat the revenues while I am away. My duty is right here, and I am determined to stay and attend to it."

"Well, then, hadn't you better pray more secretly? You have a habit, that is all well enough in ordinary times, of going up to your chamber, where the windows open toward Jerusalem, and saying your prayers there three times a day. And sometimes you pray pretty loudly, and people outside can hear you. Now, for the next thirty days, just shut your windows while you pray. These princes are sure to have some spies watching you at your prayers. You had better stop up the keyhole of your door, also, for these mean fellows are not above peeping in to watch you. It would be still better, Daniel, if you wouldn't kneel down at all, but say your prayers after you get into bed."

Ah! How many young people have gone to college, or to some strange place of business, and lost their peace of mind and their hope in Christ, because they were afraid to pray before their roommates!

And what does Daniel say to such advice as this? He scouts it; he tramples it under his feet. No man shall hinder him from praying. No king shall frighten him out of his duty. He attends to his morning's work. Looks over the accounts as usual. When twelve o'clock comes he goes to his chamber, puts the windows wide open, kneels down, and prays, not to Darius, but to the God of Abraham, Isaac, and Jacob.

His windows are opened toward Jerusalem, and his face is turned that way; for Jerusalem is dearer to him than his life, and the God of his fathers is his sure defense. I can seem to see him kneeling there—that old man with his white locks and beard, praying at the probable cost of his life; but he does not seem to be troubled by the danger. Neither is he angry at the command of the king or the manifest wickedness of those hundred and twenty princes. He prays for the king, his friend, who, he is sure, has done this wickedness in some thoughtless moment. He also prays for his enemies, the princes, who are wickedly seeking to destroy him.

Those evil men have taken care that two witnesses shall be underneath Daniel's windows at the time when he usually goes to pray. "Hark!" says one to the other, "Did you hear that? The old man is up there praying, sure enough! Listen: he is not praying to King Darius."

"No," says the other, "he is praying to the God of the Hebrews."

So they listen till the prayer is finished, and then they hurry away to the princes to give their evidence against Daniel; and the princes lose no time in laying the matter before the king. "O King Darius! Live forever. Is it not written that the laws of the Medes and Persians change not?"

"It is," said Darius. "Anything that is stamped with the king's seal cannot be changed."

"That is what we thought," said the princes. "Did you not make a decree that, for the next thirty days, no man should pray to any other god but the king?"

"Yes, I did," said Darius.

Then they tell him that the chief of the presidents—this Daniel the Hebrew—has refused to obey the king's command. Poor Darius! "What a mistake I have made!" says he. "I might have known that Daniel would never obey such a command as that. I know that Daniel worships the God of heaven. I had quite forgotten about him when I made it."

There is not a man in all Babylon who is as troubled as King Darius. The account says that "he labored till the going down of the sun to deliver Daniel." But the command had gone forth, the law had been made, and it could not be changed, even for the sake of Daniel himself.

If Darius had loved his friend as Christ loves us, he would have gone down into the den of lions for him. Our Darius, our King Jesus, counted not his life dear unto himself, but freely gave it up for us.

At sundown the king's officers take the old man away to the lions. They bind his hands behind him, and lead him along the streets of Babylon toward the den. The whole city goes out to see the sad procession. The princes rub their hands and laugh over the success of their wicked plot. The people look on in wonder, to see such a sweet-faced old man led away to die like a criminal. Poor Darius walks the chamber of his palace, wringing his hands in agony, saying, "Ah me! I have destroyed my friend."

Daniel Saved from the Lions

But Daniel walks with a firm step. His old knees don't shake a bit. The wind of the evening plays with his white locks, and with a smile upon his face he goes to face the lions. He has served his God for seventy years, and he feels sure that God will not desert him now. I can imagine him saying, "My God can bring me out of the jaws of the lions just as easily as he saved my three friends from the furnace of fire. But even if they eat me, I shall only die for my God."

And when they put him into the den, God sent one of his angels to shut the mouths of the lions. At the hour of the evening prayer Daniel kneels in the den; and, if he can get the points of the compass down there, he prays with his face toward Jerusalem. Then, taking one of the lions for his pillow, he lies down and sleeps as sweetly as any man in Babylon.

The king sits up all night, thinking what his folly has cost him—even the life of his most faithful servant. But he remembers that the God of Daniel has done strange things for those who trusted him. He has heard of Shadrach and his friends coming out of the fiery furnace. He knows that Daniel went into the den feeling that his God would go with him and save him. At the first dawn of day he orders out his chariot, and you can hear the wheels rattling over the pavements of Babylon before the people are up.

Away he goes, with his horses on the run, to the door of the lions' den, springs out of the chariot, looks down into the den, and, with a voice trembling with anxiety, cries out, "O Daniel, servant of the living God, is thy God, whom thou servest continually, able to deliver thee from the lions?"

Hark! There comes up a voice out of the den. It is the voice of Daniel to whom this morning is like the morning of the resurrection. He has been down to the gates of death, and yet he is alive. "O king, live forever! My

God hath sent his angel and hath shut the lions' mouths, that they have not hurt me."

How glad King Darius is to hear the voice of his friend once more! He has him brought up out of the den, takes him up in his arms, and into his chariot, and away they go, home to the palace to breakfast together, and to talk over this wonderful deliverance. Then King Darius publishes another decree. The experience of Daniel has thoroughly converted him; and now he ordains, that in every dominion of his kingdom "men tremble and fear before the God of Daniel; for he is the living God, who worketh signs and wonders in heaven and in earth," and "who hath delivered Daniel from the power of the lions."

Daniel Beloved by God

Three times a messenger comes from God to say to Daniel that he is greatly beloved (Dan. 9:23; 10:11, 19). I love to think of those precious words in Daniel 11:32, "But the people that do know their God shall be strong, and do exploits." There is another verse like it which says, "They that be wise shall shine as the brightness of the firmament; and they that turn many to righteousness as the stars for ever and ever" (Dan. 12:3).

Where are the great men who did not know Daniel's God? Did they shine long? Why, we know of Nebuchadnezzar and the rest of them scarcely a thing, except as they fill in the story about these humble men of God. We are not told that statesmen shall shine. They may, for a few days or years, but they are soon forgotten. Look at those great ones who passed away in the days of Daniel. How wise in council they were! How mighty and victorious over hundreds of nations! What gods upon earth they were! Yet their names are forgotten, written only in the grave.

Philosophers, falsely so-called—do they live? Behold men of science— scientific men they call themselves—going down into the bowels of the earth, digging away at some carcass and trying to make it talk against the voice of God! They shall go down to death, by and by, and their names shall rot.

But the man of God shines. Yes, he it is who shall shine as the stars for ever and ever. This Daniel has been gone for two thousand five hundred years, but still increasing millions read of his life and actions. And so it shall be to the end. He will only be better known and better loved. He shall ever shine the brighter as the world grows older. Of a truth, they that be wise and turn many to righteousness shall shine on, like stars, to eternity.

May the God of Daniel be with us, the courage of Daniel be in us. May we have grace to confess the Lord, to go through the fire, or among the lions, if need be, for the sake of his truth; and when the Savior comes, in the day that he makes up his jewels, may the Lord give each of us a place with Daniel and the shining ones.

Demoniac of Gedara

Mark 5:1–20

The demoniac was that wild man who lived among the tombs. He was the terror of all the women and children for ten miles round, and a good many of the men besides. They had tried to bind him even with chains, but he tore off the bands as Samson did the green withes and new ropes. He was absolutely full of devils; but when Christ comes to him he has only to speak the word and the legion of devils is cast out.

The cure of this maniac made a great excitement all over that country, not so much because the poor man was freed from satanic influence and made sane, as because of the loss of that great herd of swine that the devils got into and drowned.

It seems to me that is just the case with a great many people in Chicago—they are more interested in swine than in salvation. You let the price of pork go up tomorrow, and there would be a much greater excitement over it than there is over all the sinners who are getting converted at the Tabernacle.

After the man is cured he wants to follow Christ—wants to be with him—is ready to follow him to the end of the earth; but Christ sends him home.

I can imagine the children see him coming, and they run to tell their mother, "Oh, mother, mother, father is coming!"

"Is he? Run and fasten all the doors and windows! Quickly!"

They are all afraid of him. When he has been there before he has acted like a madman—broken the chairs, tipped over the tables, dashed the furniture about, driven his wife out of doors, and nearly frightened the children to death. Now they fasten him out, and the children hide behind their mother's dress and listen.

Hark! He knocks at the door; but they dare not let him in. He tries the door and finds it fastened. Then he calls, "Mary! Mary!"

"Why," says his wife, "that sounds as his voice used to when I first married him! What can have happened to him?" Then she goes to the door, and says softly, "James, is that you?"

"Yes, Mary, I have come home; you needn't be afraid of me any more. I am in my right mind now."

The woman opens the door just a little, looks into his eyes, and sees that he is gentle and kind. Then she throws it wide open, and springs into his arms, weeping for joy, and saying, "O James! James! What has happened to you?"

"Jesus of Nazareth cast all the devils out of me, and then sent me home to you all safe and well," answers the man.

"Who is this Jesus that you say has cured you?" asks his wife.

"Jesus—did you never hear of him? He is the great Galilean prophet. The people think he is the Christ. He goes all about healing sick folks and casting out devils from people just like me. Only the other day he opened the eyes of a man who was born blind. You must go and see him, Mary, and take the children, and hear the wonderful words he speaks. Maybe he would take up Johnny and Sarah in his arms and bless them, as he did some other little children."

I see them talking together of the great joy that has come to them through this Jesus of Nazareth, and I am sure they love him very much in that household for what he has done for them. Pretty soon the children begin to get confidence in their father, and one after another they steal up to him and climb up into his arms. And now all that brokenhearted family is united once more. He kisses them all, hugs them, and tells them how glad he is to get back to them.

Then after a little they run out to see their playmates, shouting, "Papa is come! Papa is come! And he is good and gentle like your papa. Jesus did it! Jesus did it!"

Ah, my friends, Jesus is the great deliverer. I like to think of him as a physician who can cure everything. He never lost a patient, and that is more than the most skilled doctors in Chicago can say.

16 Elder Brother

Luke 15:25–32

I have selected a very difficult subject to get people interested in. I am afraid you may get the chills before I am through, for I think it is one of the coldest subjects you can find in the whole Bible. It is about that elder brother of the prodigal son.

When I was in Europe once, Mr. Spurgeon gave me a copy of his sermons, and out of the whole volume, between thirty and forty, I couldn't find one sermon he had ever preached about that elder brother. I have tried a number of times to get interested, but I must confess that it is hard to get my heart warmed up toward it.

A Negative Attitude

This elder brother thought he was all right. I heard of a man when I was across the sea who thought so much of himself that he used to shake hands with himself every morning. He was an elder brother. Now, if you ever had to live in a house with a man that never did wrong, I pity you. If you wives have a husband that never does wrong, I pity you. Do you know why? Because if anything goes wrong it is you that has to suffer; he doesn't. All the blame falls upon you. He is an elder brother.

There has been a hot discussion for ages about who those ninety-nine are that we read about in this fifteenth chapter of Luke (v. 7). Some think they are the angels that have never fallen. Some think they are a sort of angelic people and don't need to be converted; they are so pure and upright naturally. I believe they are the people who think they are all right. You will notice that the chapter begins with a murmur and closes in the same way. They were finding fault with Christ because he was receiving sinners and saving the lost.

Now, this elder brother was angry because the wanderer had come home. A lady came to me some years ago and wanted me to get her daughter into a seminary with which I was connected. But she said, "I want to be frank with you. I want you to know that I do not believe in your theology."

"My theology! I didn't know I had any. I wish you would tell me what my theology is."

"Well," she said, "I don't agree with your preaching."

"What is it you don't agree with?"

"Well," she said, "your views about that elder brother are the most abominable I ever heard of."

I said, "You are the first person I ever heard try to uphold him. What are his good traits? What are his noble qualities?"

"He stayed at home with his father and took care of him, and his younger brother ran off and left him."

"Took care of his father! The last I read about him he was outside of the house in a mad fit and his father couldn't get him in."

Oh, yes, he took care of his father! These elder brothers are the hardest people in the world to get in, because they think they are already there. It is said that in Berlin one day a German minister had this question up for discussion—who the ninety-nine were and who the elder brother was. He was a great preacher and he got up in a meeting and said he had seen the elder brother the day before.

"Saw him! Where did you see him? Saw the elder brother!"

"Yes, when I looked into my mirror I saw him. I saw myself." He found himself envious of another minister, and he was an elder brother.

I tell you what, there are a good many more elder brothers than prodigals, after all. There are a lot of us pretty near kin to that elder brother. Men go to church regularly, but I tell you a man that gets angry because the usher puts a man into his pew who isn't dressed in the height of fashion, I believe, belongs to this school. If you want to find out where they are, just tell them of a poor drunkard that has been reclaimed, and see their eyes open and hear them say, "I don't believe in that kind of thing."

Measured against the Beatitudes

You follow this elder brother down through all the beatitudes, and you will find that he fails in every one of them. Now just hear what Christ says: "Blessed are the poor in spirit" (Matt. 5:3). He poor in spirit? Not he! The Lord says, "Blessed are the poor in spirit." A man may be rich and have a broken heart, but there is a blessing upon him if he has. "Blessed are they that mourn" (Matt. 5:4). Did this man mourn? For what? He had nothing to mourn over; he had never done a wrong thing in all his life.

"Blessed are the meek" (Matt. 5:5). Was he meek? There was not a single trace of meekness about him. That Pharisee that went up to the temple to pray with the poor publican, did he know anything about meekness? "I thank thee, Lord, that I am not as other men. . . . I fast twice in the week, I give tithes of all that I possess" (Luke 18:11–12). I . . . I . . . I— five great capital I's in a little prayer of only a few words. That was not a prayer. He was just boasting and bragging. That is just what this elder brother of the prodigal was doing.

"Blessed are they which do hunger and thirst after righteousness" (Matt. 5:6). He hunger and thirst after righteousness? He had so much he didn't know what to do with it. "Blessed are the merciful" (Matt. 5:7). He merciful? He was very merciful to his old father, wasn't he? He was kind to his old father, wasn't he? Oh! I pity a father who has to be taken care of by such a son as that, sticking thorns into his old father's heart in the evening of life.

"Blessed are the pure in heart" (Matt. 5:8). Was he pure in heart? "Blessed are the peacemakers" (Matt. 5:9). Was he a peacemaker? Breaking up the most peaceful scene this world ever saw! That old father sitting at the table with a peace and joy that had never before come to him, and that elder brother just broke it up. I see that father's face just beaming with joy and delight when the servants whisper that Levi is outside mad and will not come in. And I see the old man get up, all the joy gone from his face, and go out and entreat his son to come in. But he is in a mad fit and the old man can't get him into the house. I tell you I think he had a mighty mean son. Don't you? That is my opinion.

"Blessed are they which are persecuted" (Matt. 5:10). And that is the kind of religion that this world believes in. The whole country talked about the nobility of this young man. I am afraid that if we had him now we would make him a deacon or elder in the church. He is all right. All right in the sight of the world. He is never persecuted.

But now, read about that man's life, and what do you find? You find that he was sour. Oh, how many sour ones you meet now! They growl and grumble all the time. Sour! He was a touchy young man. Have you any touchy people among your acquaintances? That is just what this young man was—touchy. He was very angry. Why? Because his brother had come back.

Rejoicing in Heaven

Did you ever know what caused the thrill of joy in heaven and the thumps in that old man's breast? I believe that Luke 15 is the only chapter in the whole Bible that tells what causes joy in heaven. That elder brother was self-righteous. He was selfish, and supremely so. There is not a thing in that man's character that is lovely after all. But how grandly that father shines out.

"Son!" (He didn't call him any bad names.) "Son, thou art ever with me, and all that I have is thine" (Luke 15:31). Oh, it makes me feel rich when I read that. That is liberty. You know in France, when anarchy was overthrown, they selected for their motto, "Fraternity, Equality, Liberty." That was what they wanted, and that is just what this father wanted with those two boys. He wanted them to be with him. That is what God wants every sinner to do.

I remember once I was very busy getting up a sermon, and my little boy came into my room. I wanted to get rid of him just as quickly as possible. And I said to him, "My son, what do you want?" He threw his arms around my neck and kissed me and said, "I don't want anything, I just love you." I couldn't send him away, and I got down all his toys for him and let him stay in the room with me; and every once in a while I looked over my book and saw him just as happy as he could be.

That is just what the Lord wants, he wants the elder brother to come in and just have liberty and fraternity. "Son, all I have is thine." And that is just what the younger brother did not want when he went away. But he came back and wanted it, and when he wanted it, the elder brother didn't want it. Now, one went down through the sin of his licentiousness, and the other went down through the sin of pride and self-conceit, and one is just as black and vile as the other. There is no difference. I tell you what! It is a good thing to take a mirror and get a good look at ourselves once in a while and see what we are, for it is a sort of family disease.

But I am not going to dwell any longer upon that elder brother, for I must confess it is not a very interesting subject. But I just want to say that I have had that man brought up to me very often in the most ridiculous ways. Some say that certain people don't need to be converted. "That kind of preaching that Mr. Moody is doing here is out of place. If he would go among the slums of our large cities and preach it to those lost souls, it would be all right. But we don't need it. We are cultured and refined and we do not need any such preaching." They think they are all right. "We are piling up a righteousness of our own."

I want to say that elder brother needed to be converted just as much as the younger. You put a man that has been living in wickedness and sin on the crystal pavement, and it would be hell to him. Put a man under the very shadow of the tree of life with the spirit of the elder brother, and it would be hell to him. I can imagine that the first man he sees he greets with the question, "Who were you when you were on earth?"

"The thief on the cross."

"I never associated with thieves or murderers when I was upon earth, and I shall not up here."

And to the first woman he meets he says, "Who were you when on earth?"

And with a beautiful smile on her face, she replies, "I was Mary Magdalene."

"That woman that had seven devils in her? I never associated with such people on earth, and I won't up here." He couldn't associate with the blood-bought up in heaven. He couldn't sing the song of Moses and the Lamb with such people. He must have a little heaven of his own. He climbed up some other way. The Lord said they are "thieves and robbers" (John 10:8).

I think once in a while it would be good to preach to the elder brothers, and I think there are a great many of them in the churches. They think because they live a so called moral life they are all right. They can be proud and as vile and black as hell itself, not fit for the kingdom of God.

Now did you ever notice that four times Christ uses this word "except." "Except your righteousness shall exceed the righteousness of the scribes and Pharisees, ye shall in no case enter the kingdom of heaven" (Matt. 5:20). That was said to the elder brother school of men when Christ was on earth. Then again he said to the same class of people, "Except ye repent, ye shall all likewise perish" (Luke 13:3, 5). Another time he said to that same class, "Except ye become converted, and become as little children ye shall not enter the kingdom of heaven" (Matt. 18:3).

Don't you trust in your moral life—that is not going to save you. God will strip you of every rag of your own righteousness. You must have the righteousness of another. It was to Nicodemus, not to the poor woman at the well, that Christ said, "Except ye become converted and become as little children ye cannot see the kingdom of God."

Now it is clearly taught that there must be a new spirit and new life before we can see the kingdom of God. You can see a great many things, but there is one thing you cannot see, you cannot see the kingdom of God, you cannot buy or educate yourself into the kingdom. There is only one way and that is to be born into it.

You may go across this continent to the Pacific coast and see there trees that have been growing for ages, but that tree that grows in the midst of the paradise of God your uncircumcised eye shall never rest upon unless you are born again. You may see the Prince of Wales and the crown prince of Russia, but I tell you the Prince of Peace who is going to sit in glory you shall never see as your Prince unless you are born again. You may see the rivers of earth, but there is one river that flows through the paradise of God that your uncircumcised eye shall not see until you are born again.

You may look that sainted mother in the face today, but bear in mind that the time is coming when you are going to be separated. You may look at your little innocent child, but remember that a separation is going to come. If that child dies in early childhood, the Master will take it to himself, and you will not be permitted to sit in the kingdom with that child until you are born again.

"Joy shall be in heaven over one sinner that repenteth" (Luke 15:7). There must be true repentance before we can be born again. Now I can imagine some of you say, "I have known that for years, but I wish I could be converted this afternoon." A lady told me once that a long time ago she had made up her mind to be converted, and that she believed that if she was converted she could overcome the temptation that had crossed her path.

You can be converted before I get through speaking. "Look unto me, and be ye saved, all the ends of the earth: for I am God, and there is none else" (Isa. 45:22). I thank God that Christ has been offered as a sacrifice for the sins of the world, and every soul can be saved now if he will. Christ will save you even if you are that elder brother!

Elijah

1 Kings 18

"Did you ever see such a sight?" asked a gentleman on the platform of the great Chicago Tabernacle, pointing to the crowd of young men which entirely filled the first floor. A severe snowstorm was raging, but this did not prevent the attendance of an immense congregation of young men to whom Mr. Moody had announced a special sermon. There were many ladies in the galleries, and on the platform a large number of the leading businessmen of Chicago with their families. Whenever Mr. Moody announces a sermon to young men it is well understood that he is to speak to a class of people with whose needs he is intimately acquainted, hence the desire on the part of all classes to hear the good advice he gives them.

Unlike many who preach to the young, Mr. Moody does not forget the time when he was a young man himself. It is partly on this account, and partly on account of the manly Christian wisdom which has accumulated in him, that the young men respond by the thousands to his invitation to come and hear what he has to say.

On this occasion he chose for his text these words from 1 Kings 18:21: "And Elijah came unto all the people, and said, How long halt ye between two opinions? If the LORD be God, follow him: but if Baal, then follow him."

Alexander the Great was once asked how he had been able to conquer the world. "By not delaying," was his reply.

Now, here is a matter which I want you all to decide without delay, "If the LORD be God, follow him" (1 Kings 18:21). A man that is undecided cannot have any peace. He may intend some day to settle the question of his duty to God, and to make his arrangements to reach heaven at last, but Satan is all the while tempting him to put it off. There is nothing that Satan hates in a man worse than prompt decision.

Avoid Lukewarmness

What was it that made Moses so great? It was that he decided for God. What was it that made Daniel not only a prince in Babylon, but a prince of God's people for all time? It was because he purposed in his heart to serve his God. What made the poor prodigal son so happy? It was his decision to arise and go to his father.

Oh, how many a man is lost for want of decision! How was it with Agrippa? He hesitated, almost persuaded to be a Christian. Look at Pilate—lost for want of moral courage and decision. Thousands upon thousands of men and women have gone down to the same ruin for want of prompt decision in matters of duty to God.

Now, young man, if there is anything in this religion there is everything in it. If it is false let us find it out, and the sooner the better. If Christianity is a myth, let us denounce it. If it is a divine revelation, let us accept it. If the Bible is not true, let us burn it. What is the use of publishing so many millions of copies and sending them out over the wide world? If Christianity is a sham, then let us build its tomb and shout over it, "There is no heaven, there is no hell! Man dies like the dog!" But if the Bible is true, let us take our stand upon it; if Christ is the Son of God, let us believe on him.

If bad men had written this Bible they wouldn't have said so much about God; and if good men wrote it without any help from God they wouldn't have ventured to tell a lie and to claim that God inspired them. So, then, the question comes to you which Elijah put to those men on Mount Carmel, "If the LORD be God, follow him: but if Baal, then follow him" (1 Kings 18:21).

Elijah's Challenge: God vs. Baal

Now let us look at the surroundings of this case. King Ahab had forsaken the God of Israel, and all the court people and "upper ten" had followed his example. But there was an old prophet out in the mountains to whom God said, "Go to Ahab, and tell him the heavens shall be shut up, and there shall be no rain."

Away he goes to the wicked king, bursts in upon him like a clap of thunder, gives his message, and hurries away.

I suppose Ahab laughed at the old prophet. "What! No more rain? Why, the fellow must be crazy!"

Pretty soon the weather gets very dry. The earth is parched and begins to crack open. The rivers have but little water in them, and the brooks dry up altogether. The trees die; all the grass perishes, and the cattle die too. Famine, starvation, death! If rain doesn't come pretty soon there won't be a live man or woman left in all the kingdom.

One day the king is talking with the prophet Obadiah. You see he did have one good man near him, along with all the prophets of the false gods. Almost everyone likes to have some good man within reach, even if he is ever so bad himself. He may be wanted in a hurry sometime.

"See here, Obadiah," says King Ahab. "You go one way and I'll go another, and we'll see if we can't find some water somewhere."

So Obadiah started off to find water, but he hadn't gotten a great way before Elijah bursts out upon him.

"O Elijah! Is that you? Ahab has been hunting for you everywhere, and couldn't find you. He has sent off into all the kingdoms to have them fetch you, if you were there."

"Yes, I'm here," says Elijah. "You go and tell Ahab I want to see him."

"I dare not do that," says Obadiah. "For just as soon as I tell him you are here the spirit will catch you away and take you off somewhere else; and then the king will be very angry, and maybe he'll kill me."

"No," says Elijah. "As the Lord liveth, I will meet Ahab face to face this day."

So Obadiah hurries off to find Ahab, and tells him he has seen the prophet.

"What! Elijah?"

"Yes."

"Why didn't you bring him along?"

"He wouldn't come. He says you must come to him."

Ahab isn't used to having people talk that way to him; but he is anxious to see the prophet, so he goes.

When he sees him he is very angry, and cries, "Art thou he that troubleth Israel?"

"Not at all," says Elijah. "You are the man that is troubling Israel—going off after Baal, and leading ever so many of the people with you. Now, we have had enough of this sort of thing. Some are praying to Jehovah, and some are praying to Baal, and we must have this question settled. You just bring all your prophets and all the priests of Baal up to Mount Carmel, and I also will come. We will make us each an altar, and offer sacrifice on it; and the God that answereth by fire, let him be God."

"Agreed," says Ahab, and off he goes to tell his priests to get ready for the trial.

The Stage Is Set

I fancy that was a great day when that question was to be decided. All the places of business were closed, and everybody started for Mount Carmel. There must have been more people on Mount Carmel than there are today at the races. They were a better class of people too. There were eight hundred and fifty of the prophets and priests of Baal altogether. I fancy I can see them going up in a grand procession, with the king in his chariot at their head.

"Fine-looking men, ain't they?" says one man to another as they go by. "They'll be able to do great things up there on the mountain."

But there Elijah marches, all alone, a rough man, clad in the skins of beasts, with a staff in his hand. No banners, no procession, no great men in his train! But the man who could hold the keys of heaven for three years and six months isn't afraid to be alone.

Then says Elijah to the people, "How long halt ye between two opinions? Let the priests of Baal build them an altar and offer sacrifice, but put no fire tinder and I will do the same: and the God that answereth by fire let him be God."

Baal Doesn't Answer

So the priests of Baal built their altar, and offered their sacrifice. I am sure if God hadn't held him back, Satan would have brought up a little spark out of hell to set that sacrifice on fire. But God wouldn't let him. Then the priests begin to pray, "O Baal, hear us! O Baal, hear us!"

Elijah might have said, "Why haven't you prayed to Baal for water this dry weather? You might just as well ask him for water as for fire." After a long time they begin to get hoarse.

"You must pray louder than that if you expect Baal to hear you," says the old prophet. "Maybe he is asleep. Pray louder, so as to wake him up."

Poor fellows! They haven't any voice left, so they begin to pray in blood. They cut themselves with knives and lift their streaming hands and arms to Baal. But no fire comes down.

Elijah Calls Fire from God

It is getting toward sundown. The prophet of the Lord builds an altar. Mind, he doesn't have anything to do with the altar of Baal but builds an entirely different one, on the ruins of the altar of Jehovah which had been broken down. "We won't have anybody saying there is any trick about this thing," says the prophet.

So they bring twelve barrels of water and pour them over the altar. I don't know how they managed to get so much water, but they did it. Perhaps God provided a spring of water for the occasion.

Then Elijah prays, "Lord God of Abraham, Isaac, and of Israel, let it be known this day that thou art God in Israel" (1 Kings 18:36).

God Is Victorious

He didn't have to pray very long. God heard him at once, and down came the fire! It burnt up the sacrifice, burnt up the wood, licked up the water, and burnt up the very stones of the altar.

Nobody could halt any longer. The people cried, "The Lord, he is the God; the Lord, he is the God" (1 Kings 18:39).

Ah, but some of you say, "I too would have decided for God if I had been on Mount Carmel that day."

Oh, young man, I'll take you to another mountain, Mount Calvary. It is more wonderful than Carmel. The story of the cross is the great wonder of the world.

A man once tried to sell me a book of wonders. I looked it over, and then asked him if it had anything about the cross of Calvary in it. He said, "No."

"What," said I, "a book of wonders, and the greatest of all wonders left out!" There the sun refused to shine, the rocks were rent, the earth shook, the graves were opened, and the dead came forth. How wonderful!

So now there are wonders here. The Son of God stoops down and gives these inquirers victory; drunkards are converted, and publicans and harlots are coming into the kingdom of God.

Now hundreds and thousands are convinced, but they are holding on to some darling sin. A man could not decide to give his heart to Christ the other day because he had a bet. Now, suppose that man dies, what will become of his soul? Oh, why not come out now? Why not come out tonight? Just ask yourselves, "What stands in the way?"

"Oh," you say, "I can't stand those jeers." But can't you set your face like a flint against Satan and decide tonight? You can't find a man who has decided for Christ who ever regretted it. I have stood at the bedside of many who were dying, and I never saw one that regretted that he had decided for Christ.

Decide now. Now is the accepted time. The last night I preached in the church in Chicago I made the greatest mistake of my life. I told the people to take this text home with them and pray over it. But as we went out the firebells were ringing, and I never saw that audience again. The Chicago fire had come. The city was in ashes and some of those very people that I had not challenged to decide were burned up in it. There is no other time to be saved but now.

Elisha and the Widow

18

2 Kings 4:1-7

A man said to me, "Moody, have you got grace to go to the stake as a martyr?"

"No, what do I want to go to the stake for?"

A person said to me, "Moody, if God should take your son, have you grace to bear it?"

I said, "What do I want that grace for? I don't want grace to bear that which has not been sent. If God should call upon me to part with my boy, he would give me strength to bear it." What we want is grace for the present, to bear the trials and temptations for every day. "In the day when I cried thou answeredst me, and strengthened me with strength in my soul" (Ps. 138:3).

A widow went to Elisha with a story that would move the heart of Elisha or anyone else. Her husband had died bankrupt, and the creditors were preparing to sell her boys into slavery. She came to Elisha and told her story. He asked her what she owned with which to make payment. She replied, "One pot of oil."

Elisha told her to go home, borrow vessels, take oil, and pour into the empty vessels.

Men in these times wouldn't believe in this. They would say, "What, take a pot of oil and pour into all these vessels? What good will that do?"

Not so with this poor widow. She has faith and does as she is told. She goes to her neighbors and asks for vessels they can lend her. She takes all they have and goes on. She clears out the next house, and the next, and the next. Borrow, says the prophet, and she goes on until her house is filled with vessels. "Now, close the doors," she says to her sons.

And she pours oil into the first vessel and fills it full, and the next, and the next, and the next, in the same way. She pours it in and pours it in, and the boys run and get more vessels until the house is full of oil. Then she goes to Elisha, and asks what she shall do. He tells her, "Go sell the oil and pay the debt."

Now, Christ pays the debt and gives us enough to live on besides. He doesn't merely pay our debt, he gives us enough to live on. He gives according to our need. As thy days so shall thy strength be.

Rowland Hill used to tell a good story of a rich man and a poor man in his congregation. The rich man desired to do an act of benevolence, and so he sent a sum of money to a friend to be given to this poor man as he thought best. The friend just sent him five pounds, and said in the note, "This is yours. Use it wisely. There is more to follow." After a while he sent another five pounds, and said, "More to follow." Again and again he sent the money to the poor man, always with the cheering words, "More to follow." So it is with the wonderful grace of God. There is always "more to follow."

19 **Gideon**

Judges 6–7

I believe this man Gideon was called an enthusiast in the camp of Israel. The very idea of his going out to meet a hundred and thirty-five thousand men with three hundred men bearing pitchers and torches! How many people would have said, "The man has gone clean mad." Yes, he was an enthusiast, but the Lord was with him.

If we lean upon ourselves we will have failure, but if we lean upon the arm of God we will see how swiftly God will give us victory. God wants the glory, and no flesh shall glory in his stead.

Gideon had called in an army of thirty-two thousand men. The Lord said to him, "You have too many men. If I give you victory, Israel will vaunt themselves against me, saying: 'My own hand hath saved me.' You cannot work with so many, because I must have the glory. Just say to all that are fearful: 'Depart if you want to.'"

So Gideon proclaimed, in accordance with God's command, "Whosoever is fearful and afraid, let him return and depart early from Mount Gilled. And there returned of the people twenty and two thousand, and there remained ten thousand" (Judg. 7:3).

I can imagine that Gideon became a little frightened at first. Only ten thousand left! But the Lord came again, and said, "Gideon, you have got too many men. If I work with them, you will take the glory." So he brought down the people unto the water, and the Lord said unto Gideon, "Every one that lappeth of the water with his tongue, as a dog lappeth, him shalt thou set by himself; likewise every one that boweth down upon his knees to drink" (Judg. 7:5).

Three hundred lapped and ninety-seven hundred wheeled out of line. I can imagine they were like many Christians. What can God do with those who are like those of Gideon's army who were full of fears and doubts? Look at the reduction in that great army. But three hundred men with the Almighty! Three hundred men on that side with God can be a power for God. Three hundred like Gideon's men will move any city. What a routing there was before that band! They fly like chaff before the wind. Do not call anything of God small.

20 **Good Samaritan**

Luke 10:25–37

The following sketch of the good Samaritan is taken from Mr. Moody's sermon on the text, "Who is my neighbor?" It forms a part of his list of what may be called preparatory discourses—sermons with which he opened his revival campaigns. Their purpose is to awaken the church to a sense of its privilege and duty, and to prepare Christian workers for the service of the inquiry room. Christian helpfulness and sympathy were themes very precious to Mr. Moody, because so large a portion of his own life and labor had been in that direction.

Who Is My Neighbor?

We are taught in this chapter (Luke 10) that a lawyer once stood up and asked the Lord what he should do to inherit eternal life. Christ answered his question by asking him another, "What is written in the law?" He answered and said, "Thou shalt love the Lord thy God with all thy heart, and with all thy soul, and with all thy strength, and with all thy mind; and thy neighbor as thyself."

It would seem that the lawyer wasn't very well satisfied with the Lord's answer, so he asked another question, "Who is my neighbor?" Then Christ tells him this little story of a man who went down from Jerusalem to Jericho and fell among thieves.

Who our neighbor is, is something we have to find out before we can accomplish much for Christ. The church has been nearly nineteen hundred years finding out the answer to that question, and very few have found out yet who is their neighbor.

Jerusalem was called the city of peace, God's city. Jericho stood not far from ancient Jericho, the city that Joshua cursed. It was about twenty miles from Jerusalem, and all the way downhill.

This man started from Jerusalem to go down to Jericho, and on his way down he fell among thieves. A great many have traveled from Jerusalem to Jericho. I think there are some in this audience that will understand what I mean when I say that this poor fellow fell among thieves. I don't think Jericho is a great ways from here. I think you will find a good many that have been stripped and wounded, and then left for dead right here in the streets of Boston.

Not less than eight or ten Christians have been to me today and wanted me to set them to work. I looked at them in perfect amazement. People that have been living in Boston for ten or fifteen years want me, a stranger, to set them to work! Why, you will find enough to do without my telling you if you just keep your eyes open. There are a great many men that are waiting for someone to come and help them up. Satan has tripped them. They have fallen among thieves, and they are not only half dead, but many of them are altogether dead in trespasses and sins.

The Priest That Passed By

Now, the cases of these three men that Christ mentions here are cited for our profit, so let us take a look at them. The first man was a priest. He belonged to the temple up there in Jerusalem. He was on his way down to Jericho, perhaps on some very important business. Maybe they were going to dedicate a new synagogue, and he was on his way down to open the service.

When he gets about ten miles from Jerusalem, as he is passing along thinking about his sermon, he hears somebody groan. He is in a great hurry, but he turns and looks to see who it is. It was a Jew, not a Samaritan; and I don't doubt but he feels very sorry for him. No doubt he said to himself, "Why, that man is a Jew! He belongs to the seed of Abraham. If I remember aright, I saw him in the synagogue last Sabbath. I pity him; but I have too much business, and I cannot attend to him. Poor fellow; it was a pity he took this way. He ought to have gone some other way down to Jericho." Or, "He ought not to have been out late at night. Perhaps he's been drinking too much."

"Poor fellow, I pity him!" thought the man, and then passed along down to Jericho. If he did pity him, he didn't have compassion enough to give him even one kind word. He might have just given him something to rest his dying head upon, or brought him just one drop of water. In that hot country no doubt the man was crying for water. Perhaps that was the first cry that fell upon his ears, "Water! Water!" For that is usually the first cry of a wounded man; but he was too busy. He couldn't stop even to give him a drop of water. He must attend to his professional duties: so on he went.

The Levite Who Passed By

The next man who came along was a Levite. He was a deacon, and he did more than the priest, for he did stoop to look at the poor fellow. He gave him a good look, saw he was a Jew, saw he couldn't help himself, saw he was wounded, and heard his groans. But his business was also very important, and very pressing. Perhaps he was going down to Jericho to help the priest. Or, maybe, he was going the other way, up to Jerusalem, to attend to some very important duties at the temple. The wounded man might have been his next-door neighbor. He may have said, "I saw him in the temple last Sunday. He has always done all he could to keep up the temple service. I wish I had time to help him; but I have not. My business is pressing. If I see a policeman on the way I will send him back to look after him; and I think when I get to Jerusalem we will start some society to look after this sort of unfortunates."

There are a great many of that group of people now. They are willing, if they have a great deal of money, to give a few dollars, but how few are ready to take off their coats and go right into the vineyard and go to work themselves!

He follows in the footsteps of the priest. Perhaps for some ways on he can hear the groans of the dying man, and then he begins to reason with himself what he shall say to that man's wife. If he should see her at the temple on Sabbath she might ask him if he had seen her husband. And those two boys of his. "I know Johnny and Jimmy. They have been watching and waiting for their father to come home, and what will they say if I tell them I met him on the way down to Jericho, wounded and dying."

But he goes on. I don't know how he eased his conscience, but on he went. Perhaps he hadn't gone but a short distance before he met the Samaritan. He wouldn't speak to that Samaritan; he wouldn't bow to him; he wouldn't look at him; he wouldn't even allow his dog to follow him. He would be cast out of the synagogue if he did.

The Good Samaritan Knows His Neighbor

Now look at that Samaritan. He has got a good face; he is a benevolent-looking man. I can see him coming along, perhaps whistling, or singing, for men who like to do good deeds are generally cheerful. I will guarantee there were not many wrinkles on his brow, even if the Jew did despise him.

All at once he hears the groans of this poor, wounded man. He reins up his horse and stops to listen. He says, "Yes, I hear the groans of a man; that is a human voice." He dismounts and seeks the man till he finds him; for we are told he came to where he was. We are told the priest and Levite came upon him by chance; but the good Samaritan came on purpose; he represents your Master and mine. The Son of God didn't come into this world by chance; God sent him into this world. He came where we sinners were.

Some people tell us—I heard someone say not long ago—that if a man was willing to meet God halfway God would meet him there, and he would be blessed. Suppose that this is true, how was this poor, wounded, dying man going to be saved?

Supposing that the good Samaritan had ridden up on his horse and said, "Now come, my good friend, jump up here and I will take you to an inn. Come, give me your hand, and I will help you." That wouldn't have helped him any.

"He came to where he was." Christ comes to where the sinner is. The first thing this good Samaritan did wasn't to scold him, not to condemn him for coming that way. He didn't begin to appeal to his prejudice and say, "Here, you are a Jew; you are a man who hates us Samaritans. I have a chance now to heap coals of fire on your head, and I will do it." He didn't go at him that way. He never said anything about that old quarrel between the Jews and the Samaritans.

He first poured oil into his wounds. That is what the gospel does. Then he gave him water, and then a little wine, emblem of joy, to revive him, and I can imagine he tears off one of the sleeves of his garment to bind up a wound; and then, after he has made him comfortable, he takes him up in his own strong arms and puts him on his own beast. That is our gospel; that is what Christ does. He takes him to an inn, leaves some money, and says if the charge is more he will pay it.

Then Christ puts the question to the lawyer, "Which one is neighbor to the man that fell among the thieves?"

The man was convicted right there. He had his eyes opened, and he had to tell the truth, and reply, "He that showed mercy."

Now, my friends, have we got the spirit of the good Samaritan? Are we ready to go out and lift those men out of the gutter? Have we found out who our neighbor is? I don't know but I overdraw the picture when I say this seems to be a good deal like the spirit of the present day. Suppose a Methodist had been down there trying to get that poor fellow onto his beast, and wasn't quite strong enough to lift him up, and a Presbyterian had come along, and the Methodist says, "Help me get him on the beast."

"What are you going to do with him? What church is he going to join?" asks the Presbyterian.

"I haven't thought of that," says the Methodist. "I am going to save him first."

"I won't do it. I won't help him till I know what church he is going to join."

An Episcopal brother comes along and wants to know if he has been confirmed.

"We haven't time to talk about that," says this Methodist good Samaritan, "let us save him."

"What inn are you going to take him to?" asks another. "A Congregationalist, Methodist, Baptist, or Episcopal inn?"

Isn't that the spirit of our age? Haven't we a good deal of that spirit in the church—not ready to help a poor man out of the gutter, because we are not sure he will join our sect? Oh, that God would lift us above that party feeling! It won't take us long to find out who our neighbor is if we read the gospel aright. We shall find that these men who feel bitter against us and talk against us are our neighbors; and let us go and try to do them good.

Satan has deceived them, sin has blinded them, and they don't know the gospel of Jesus Christ. They don't know the love of God, and if we don't tell them who will? Now, my friends, should we not ask God from the very depths of our hearts to show us who our neighbor is, and then go and try to bring him to God, that he may walk in newness of life?

Live a Life of Sympathy

I am coming to the conclusion, the longer I live, that what this poor perishing world wants is Christians who have sympathy for their fellow men. Men want compassion more than sermons. As I said the other night, there have been sermons enough preached to convert them. But it is not some fine written essay, it is not some oratorical effort, that is going to save these men. We want to get out of the pulpit and off these high platforms, and go down among them, and show them we love them, and speak to them a kind word here and there; show them some act of kindness, and convince them that we have a love for their souls.

What we want is a gospel of acts, and not a gospel of resolves and creeds and dogmas. We have had too many of them. We want people who are going to carry out the principles that Christ taught, hunting out the fallen and degraded, and trying to lift them up in the name of our Master. But if we haven't sympathy with them we can't do it. A sermon may be keen, it may be very logical, it may be full of real intellectual power, it may be as sharp and beautiful as an icicle, and just as cold, and if it is, it never will reach the hearts of the people. What we have got to have in our own hearts is sympathy with the Master, and with the people that we want to reach. If we have it, it won't be long before they find it out. You can't reach a man if you have no sympathy with him.

When I was a boy and left home for the first time, and went thirteen miles away—I often think that I never was so far away from home since—I was very lonesome. I had gone into a neighboring town to spend the winter and to do chores, as we call it in New England, for my board. My older brother had gone to that same town a year before, and as we were walking down the street I was crying, and my brother was trying to cheer me up. Presently we saw an old man coming down the street, and my brother said, "There, there, that man will give you a cent."

"How do you know he will?"

"He gives every new boy that comes to town a cent. He gave me one when I came."

I looked at him and thought he was the best looking man I ever saw. He had long white hair, and he looked so good as he came along. But I thought he was going by me without saying a word. I think it would have broken my heart if he had, for my brother had raised my hopes so high. When he got right opposite he said, "You are a new boy in town, aren't you?"

My brother was afraid I would lose the cent, so he straightened up, and said, "Yes, came here today."

The old man knew my brother and I were fatherless, and so he took my hat off and put his trembling hand on my head, and said I had a Father in heaven who would care for me. And then he gave me a brand new cent.

I don't know what has become of the cent, but I can feel the pressure of the old man's hand on my head tonight. It has followed me all through life. Those kind words didn't cost him much, but they have been a life-long blessing to me. Let us go to those who are fallen, those that have been taken captive by Satan, those that have fallen among thieves and have been stripped and wounded, and let us tell them that the Son of God will have compassion on them, and that he will save them if they will only trust him.

May the God of heaven give us the spirit of his Son!

Herod and John the Baptist

If someone had told me a few years ago that he thought Herod at one time came near the kingdom of God, I should have been inclined to doubt it. I would have said, "I don't believe that the bloodthirsty wretch who took the life of John the Baptist ever had a serious thought in his life about his soul's welfare."

I held that opinion because there is one scene recorded in Herod's life that I had overlooked. But some years ago, when I was going through the Gospel of Mark, making a careful study of the book, I found this verse: "Herod feared John, knowing that he was a just man and an holy, and observed him; and when he heard him, he did many things, and heard him gladly" (Mark 6:20).

This caused me to change my views about Herod. I saw that he was not only brought within the sound of John's voice, but under the power of the Spirit of God. His heart was touched and his conscience awakened. We are not told under what circumstances he heard John; but the narrative plainly states that he was brought under the influence of the Baptist's wonderful ministry.

John's Ministry

Let me first say a word or two about this preacher. I contend that John the Baptist must have been one of the grandest preachers this world has ever had (Matt. 3:1–12). Almost any man can get a hearing nowadays in a town or a city, where the people live close together; especially if he speaks in a fine building where there is a splendid choir, and if the meetings have been advertised and worked up for weeks or months before-hand. In such circumstances any man who has a gift for speaking will get a good audience.

But it was very different with John. He drew the people out of the towns and cities away into the wilderness. There were no ministers to back him, no businessmen interested in Christ's cause to work with him, no news-paper reporters to take his sermons down and send them out. He was an unknown man, without any title to his name. He was not the Right Rev-erend John the Baptist, D.D., or anything of the kind, but plain John the Baptist. When the people went to inquire of him if he were Elias or Jere-miah come back to life, he said he was not. "Who are you then?" they asked.

"I am the voice of one crying in the wilderness."

He was nothing but a voice to be heard and not seen. He was Mr. Nobody. He regarded himself as a messenger who had received his com-mission from the eternal world.

How he began his ministry, and how he gathered the crowds together we are not told. I can imagine that one day this strange man makes his appearance in the valley of the Jordan, where he finds a few shepherds tending their flocks. They bring together their scattered sheep, and the man begins to preach to these shepherds. The kingdom of heaven, he says, is about to be set up on the earth; and he urges them to set their houses in order—to repent and turn away from their sins. Having deliv-ered his message, he tells them that he will come back the next day and speak again.

When he has disappeared into the desert, I can suppose one of the shepherds says to another, "Was he not a strange man? Did you ever hear a man speak like that? He did not talk as the rabbis or the Pharisees or the Sadducees do. I really think he must be one of the old prophets. Did you notice that his coat was made of camel's hair, and that he had a leather girdle round his loins? Don't the Scriptures say that Elijah was clothed like that?"

Says another, "You remember how Malachi says that before the great and dreadful day of the Lord, Elijah should come? I really believe this man is the old prophet of Carmel." What could stir the heart of the Jewish peo-ple more than the name of Elijah?

The tidings of John's appearance spread up and down the valley of the Jordan, and when he returned the next day, there was great excitement and expectation as the people listened to the strange preacher. Perhaps till Christ came he had only that one text, "Repent, for the kingdom of heaven is at hand."

Day after day you could hear his voice ringing through the valley of the Jordan, "Repent! Repent! Repent! The King is at the door; I do not know the day or the hour, but he will be here very soon."

By and by some of the people who flocked to hear him wanted to be baptized, and he took them to the Jordan and baptized them.

The news spread to the surrounding villages and towns, and it wasn't long before it reached Jerusalem. Then the people of the city began to flock into the desert to hear this prince among preachers. His fame soon reached Galilee, and the people in the mountains began to flock down to hear him. Men left their fishing smacks on the lake, that they might listen to this wonderful preacher. When he was in the zenith of his popularity, as many as twenty or thirty thousand people perhaps flocked to his ministry day after day.

John Denounces Sin

No doubt there were some old croakers who said it was all sensation. "Catch me there! No, sir; I never did like sensational preaching."

Just as some people speak nowadays when any special effort is made to reach the people! "Great harm will be done," they say. I wish all these croakers had died out with that generation in Judea. But we have plenty of their descendants still. I venture to say you have met with them. Why, my dear friends, there is more excitement in your whisky shops and beer saloons in one night than in all the churches put together in twelve months. What a stir there must have been in Palestine under the preaching of John the Baptist, and of Christ! The whole country reeled and rocked with intense excitement. Don't be afraid of a little excitement in religious matters. It won't hurt.

One might hear those old Pharisees and scribes grumbling about John being such a sensational preacher. "It won't last." And when Herod had John the Baptist beheaded, they would say, "Didn't I tell you so?"

Let's not be in a hurry in passing judgment. John the Baptist lives today more than ever he did. His voice goes ringing through the world yet. He only preached a few months, but for more than eighteen hundred years his sermons have been repeated and multiplied, and the power of his words will never die as long as the world lasts.

John's Preaching Reaches Herod

I can imagine that just when John was at the height of his popularity, as Herod sat in his palace in Jerusalem looking out toward the valley of the Jordan, he could see great crowds of people passing day by day. He began to make inquiries as to what it meant, and the news came to him about this strange and powerful preacher. Someone, perhaps, reported that John was preaching treason. He was telling of a king who was at hand, and who was going to set up his kingdom.

"A king at hand! If Caesar were coming, I should have heard of it. There is no king but Caesar. I must look into the matter. I will go down to the Jordan and hear this man for myself."

So one day, as John stood preaching, with the eyes of the whole audience upon him, the people being swayed by his eloquence like treetops when the wind passes over them, all at once he lost their attention. All eyes were suddenly turned in the direction of the city. One cries, "Look, look! Herod is coming!"

Soon the whole congregation knows it, and there is great excitement.

"I believe he will stop this preaching," says one.

And if there were in those days some of the compromising, weak-kneed Christians we sometimes meet, they would have said to John, "Don't talk about a coming King; Herod won't stand for it. Talk about repentance, but any talk about a coming King will be high treason in the ears of Herod."

I think if anyone had dared to give John such counsel, he would have replied, "I have received my message from heaven; what do I care for Herod or anyone else?"

As he stood thundering away and calling on the people to repent, I can see Herod, with his guard of soldiers around him, listening attentively to find anything in the preacher's words that he can lay hold of. At last John says, "The King is just at the door. He will set up his kingdom and will separate the wheat from the chaff."

I can imagine Herod then saying to himself, "I will have that man's head off inside of twenty-four hours. I would arrest him here and now if I dared. I will catch him tomorrow before the crowd gathers."

By and by, as Herod listens, some of the people begin to press close up to the preacher and to question. Some soldiers are among them, and they ask John, "What shall we do?"

John answers, "Do violence to no man, neither accuse any falsely; and be content with your wages."

"That is pretty good advice," Herod thinks, "I have had a good deal of trouble with these men, but if they follow the preacher's advice, it will make them better soldiers."

Then he hears the publicans ask John, as they come to be baptized, "What shall we do?"

The answer is, "Exact no more than that which is appointed you."

"Well," says Herod, "that is excellent advice. These publicans are all the time overtaxing the people. If they would do as the preacher tells them, the people would be more contented."

Then the preacher addresses himself to the Pharisees and the Sadducees in the crowd, and cries, "O generation of vipers, who hath warned you to flee from the wrath to come? Bring forth therefore fruits worthy of repentance" (Matt. 3:7–8).

Says Herod within himself, "I like that. I am glad he is giving it pretty strongly to these men. I do not think I will have him arrested just yet."

So he goes back to his palace. I can imagine he was not able to sleep much that night. He kept thinking of what he had heard. When the Holy Ghost is dealing with a man's conscience, very often sleep departs from him. Herod can't get this wilderness preacher and his message out of his mind. The truth had reached his soul. It echoed and reechoed within him, "Repent, for the kingdom of heaven is at hand."

He says, "I went out today to hear for the Roman government. I think I will go tomorrow and hear for myself."

So he goes back again and again. My text says that he heard him gladly, that he observed him and feared him, knowing that he was a just and holy man. He must have known down in his heart that John was a heaven-sent messenger. Had you gone into the palace in those days, you would have heard Herod talking of nobody but John the Baptist. He would say to his associates, "Have you been out into the desert to hear this strange preacher?"

"No, have you?"

"Yes."

"What! You, the Roman governor, going to hear this unordained preacher?"

"Yes, I have been quite often. I would rather hear him than any man I ever knew. He does not talk like the regular preachers. I never heard anyone who had such influence over me."

You would have thought that Herod was a very hopeful subject. "He did many things." Perhaps he stopped swearing. He may have stopped gambling and getting drunk. A wonderful change seemed to have passed over him. Perhaps he ceased from taking bribes for a time. We catch him at it afterwards, but just then he refrained from it. He became quite virtuous in certain directions. It really looked as if he were near the kingdom of heaven.

I can imagine that one day, as John stands preaching, the truth is going home to the hearts and consciences of the people, and the powers of another world are falling upon them. One of John's disciples stands near Herod's chariot, and sees the tears in the eyes of the Roman governor. At the close of the service he goes to John and says, "I stood close to Herod today, and no one seemed more impressed. I could see the tears coming, and he had to brush them away to keep them from falling."

Have you ever seen a man in a religious meeting trying to keep the tears back? You noticed that his forehead seemed to itch, and he put up his hand. You may know what it means—he wants to conceal the fact that the tears are there. He thinks it is a weakness. It is no weakness to get drunk and abuse his family, but it is weakness to shed tears. So this disciple of John may have noticed that Herod put his hand to his brow a number of times. He did not wish his soldiers, or those standing near, to observe that he was weeping.

The disciple says to John, "It looks as if he were coming near the kingdom. I believe you will have him as an inquirer very soon."

When a man enjoys hearing such a preacher, it certainly seems a hopeful sign. Herod might have been present that day when Christ was baptized. Was there ever a man lifted so near to heaven as Herod must have been if he were present on that occasion? I see John standing surrounded by a great throng of people who are hanging on his words. The eyes of the preacher, that never had quailed before, suddenly began to look strange. He turned pale and seemed to draw back as though something wonderful had happened, and right in the middle of a sentence he ceased to speak. If I were suddenly to grow pale and stop speaking, you would ask, "Has death crept onto the platform? Is the tongue of the speaker palsied?"

There must have been quite a commotion among the audience when John stopped. The eyes of the Baptist were fixed upon a stranger who pushed his way through the crowd and, coming up to the preacher, requested to be baptized. That was a common occurrence; it had happened day after day for weeks past. John listened to the stranger's words, but instead of going at once to the Jordan and baptizing him, he said, "I need to be baptized of thee!"

What a thrill of excitement must have shot through the audience! I can hear one whispering to another, "I believe that is the Messiah!"

Yes, it was the long-looked-for One, for whose appearing the nation had been awaiting these thousands of years. From the time God had made the promise to Adam, way back in Eden, every true Israelite had been looking for the Messiah; and there he was in their midst!

He insisted that John should baptize him, and the forerunner recognized his authority as Master, took him to the Jordan, and baptized him. As he came up from the water, lo! the heavens opened, and the Spirit of God in the form of a dove descended and rested on him (Matt. 3:13–17). When Noah sent forth the dove from the ark, it could find no resting place; but now the Son of God had come to do the will of God, and the dove found its resting place upon him. The Holy Ghost had found a home. Now God broke the silence of four thousand years. There came a voice from heaven, and Herod may have heard it if he was there that day, "This is my beloved Son, in whom I am well pleased."

Herod Responds to John's Preaching

Even if Herod had not witnessed this scene and heard the voice, he must have heard about it; for the thing was not done in a corner. There were thousands to witness it, and the news must have been taken to every corner of the land.

Yet Herod, living in such times, and hearing such a preacher, missed the kingdom of heaven at last. He did many things because he feared John. Had he feared God he would have done everything. "He did many things"; but there was one thing he would not do—he would not give up one darling sin. The longer I preach, the more I am convinced that that is what keeps men out of the kingdom of God. John knew about Herod's private life, and warned him plainly.

If those compromising Christians of whom I have spoken had been near John, one of them would have said, "Look here, John, it is reported that Herod is very anxious about his soul, and is asking what he must do to be saved. Let me give you some advice; don't touch on Herod's secret sin. He is living with his brother's wife, but don't you say anything about it, for he won't stand it. He has the whole Roman government behind him, and if you allude to that matter it will be more than your life is worth. You have a good chance with Herod; he is afraid of you. Only be careful, and don't go too far, or he will have your head off."

There are those who are willing enough that you should preach about the sins of other people, so long as you do not come home to them. My wife was once teaching my little boy a Sunday school lesson. She was telling him to notice how sin grows till it becomes habit. The little fellow thought it was coming too close to him, so he colored up, and finally said, "Mama, I think you are getting a good way from the subject."

John was a preacher of this uncompromising kind, for he drove the message right home. I don't know when or how the two were brought together at that time, but John kept nothing back; he boldly said, "Herod, it is not lawful for thee to have thy brother's wife."

The man was breaking the law of God, and living in the cursed sin of adultery. Thank God, John did not spare him! It cost the preacher his head, but the Lord had got his heart, and he did not care what became of his head. We read that Herod feared John, but John did not fear Herod.

I want to say that I do not know of a quicker way to hell than by the way of adultery. Let no one flatter himself that he is going into the kingdom of God who does not repent of this sin in sackcloth and ashes. My friend, do you think God will never bring you into judgment? Does not the Bible say that no adulterer shall inherit the kingdom of God?

Do you think John the Baptist would have been a true friend of Herod if he had spared him, and had covered up his sin? Was it not a true sign that John loved him when he warned him, and told him he must quit his sin? Herod had before done many things, and heard John gladly; but he did not like him then. It is one thing to hear a man preach down other people's sins. Men will say, "That is splendid," and will want all their friends to go and hear the preacher. But let him touch on their individual sin as John did, and declare (as Nathan did to David in 2 Samuel 12:7), "Thou art the man," and they say, "I do not like that." The preacher has touched a sore place.

When a man has broken his arm, the surgeon must find out the exact spot where the fracture is. He feels along and presses gently with his fingers.

"Is it there?"

"No."

"Is it there?"

"No."

Presently, when the surgeon touches another spot, "Ouch!" says the man. He has found the broken part, and it hurts. John placed his finger on the diseased spot, and Herod winced under it. He put his hand right on it, "Herod, it is not lawful for thee to have thy brother Philip's wife!" Herod did not want to give up his sin.

Many a man would be willing to enter into the kingdom of God, if he could do it without giving up sin. People sometimes wonder why Jesus Christ, who lived six hundred years before Mohammed, has fewer disciples than Mohammed today. There is no difficulty in explaining that. A man may become a disciple of Mohammed and continue to live in the foulest, blackest, deepest sin; but a man cannot be a disciple of Christ without giving up sin.

If you are trying to make yourself believe that you can get into the kingdom of God without renouncing your sin, may God tear the mask from you! Can Satan persuade you that Herod will be found in the kingdom of God along with John the Baptist, with the sin of adultery and of murder on his soul?

And now, let me say this to you. If your minister comes to you frankly, tells you of your sin, and warns you faithfully, thank God for him. He is your best friend. He is a heaven-sent man. But if a minister speaks smooth, oily words to you, tells you it is all right, when you know, and he knows, that it is all wrong and that you are living in sin, you may be sure that he is a devil-sent man.

I want to say I have a contempt for a preacher that will tone his message down to suit someone in his audience; some senator, or big man whom he sees present. If the devil can get possession of such a minister and speak through him, he will do the work better than the devil himself. You might be horrified if you knew it was Satan deceiving you, but not if a professed minister of Jesus Christ preaches this doctrine and says that God will make it all right in the end, that though you go on living in sin, it is just the same. Don't be deluded into believing such doctrine—it is as false as any lie that ever came from the pit of hell. All the priests and ministers of all the churches cannot save one soul that will not part with sin.

There is an old saying that "every man has his price." Esau sold his birthright for a mess of pottage; pretty cheap, was it not? Ahab sold out for a garden of herbs. Judas sold out for thirty pieces of silver—less than seventeen dollars of our money. Pretty cheap, was it not? Herod sold out for adultery.

What is the price that you put upon your soul? You say you do not know. I will tell you. It is the sin that keeps you from God. It may be whisky; there is many a man who will give up the hope of heaven and sell his soul for whisky. It may be adultery. You say, "Give me the harlot, and I will relinquish heaven with all its glories. I would rather be damned with my sin than saved without it." What are you selling out for, my friend? You know what it is.

Do you not think it would have been a thousand times better for Herod today if he had taken the advice of John the Baptist instead of that vile, adulterous woman? There was Herodias pulling one way, John the other, and Herod was in the balance. It's the same old battle between right and wrong; heaven pulling one way, hell the other. Are you going to make the same mistake yourself?

We have ten thousandfold more light than Herod had. He lived on the other side of the cross. The glorious gospel had not shone out as it has done since. Think of the sermons you have heard, of the entreaties addressed to you to become a Christian. Some of you have had godly mothers who have prayed for you. Many of you have godly wives who have pleaded with you and with God on your behalf. You have been surrounded with holy influences from year to year, and how often you have been near the kingdom of God! Yet here you are today, further off than ever!

It may be true of you, as it was of Herod, that you hear your preacher gladly. You attend church, you contribute liberally, you do many things. Remember that none of these avail to cleanse your soul from sin. They will not be accepted in the place of what God demands—repentance and the forsaking of every sin.

A child was once playing with a vase and put his hand in and could not draw it out again. His father tried to help him, but in vain. At last he said, "Now, make one more try. Open your fingers out straight, and let me pull your arm."

"Oh, no, papa," said the son, "I'd drop the penny if I opened my fingers like that."

Of course he couldn't get his hand out when his fist was doubled. He didn't want to give up the penny. Just so with the sinner. He won't cut loose from his sins.

Your path and mine will perhaps never cross again. But if I have any influence with you, I beseech and beg of you to break with sin now, let it cost you what it will. Herod might have been associated with Joseph of Arimathea, and with the twelve apostles of the Lamb, if he had taken the advice of John. There might have been a fragrance around his name all these centuries.

Herod Rejects John's Preaching

But alas! When we speak of Herod, we see a sneer on the faces of those who hear us. If one had said to Herod in those days, "Do you know that you are going to silence that great preacher, and have him beheaded?" he would have replied, "Is thy servant a dog that he should do such a thing? I never would take the life of such a man." He would probably have thought he could never do it. Yet it was only a little while after that he had the servant of God beheaded.

Do you know that the gospel of Jesus Christ proves either a savor of life unto life, or of death unto death? (2 Cor. 2:16). You sometimes hear people say, "We will go and hear this man preach. If it does us no good, it will do us no harm."

Don't you believe it, my friend! Every time you hear the gospel and reject it, the hardening process goes on. The same sun that melts the ice hardens the clay. The sermon that would have moved you a few years ago would make no impression now. Do you not recall some night when you heard a sermon that shook the foundations of your skepticism and unbelief? But you are indifferent now.

I believe Herod was seven times more a child of hell after his conviction had passed away than he was before. There is not a true minister of the gospel who will not say that the hardest people to reach are those who have been impressed, and whose impressions have worn away. It is a good deal easier to commit a sin the second time than it was to commit it the first time, but it is a good deal harder to repent the second time than the first.

If you are near the kingdom of God now, take the advice of a friend and step into it. Don't be satisfied with just getting near to it. Christ said to the young ruler, "Thou art not far from the kingdom," but he failed to get there. Don't run any risks. Death may overtake you before you have time to carry out your best intentions if you put off a decision.

It is sad to think that men heard Jesus and Paul, and were moved under their preaching, but were not saved. Judas must many times have come near the kingdom, but he never entered in. I saw it in the army men who had almost decided to become Christians, then were cut down in battle without having taken the step that would have made them sure of eternal life. I confess there is something very sad about it.

In one of the tenement houses in New York city, a doctor was sent for. He came, and found a young man very sick. When he got to the bedside the young man said, "Doctor, I don't want you to deceive me; I want to know the worst. Is this illness to prove serious?"

After the doctor had made an examination, he said, "I am sorry to tell you cannot live out the night."

The young man looked up and said: "Well, then, I have missed it at last!"

"Missed what?"

"I have missed eternal life. I always intended to become a Christian some day, but I thought I had plenty of time, and put it off."

The doctor, who was himself a Christian man, said, "It is not too late. Call on God for mercy."

"No. I have always had a great contempt for a man who repents when he is dying; he is a miserable coward. If I were not sick I would not have a thought about my soul, and I am not going to insult God now."

The doctor spent the day with him, read to him out of the Bible, and tried to get him to lay hold of the promises. The young man said he would not call on God, and in that state of mind he passed away. Just as he was dying the doctor saw his lips moving. He reached down, and all he could hear was the faint whisper, "I have missed it at last!"

Dear friend, make sure that you do not miss eternal life at last. Will you go with Herod or with John? Bow your head now and say, "Son of God, come into this heart of mine. I yield myself to you, fully, wholly, unreservedly." He will come to you, and will not only save you, but will keep you to the end.

22 Ittai

Then said the king to Ittai the Gittite, Wherefore goest thou also with us? Return to thy place, and abide with the king; for thou art a stranger, and also an exile. Whereas thou camest but yesterday, should I this day make thee go up and down with us? Seeing I go whither I may, return thou, and take back thy brethren: mercy and truth be with thee.

And Ittai answered the king, and said: As the LORD liveth, and as my lord the king liveth, surely in what place my lord the king shall be, whether in death or life, even there also will thy servant be.

And David said to Ittai: Go and pass over. And Ittai, the Gittite, passed over, and all his men, and all the little ones that were with them.

And all the country wept with a loud voice, and all the people passed over: the king also himself passed over the brook Kidron, and all the people passed over, toward the way of the wilderness.

2 Samuel 15:19–23

What must have been the feeling of David when he got outside the city and found this foreigner and stranger out there with six hundred men, ready and willing to go with him! He had had three men who sat at his table and in the hour of trial, in the hour of trouble, they had deserted him. It is in the time of darkness that we find out our friends. You find then who are your friends.

Now, David was in trouble, and here was this Ittai standing right by him. How that must have cheered the heart of the king! He had been driven from the throne by Absalom, and the whole kingdom seemed to be going with Absalom. Absalom and those who were with him were planning to take the life of David, but here we find this stranger—this man Ittai—just following David. And when David told him to go back, see what he says: "As the LORD liveth, and as the lord my king liveth, surely in what place my lord the king shall be, whether in death or life, even there also will thy servant be" (2 Sam. 15:21).

I think it is one of the sweetest things in the whole life of David. Then David invited Ittai, the Gittite, to go with him (2 Sam. 15:22).

Here was a man who was attached to a person. That is the point I wanted to call to your attention. We are living, I think, in the day of shams. There are a good many people who are attached to creeds, denominations, and churches. They are attached to this and to that, instead of a person. Creeds and churches are all right in their places, but if a man puts them in the place of the Savior and the personal Christ, then they are but snares. He would be willing to give up everything but Christ in the hour of trouble, and if he is attached to Christ he will be able to say, "Wherever thou goest I go." David had nothing to offer this man. There he was, barefooted and leaving the throne. Ittai was attached to the man.

David was everything to Ittai, and life was nothing. No man had better friends than David had in his day. What we should desire is to be attached to the Lord Jesus Christ as Ittai was attached to David.

23 Jacob

Genesis 25–35

The freedom with which God points out the faults in Bible characters may be somewhat surprising to those who have been accustomed to think that all the men and women whose history God narrates in his book must necessarily be good men and women. This was formerly my view of Bible characters, but I have discovered my error. The men and women of the Bible were just such men and women as were to be found outside of it. Their virtues were of the same kind, and their faults of the same kind, as characterize persons we find in the church today. We can take as much warning from characters such as Jacob as encouragement in the study of the character of Joseph.

Jacob's Key Problem

The key to all Jacob's difficulties may be found in this story of the laborers in the vineyard, in the twentieth chapter of Matthew (vv. 1–16). In the second verse we are told that the first men who were hired made an agreement to work for a penny a day, while the men who came afterward made no bargain but accepted the word of the lord of the vineyard that he would pay them what was right. When the lord of the vineyard came to pay the laborers for their day's work he gave them all a penny, though some had worked only half a day, or a quarter of a day, and some had worked only an hour.

When those who had been hired first came to get their money they thought they should have received more; but they only got a penny, according to their bargain. They received only their legal wages. I can see them scowling when they receive the penny.

"Is that all you are going to give me?" says one. "There is that man over there who only worked an hour, and you have paid him as much as you have us who have borne the burden and heat of the day."

"That is true," says the lord of the vineyard, "I am paying that man according to my views of the case, and I am paying you according to the bargain you made."

Jacob was all the time making bargains. The Christians who are making bargains with the Lord do not get as much as those who trust him. You see, my friends, it doesn't pay to make bargains with the Lord.

Jacob is a twin brother to the most of us. You will find a hundred Jacobs where you will find one Joseph or one Daniel. Joseph was willing to trust everything to God, but Jacob wasn't willing to trust him any further than he could see him.

Jacob and His Mother

No doubt Jacob got much of his weakness from his mother. There was a division in that home. There is always trouble in a family where there are any favorites. Petting one child and finding fault with another is sure to bring out the old Adam. It looks as if Esau was the favorite son of his father, while Jacob was the favorite of his mother (Gen. 25:27–28).

By nature Esau was the better man of the two; and if such a mean, contemptible person as Jacob can be saved, then there is hope for all of us. Sometimes when a man has a marked peculiarity we say he got it from his father or his mother. I think Jacob took after his mother. She wasn't willing to wait on the Lord, but wanted to arrange everything connected with her children's future herself, and in this she was like a good many parents in these days.

Jacob and Esau

You remember that Rebecca formed a plan to get Jacob into the good graces of his father, and to obtain for him the birthright of his brother (Genesis 27). But you will notice that it got him into great trouble. Jacob had to leave home, and his mother died before he returned. Rebecca tried to get something for Jacob by fraud, and he acted out the lie.

Jacob at Bethel

Up to the time of Jacob's departure from home there was little that was lovely in his character. He had a mean, miserable nature, but God gave him grace to subdue it. The Lord, from the top of the ladder which Jacob saw reaching up to heaven, promised him what he should have in the future (Gen. 28:13–15). Then Jacob gets up and begins to make a bargain with God, and says, "If you will do such and such with me—if you will be with me, and keep me, and clothe me—then you shall be my God."

What a contemptible speech! God had promised him all from Dan to Beersheba, but he is not satisfied without making some special terms of his own. That is just the way with a great many of us. If God will bless us in our basket and our store we will have him for our God; but the minute we fail to get something we want, we begin to find fault with him.

Jacob in Haran

Now look at Jacob down there in Haran. He is driving bargains all the time, and always gets the worst of it (Genesis 29–30). He works seven years for his wife, and then gets another woman in her place. He had started out wrong with a lie on his lips, and now he gets paid back in his own coin. But we do not hear that he made any confession. One would have thought that when God met him at Bethel he would have confessed his sins, but he did not.

Some people seem to think, that because God chose Jacob instead of Esau, Jacob must have been a very good man and Esau a very bad one; but we must not forget that some of God's promises are conditional and others unconditional. The promise which he made to Jacob was of the latter class. God was dealing in sovereign grace with him, for God is sovereign and has the right to do what he pleases. The Bible says that Jacob was chosen before he was born (Mal. 1:2; Rom. 9:13). That was the election in his case. But it doesn't say that his soul was saved or that Esau's soul was lost. It was a question of an entirely different kind.

After Jacob has been in Haran for some years God says to him, "I am the God of Beth-el . . . arise, get thee out from this land, and return to the land of your kindred" (Gen. 31:13). And now we find him stealing away from Haran like a thief, pursued by his father-in-law who was also his uncle.

Jacob ought to have been proud, and should have left Haran like a prince, but instead he steals away like a thief. He starts off, and his uncle and father-in-law pursues. God took care of him. God was determined to keep his vows, and there is no doubt that, had not God interfered, Jacob would have been slain. We find that Jacob stays behind, like a miserable coward, after he had sent his effects away. A man out of communication with God is a coward always.

Jacob Wrestles with the Angel

Then, again, when he hears that Esau is coming to meet him he makes another cowardly exhibition of himself. I suppose he had gotten out of communion with God again. A man out of communion with God is always a coward.

In the midst of his trouble, while he is trembling with fear at the thought of meeting his brother whom he has wronged, he meets an angel, who wrestles with him until the break of day, and who at length touches his thigh and puts it out of joint (Gen. 32:24–25). By this miracle Jacob understands that this is the angel of the Lord. I suppose it was the Jesus Christ of the Old Testament.

There is this to be noticed, that as long as Jacob was able to wrestle in his own strength he did not prevail; but when his thigh was out of joint, and all he could do was to hold on to the Lord, he got the blessing. It is the man who is lowest down that God is most willing to lift up. The man that has the greatest humility is the one to be most exalted.

Jacob after Peniel

Some people tell us that after this Jacob was a very different man. But not long after he has escaped the danger he feared from his brother, we find him going down to Shechem and building an altar and calling it by a high sounding name, El-elohe-Israel, that is, the God of Israel (Gen. 33:18–20). But Jacob in Shechem, with his high altar, was no better than Jacob in Haran without any altar. The Lord did not tell him to go to Shechem.

I think the trouble with a great many people is that they have gone down to Shechem instead of going to Bethel. We find Jacob's children getting into trouble here, and that is where the children of the members of the church are very apt to get into trouble. They stay away from the place of the Lord's appointment and choose out places for themselves. But just the moment Jacob came to Bethel the Lord met him (Gen. 35:1–15). And just as soon as the church leaves Shechem and comes to Bethel the Lord will meet it.

The next thing we hear is the death of his favorite wife, Rachel. Not long afterward comes the famine, when he is obliged to send down to Egypt for corn. You remember how his sons sold Joseph into slavery, and came back to their father and said they had found his torn and bloody coat (Genesis 37). The old man mourned him as dead for twenty long years. He had deceived his own father, and now his sons deceive him. Surely he might say to Pharaoh, "Few and evil have the days of the years of my life been" (Gen. 47:9).

Poor man! He started out with a lie in his mouth, and after a life of trouble and mourning he dies an exile in Egypt instead of in the land that God had promised him.

He would not let God choose for him, and that is the cause of the failure of his life. I suppose Jacob was saved by fire, or, as Job says, by the skin of his teeth (Job 19:20). But his life ought to be a warning to show us that it is best to let God do the choosing and planning for us. We should be satisfied and wait upon him, saying, "Thy will, not ours, be done." We gain nothing by trying to drive sharp bargains with God, and we gain just as little by doing the same thing with men.

Jacob's Sons

Look at the sons of Jacob. Look at them when they took away their brother, and after they had delivered him into slavery see them coming back (Gen. 37:12–36). How much they must have suffered with their secret during those twenty years! What misery they must have endured as they looked, during all those years, at their old father sorrowing for his son, Joseph! They knew the boy had not been killed. They knew he was in slavery.

For twenty years the sin was covered up, but at last it came back upon them. God had, in the meantime, been doing everything for Joseph. He had raised him nearly to the throne of Egypt. A famine struck the land of the father, and the old man sent his sons down into Egypt to purchase corn (Genesis 42). God was at work. He was making these men bring their own sin home to themselves.

Their consciences smote them, and they confessed, in the presence of Joseph, that their sin had found them out. Twenty years after it was committed that sin was resurrected and they were brought face to face with it. "He that covereth his sins shall not prosper" (Prov. 28:13).

24 John the Baptist

Matthew 3; Mark 1:1–11; Luke 3:1–9;
John 1:19–28

The Voice in the Wilderness

Thirty years have rolled away, and it is now time that Jesus the Messiah should come unto the nation. The Scriptures have been fulfilled, and the first sound we hear of his coming is that strange voice crying in the wilderness (Matt. 3:3; Mark 1:3; Luke 3:4; John 1:23).

There had been a great many prophets and wonderful men under the Old Testament dispensation, but John was the last. He dressed like Elijah, his preaching was very much in Elijah's style; he was, in fact, in a great many respects, very much like that prophet. Many people talk about sensational preaching, but there never was such a sensational preacher as John the Baptist. He shook the whole world. He got hold of the Pharisees, those people who live on church forms, denying the power, and I tell you those are the hardest people to reach. Harlots and drunkards are much more easily converted.

I used to think I should have liked to live in the days of the prophets, but I have gotten over that. Whenever a prophet bursts out on a nation you must know that everything is in the worst condition that it can be. Everything is chaos and confusion, and the people have turned away from God.

So I would rather live when there are no prophets, because many of those men who were sent from God to bring the nation back to him were stern men, men of iron will and resolution. Jesus and John, in comparison with all the great men that have gone before, are like the sun and moon in comparison with the stars. There never was such a man as John the Baptist, except the Lord Jesus himself.

It is evident that the people believed in him. He practiced what he preached, and they believed what he said. Whenever you find a man doing that, casting out self and believing in Jesus down in his own heart, the people will believe him and flock to hear him. The great trouble with many of us is we say a great deal that we don't mean. John didn't want, and wouldn't receive, honor from men. He simply delivered his message. The result was that the Spirit of God rested upon him, and God used him to do a great work.

John's Preaching

I notice one thing about John's preaching. Up to the time that Christ came he was all the time crying, "Repent! Repent!" In view of his power and influence, there was a splendid chance for John to become an antichrist; but he was true to his mission. He never sought great things for himself, but simply performed the work that God gave him to do.

The reason there are so few today that God can use is because men are seeking great things for themselves. This man was emptied of self. Ambition was out of sight with him; but he proclaimed the message as God had given it. He didn't care what people said, but just told the Pharisees plainly what he thought of them.

But not only did he cry "repent"; he told of the coming of Messiah. You may preach repentance as long as you like, but if you don't preach a deliverance—if you do not preach Christ as coming to set men free—you will do very little good. The nation is now crying "reform." I don't know how long they are going to continue that cry. They have kept it up ever since I can remember; but there will be no true reform until Christ gets into our politics.

Men are all naturally bad, and cannot reform until the Reformer gets into their hearts. John preached Christ to come, and I suppose that was the reason why he drew such immense crowds. He preached himself down and preached Christ up; and that is what every minister ought to do. He said to the people, "I am nothing" (Matt. 3:11; Mark 1:7; Luke 3:16; John 1:27). The great trouble with most of us is that we think ourselves something. We have got so much dignity and position to keep up that the God of heaven can't use us.

I should judge from John 3:26 that some of the Baptist's disciples got a little jealous of Jesus. But there was no room in John's heart for jealousy. Thank God for such a man! Thank God the world has had one man so full of the Holy Spirit that there was no room in him for jealousy, ambition, or self!

John Represents Law

In Luke 7:18–23 we find John sending his disciples to learn if Jesus was the true Christ. I think John is misrepresented here. It may be that he had wavered because he was shut up in prison and Christ had not come to see him. But it seems to me that his disciples could not understand the two men, there was so much difference between John and Jesus. John was given to fasting; he wouldn't be seen at a publican's feast. He denounced them.

He was the representative of the law, and that was what the law always did. But Jesus Christ came to bring grace and truth (John 1:17). The disciples, however, couldn't understand this. Some think that Christ didn't treat John right in leaving him in the prison; but the fact was, John's work was finished. He belonged to the old dispensation; the new one was to commence, and he might as well be in heaven as down here.

Although Christ did not visit John in prison, he paid him the highest tribute that was ever paid to mortal man. He said of him, "Among those that are born of women there is not a greater prophet than John the Baptist" (Luke 7:28).

John Introduces Jesus

What a chance there was for John to have let self come in! When people were wondering in their hearts if he was not the true Messiah, if he was not Christ, he might have been tempted to come out and say he was more than himself—that he was Christ. But there was this commendable trait about John, he never preached up self.

John was preparing the nation to receive the Lord of Glory. He had come merely to introduce him. He was nothing. Just as a man comes and introduces a friend to you, he barely introduces him and steps aside. He does not put himself forward.

So John introduces the Son of God, and then begins to fade away, and soon is gone. He had not come to introduce himself, but to preach Christ. This is the very height of preaching. When they begin to wonder who he is, he just comes right out and says, "I am not Jesus. I am just one sent to introduce him. I have come for that purpose. I have not come to preach up myself, but him that is mighty to save."

While his star was just at its height, while he was just about at the zenith of his glory, while people were flocking in from the towns and villages to hear him, the chief rulers of Jerusalem sent down a deputation to inquire what this religion meant. They appointed some influential men to find him out, and they said to him, "We have been sent by the chief priest of Jerusalem to find out who you are. Are you Christ?"

And John answered, "No."

"Well, who are you? Are you this man or that man?"

"No."

"Are you this prophet or that prophet?"

"No."

"Well, who are you?"

Did he say, "I am Jesus"? No. "Merely Mr. Nobody—merely a voice crying in the wilderness."

What a message that was to send back to Jerusalem! He was not trying to put himself forward. He was all the time trying to get out of self. Now, this was the day, I say, when John was at the very zenith of his glory; but see how nobly he stood. He did not take any honor or glory to himself.

John Baptizes Jesus

Talk about eloquence! John was one of the most eloquent men that ever lived. He was the herald of God when the nation was in a terrible state of excitement, and the chief priests of Jerusalem, and even the king himself, went to hear him. There he stood on the banks of the Jordan. I can see the men and women on both sides of the river—little children, mothers with their babes in their arms—all intensely excited and leaning forward to catch what he says. "Now," says John, "if you believe what I say, that if you have broken the law given at Sinai you have sinned, to be forgiven you must repent and come down into this Jordan, and I will baptize you in the name of the God of Hebron."

The people went in by scores and hundreds, and there he baptized them. And as he stood there baptizing them, I can imagine about twenty thousand people hanging upon his lips. There was a man who came down through the crowd. I can imagine that John was a man who looked as though he was more like a mountain eagle, but his wings seemed to droop. That eye which had been so keen and so severe on the Israelites when he called them a generation of vipers became lusterless, his face fell and he shook his head as this stranger came.

I suppose, as he came walking along toward John, God revealed the fact to him and said, "This is my Son. This is the Savior of the world. This is the Prince of Peace." And when John saw him he quailed before him, and he said, "I have need to be baptized of thee."

What excitement! How it must have thrilled the audience as John drew back and said, "I have need to be baptized of thee." John knew him. John at once recognized him. He knew he was the promised One of the law. John said, "I have need to be baptized of thee, and comest thou to me?" (John 3:14).

But Jesus said unto him, "Suffer it to be so now, that the law may be fulfilled." Now, what excitement as these two men went down into the river together!

Oh, if Jordan could speak it could tell some wonderful stories! Wonderful scenes have taken place there. Naaman had gone into that river and washed, and had come forth clean. Elijah, going up with his mantle, struck the water and went over dry shod, as also did Elisha after Elijah had ascended. But a more wonderful scene was taking place in Jordan than ever took place before. It was of transcendent interest to all mankind.

Our Lord was going down into Jordan to be baptized, and he was going to come up on resurrection ground. So he goes down with John the Baptist, and the moment he was baptized and came up out of the water the heavens were opened unto him. The Spirit of God descended upon him like a dove, and alighted upon him. Heaven witnessed the scene. God the Father spoke then. He broke the silence of ages. The God of the Old Testament was the Christ of the New. And he heard a voice from heaven, saying, "Thou art my beloved Son, in whom I am well pleased" (Mark 1:11; Luke 3:22).

Someone says that was the first time God could look down on this old world since Adam fell and say that he was well pleased. In Hebrews 10:7 we read of our Lord Jesus, "Lo, I come (in the volume of the book it is written of me,) to do thy will, O God." He was the Son that was born from above.

John's Central Preaching Theme

John's preaching changed. But he was not like many men of the present day, who want to reform the world without Christ, who set a good example and tell men to sign pledges and to do this or that, and to trust in their own strength.

The moment John got his eye on Christ he had one text, "Behold the Lamb of God, which taketh away the sin of the world" (John 1:29). That is how you are going to get rid of your sins. Says John, "I bear record that this in the Son of God." And he told his disciples, "Now, you follow him. Go with him."

One afternoon, as he sat there with his disciples, he said, "Behold the Lamb of God!" And John's disciples left him to follow Jesus. I tell you that is something which you don't like to do, to make your friends leave you, to preach them away—your own congregation. But now this man begins to ask his disciples to leave him. "Why," said he, "I tell you I am not worthy to just unloose his shoes. He is more worthy than I am. Follow Jesus." He began to preach up Christ. "He must increase, but I must decrease" (John 3:30).

Some of his disciples came to him one day and said, "You know that man you baptized over there in the Jordan? Well, more men are coming to him than are coming to you." That was jealousy—envy rankling in those men's bosoms. But what did John say? "I told you that I was not the promised One. Why, he must increase, and I must decrease. That's right. I would rather see the crowd flocking to hear him."

John was cast into prison. Then he sent two of his disciples to inquire of Christ if he was the true Messiah, or must he look for another. I do not know, but I have an idea that he wanted his disciples to leave him and go over to Jesus. So he called two of his most influential disciples and told them, "Now, you go and ask Jesus if he is the true Messiah." He wanted them to be convinced in their own hearts as he was in his. I can't believe in John's faith wavering; but, if he was wavering, he took the very best way, and sent those men to ask the Savior.

I see his deputation arrive, and when Jesus had finished preaching these disciples come up and say, "Our master has sent us to ask if you are the true Messiah or shall he look for another?"

Jesus goes on healing the sick, causing the lame to leap, giving sight to the blind, making the deaf to hear. Then he said to John's messengers, "You go back and tell your master what you have seen and what you have heard. Go back and tell John that the blind see, the deaf hear, the lame walk, and the poor have the gospel preached to them."

When John heard that, in prison, it settled all his doubts. His disciples believed, and the poor had the gospel preached to them. That was the test, and then John's disciples, one after another, left him. And now we find him thrown into prison. There he is, in prison—awaiting his appointed time. Just bear in mind that God had sent him. His work was done. He had only just come to announce the Savior—only for that object.

Some think that Christ's treatment of John was rather hard—in fact, harsh; but the greatest tribute ever paid to any man was paid by Jesus to John.

"But what went ye out for to see? A man clothed in soft raiment? Behold, they that wear soft clothing are in kings' houses. But what went ye out for to see? A prophet? Yea, I say unto you, and more than a prophet. For this is he of whom it is written: Behold, I send my messenger before thy face, which shall prepare thy way before thee. Verily, I say unto you, among them that are born of women there has not risen a greater than John the Baptist: notwithstanding he that is least in the kingdom of heaven is greater than he."

Matthew 11:8–11

There was none greater than this same John. Our Savior knew that John was going first. He knew that he was soon to die, and that John would have to come to him; that they would soon be together in glory, and then they could talk matters over; that John must sink out of sight, and the Lord of Glory must be the central object. Jesus and John were like the sun and moon in comparison with the stars. All the prophets were like the stars in comparison with those two men. There was no prophet like John. None born of woman was greater. Moses was a mighty prophet. Elijah was the son of thunder, and a great and mighty prophet, and so was Elisha. But they were not to be compared with John.

What a character! He lost sight of himself entirely. Christ was uppermost; Christ was the all-in-all with him. He was beheaded outside the Promised Land. He was buried in Moab, somewhere near where Moses was laid away. The first and last prophets of that nation were buried near together, and there they lie, outside the Promised Land; but their bodies, by and by, will be resurrected, and they will be the grandest and most glorious in God's kingdom.

25 Joseph of Arimathea

Matthew 27:57–60; Mark 15:43–46; Luke 23:50–53; John 19:38

Now we come to Joseph of Arimathea. We read in John's Gospel that for fear of the Jews he was kept back from confessing openly. "And after this Joseph of Arimathea, being a disciple of Jesus, but secretly, for fear of the Jews, besought Pilate that he might take away the body of Jesus: and Pilate gave him leave. He came therefore, and took the body of Jesus" (John 19:38).

Read the four accounts given in the four Gospels concerning Joseph of Arimathea. There are very few things mentioned by all four of the Evangelists. If Matthew and Mark refer to an event it is often omitted by Luke and John; and, if it occurs in the latter, it may not be contained in the former. John's Gospel is made up of that which is absent from the others in most instances—as in the case of the blind man in chapter nine. But all four record what Joseph did for Christ. All his disciples had forsaken him. One had sold him, and another had denied him. He was left in gloom and darkness, when Joseph of Arimathea came out and confessed him.

The Secret Disciple

It was the death of Jesus Christ that brought out Joseph of Arimathea. Probably he was one of the number that stood at the cross when the centurion smote his breast, and cried out, "Truly, this was the Son of God."

129

It is likely that he was convinced at the same time. He was a disciple before, because we read that on the night of the trial he did not give his consent to the death of Christ. There must have been some surprise in the Council chamber on that occasion, when Joseph of Arimathea, a rich man, stood up and said, "I will never give my consent to his death."

There were seventy of those Sanhedrin members, but we have very good reason to believe that there were two of them that, like Caleb and Joshua of old, had the courage to stand up for Jesus Christ—these were Joseph of Arimathea and Nicodemus. Neither of them gave their consent to the death of Christ. But I am afraid Joseph did not come out and say that he was a disciple—for we do not find a word said about his being one until after the crucifixion.

I am afraid there are many Josephs today, men of position, of whom it could be said they are secret disciples. Such would probably say today, "I don't need to take my stand on Christ's side. What more do I need? I have everything."

We read that he was a rich and honorable counselor, a just and a good man, and holding a high position in the government of the nation. He was also a benevolent man, and a devout man too. What more could he need? God wants something more than Joseph's good life and high position. A man may be all Joseph was and yet be without Christ.

Joseph Takes a Stand

But a crisis came in his history. If he was to take his stand, now was the time for him to do it. I consider that this is one of the grandest, noblest acts that any man ever did, to take his stand for Christ when there seemed nothing, humanly speaking, that Christ could give him. Joseph had no hope concerning the resurrection. It seems that none of our Lord's disciples understood that Jesus was going to rise again. Even Peter, James, and John, as well as the rest, scarcely believed that he had risen when he appeared to them.

They had anticipated that he would set up his kingdom, but he had no scepter in his hand; and, so far as they could see, no kingdom in view. In fact, he was dead on the cross, with nails through his hands and feet. There he hung until his spirit took its flight; that which had made him so grand, so glorious, and so noble, had now left the body.

Joseph might have said, "It will be no use my taking a stand for him now. If I come out and confess him I shall probably lose my position in society and in the council, and my influence. I had better remain where I am."

There was no earthly reward for him; there was nothing, humanly speaking, that could have induced him to come out; and yet we are told by Mark that he went boldly into Pilate's judgment hall and begged the body of Jesus.

In that darkness and gloom—Jesus' disciples having all forsaken him; Judas having sold him for thirty pieces of silver; the chief apostle Peter having denied him with a curse, swearing that he never knew him; the chief priests having found him guilty of blasphemy; the Council having condemned him to death; and when there was a hiss going up to heaven over all Jerusalem—Joseph went right against the current, right against the influence of all his friends, and begged the body of Jesus.

Blessed act! Doubtless he upbraided himself for not having been more bold in his defense of Christ when he was tried, and before he was condemned to be crucified. The Scripture says he was an honorable man, an honorable counselor, a rich man, and yet we have only the record of that one thing, the one act of begging the body of Jesus. But I tell you, that what he did for the Son of God, out of pure love for him, will live forever.

That one act rises up above everything else that Joseph of Arimathea ever did. He might have given large sums of money to different institutions, he might have been very good to the poor, he might have been very kind to the needy in various ways; but that one act for Jesus Christ, on that memorable, dark afternoon was one of the noblest acts that a man ever did. He must have been a man of great influence, or Pilate would not have given him the body.

Joseph and Nicodemus

And now you see another secret disciple, Nicodemus. Nicodemus and Joseph go to the cross. Joseph is there first, and while he is waiting for Nicodemus to come, he looks down the hill; and I can imagine his delight as he sees his friend coming with a hundred pounds of ointment. Although Jesus Christ had led such a lowly life, he was to have a kingly anointing and burial. God has touched the hearts of these two noble men, and they drew out the nails, and took the body down, washed the blood away from the wounds that had been made on his back by the scourge, and on his head by the crown of thorns; then they took the lifeless form, washed it clean, and wrapped it in fine linen, and Joseph laid him in his own sepulcher.

When all was dark and gloomy, when his cause seemed to be lost, and the hope of the church buried in that new tomb, Joseph took his stand for the one "despised and rejected of men." It was the greatest act of his life; and, my reader, if you want to stand with the Lord Jesus Christ in glory, if you want the power of God to be bestowed upon you for service down here, you must not hesitate to take your stand boldly and manfully for the most despised of all men—the man Christ Jesus.

His cause is unpopular. The ungodly sneer at his name. But if you want the blessings of heaven on your soul, and to hear the "Well done, good and faithful servant, enter thou into the joy of thy lord" (Matt. 25:21,23), take your stand at once for him, whatever your position may be, or however much your friends may be against you. Decide for Jesus Christ, the crucified but risen Savior. Go outside the camp and bear his reproach. Take up your cross and follow him, and by and by you will lay it down and take the crown to wear it forever.

I remember some meetings being held in a locality where the tide did not rise very quickly, and bitter and reproachful things were being said about the work. But one day, one of the most prominent men in the place rose and said, "I want it to be known that I am a disciple of Jesus Christ, and if there is any odium to be cast on his cause, I am prepared to take my share of it." It went through the meeting like an electric current and a blessing came at once to his own soul and to the souls of others.

Depend upon it, there is no crown without a cross. We must take our proper position here, as Joseph did. It cost him something to take up his cross. I have no doubt they put him out of the council and out of the synagogue. He lost his standing, and perhaps his wealth. Like other faithful followers of Christ, he became, henceforth, a despised and unpopular man.

Our Responsibility

The blind man could not have done what Joseph did. Some men can do what others cannot. God will hold us responsible for our own influence. Let each of us do what we can. Even though the conduct of our Lord's confessed followers was anything but helpful to those who, like Joseph, had but little courage to come out on the Lord's side, he was not deterred from taking his stand.

Whatever it costs us, let us be true Christians, and take a firm stand. It is like the dust in the balance in comparison to what God has in store for us. We can afford to suffer with him a little while if we are going to reign with him forever. We can afford to take up the cross and follow him, to be despised and rejected by the world, with such a bright prospect in view. If the glories of heaven are real, it will be to his praise and to our advantage to share in his rejection now.

May the Lord keep us from halting; and may we, when weighed in the balance, not be found wanting! May God help every reader to do all that the poor blind beggar did, and all that Joseph did!

Let us confess him at all times and in all places. Let us show our friends that we are out and out on his side. Everyone has a circle that he can influence, and God will hold us responsible for the influence we possess. Joseph of Arimathea and the blind man had circles in which their influence was powerful. I can influence people that others cannot reach; and they, in their turn, can reach a class that I could not touch. It is only for a little while that we can confess him and work for him. It is only for a few months or years, and then the eternal ages will roll on, and great will be our reward in the crowning day that is coming. We shall then hear the Master say to us, "Well done, good and faithful servant, enter thou into the joy of thy Lord."

God grant it may be so!

26 Joshua

The character of Joshua, as depicted by Mr. Moody, is a lesson of godly courage. Mr. Moody himself professes to have been blessed with "a forehead of brass," and it is natural to expect in him a great admiration of this quality in other men similarly endowed. Joshua is one of Mr. Moody's favorite Bible characters, as may appear from the manner in which he speaks of him. The address containing this Bible portrait was given one Sunday morning at the Tabernacle in Chicago, where, in spite of a severe snowstorm, there were about three thousand Christian workers assembled. The singing on this occasion was "Hold the Fort," the chorus by the whole congregation, and "Who's on the Lord's Side," a solo by Mr. Sankey.

Joshua's Call to Courage

I want to call your attention this morning to one word, "courage." In this first chapter of Joshua which we have been reading God is telling him to arise and go over Jordan, and lead his people into the Promised Land, and he gives him a promise in these words:

> Every place that the sole of your foot shall tread upon, that have I given unto you, as I said unto Moses. . . . There shall not any man be able to stand before thee all the days of thy life: as I was with Moses, so I will be with thee. . . . Be strong and of a good courage: for unto this people shalt thou divide for an inheritance the land, which I sware unto their fathers to give them. Only be thou strong and very courageous. . . . This book of the law shalt not depart out of thy mouth . . . then thou shalt make thy way prosperous.
> Joshua 1:3–8

Four times over in this chapter God tells Joshua to be courageous. He doesn't tell him how to use a sword, or show him how to lay out his campaigns, or set his battles in array; but he tells him to meditate on the word of God. That was to be his power.

Courage is necessary to success in Christian work. I have yet to find a man who is easily discouraged that amounts to anything anywhere. If a minister is easily discouraged his people soon find it out and lose their courage also. If a Sunday school teacher hasn't any courage, his class finds it out and leaves him. About the most worthless set of people you can find is a lot of faint-hearted Sunday school teachers. If we are to have any success, we must be of good courage. We must also meditate upon, and believe in, and obey the Word of God. God hasn't any use for a man who is all the time looking on the dark side. What God desires is a person who isn't afraid. "Be of a good courage," says he. "Fear nothing; believe that I am willing to use you, and then I will use you."

Joshua's Development

We hear a great deal in these days about "development," but where can you find a man, with all the advantages of culture and learning, who is equal to this Joshua, brought up among the brick kilns of Egypt?

Joshua dared to be in the minority. Now, friends, there are very few men at the present time who like to be in the minority. They always want to be in the majority. They want to go with the crowd. But when a man has laid hold of the divine nature of God, and has become a product of the divine nature, he is willing then to go against the crowd of the world and be numbered with the minority.

Where Joshua met the God of Israel first we are not told. We do not catch a glimpse of him until the man is about forty years old. The first sight we get of Joshua is as he comes up out of Egypt. We are told that after Moses had struck the rock in Horeb and the children of Israel had drunk the water that came out of that rock—and that rock was typical of Christ and of God's pure throne—Amalek came out to fight them, and after they had gotten a drink of this pure water they were willing to meet him.

The first thing we hear of Joshua he is fighting against Amalek and prevailing against him (Exod. 17:9–14). He is victorious to begin with because God is with him. We find that Joshua's first battle was successful and that his last one was successful. He was successful because he believed in the Lord God of heaven—because he had strong faith in God. Moses went up into the mountain to pray, and while he was praying Joshua was down fighting Amalek. And when Moses held up his hand Israel prevailed, and when he let down his hand Amalek prevailed. "And Aaron and Hur stayed up his hands, the one on the one side, and the other on the other side; and his hands were steady until the going down of the sun" (Exod. 17:12). His hands were up until Amalek was defeated.

Joshua and Lay Preachers

It appears that Joshua didn't like lay preachers. On a certain occasion he finds two men, named Eldad and Medad, who were prophesying in the camp, but who had never been ordained. They didn't even belong to the company of the seventy elders; so Joshua reports the thing to Moses, and wants him to stop them (Num. 11:26–28).

The people of that class are not all dead yet. We find a good many who are opposed to having the laymen preach; but the word of the Lord is, "Let him that heareth say, come." And a layman can hear as well as if he had been ordained. If I saw a man fall into a river do you think I should go off and get somebody to lay hands on me before I should try to pull him out? Would you have the good Samaritan on his way to Jericho, when he finds the man wounded and half dead by the wayside, leave the poor fellow there while he goes away to get some of his priests to ordain him? By the time he would come back to the wounded man it might be too late to do him any good.

We find that Moses hadn't any such prejudice against lay preachers as Joshua had. He rebukes him, and says he wishes that everybody in the camp was able to prophesy as well as Eldad and Medad (Num. 11:29); so that is the last we hear of Joshua's complaints about lay preachers.

Joshua and Caleb's Minority Report

It looks as if God meant to have his people go over Jordan at Kadesh-barnea, and enter at once into the Promised Land, instead of wandering about in the desert for forty years. But instead of going straight over, when they come to the Jordan they stop on the wilderness side, and Moses sends out an investigating committee to spy out the country (Num. 13:1–25).

This committee consisted of twelve men, one from each tribe, who were to go through the land and inspect it. When they got back they brought in what we should call a majority and a minority report (Num. 13:26–33). Ten of them were discouraged. Like many people nowadays, they had been looking on the dark side. They said it was a good land, a rich land, a land flowing with milk and honey; but they had been looking at the strong cities, with their walls reaching up to heaven, and they had seen some of the sons of Anak, those tall giants, and they were terribly frightened at them.

"When one of those giants looked down upon us," said they, "we felt as if we were but grasshoppers. Their swords and spears are so big we could hardly lift them. One of those Anakims is equal to a score of us, who haven't any weapons to defend ourselves. We are not used to war, and it is folly for us to try to capture this Canaan from the hands of these giants who have been fighting and conquering all their lives. We are not able to go up and possess this land."

But Joshua and his friend Caleb, who were members of this investigating committee, had been looking at the subject in a different light. They had seen the giants and the cities, but they had also remembered the God of Israel. They called to mind how he had brought them up out of Egypt in spite of Pharaoh; how he had brought them through the Red Sea, which had opened its waters to let them pass; how he had rained down bread from heaven, and made the waters to flow out of the rock for them. This was the land which Jehovah had promised to give them for an inheritance. Therefore the giants were nothing but grasshoppers to them. They brought in a minority report, and said, "We are well able to go up and possess the land."

I thank God for Caleb and Joshua! Whenever a man is walking with God he looks down on the giants as if they were grasshoppers, but just as quickly as he loses sight of the Lord and begins to think of himself, he becomes a grasshopper in his own eyes, and the giants look terribly large. I would to God that every Christian in Chicago were like Caleb and Joshua! Then, instead of being discouraged at these saloons, and theaters, and gambling dens, we should all be ready to move forward in the name of God, and gloriously beat back these hosts of hell.

How many people do you suppose there were in Chicago who thought it was foolish to put up this great Tabernacle? One man said to me, "There is no use in building such a great place; it will never be full; if you get Farwell Hall full you will do better than I think you will." That man had been looking at the giants, you see. Some people say we cannot have successful meetings, because the public mind is so much taken up with politics; and there is the Chicago Exposition besides. They do not believe we can do anything in the way of revival till politics and the Exposition are out of the way. These people are looking at the giants and that is all wrong. If God is with us we shall succeed, and a wave of salvation will roll over this city that will bring a great many of its worst sinners to Christ.

But Israel did not believe in God, so they accepted the majority report, and were so angry with Caleb and Joshua that they were going to stone them to death; but the Lord preserved them, for he had great use for them by and by.

So Israel was turned back into the wilderness, and wandered there for forty years, till every man who came up out of Egypt, except these two, had laid his bones in the desert.

Joshua Replaces Moses

Now in Joshua chapter one the forty years' wilderness journey is over, and Moses is about to leave. He went up into Mount Nebo, and God kissed away his soul and buried him (Deut. 34:1–8).

Then Joshua was commanded to take charge of the army. The word of the Lord came to him, saying, "Joshua, arise and go over this Jordan. Moses, my servant, is dead."

There was no president, no general, no marshal about it. There was no title at all, but just merely, "Joshua, arise and go over this Jordan." Now, Joshua just obeyed, and here you will find the secret of his wonderful success. He did just what the Lord told him to do. He did not stand, like many people would have done, and say, "I don't know how I am going to get these people over. Hadn't you better wait, Lord, until the next day? How am I to get these three million people over this angry flood? Hadn't we better wait until the waters recede?"

No! Joshua did not say that. He had his command from God, "Arise and go." When the Lord gave orders, that was enough. He had his command, and he brings these children of Israel down in sight of the swollen stream. Faith must be tried. God will not have people whom he cannot try.

Israel Crosses the Jordan River

And now we see Israel coming up again to the Jordan (Joshua 3). It is in time of harvest, when the Jordan overflows its banks. God was going to test their faith before he took them into Canaan. Some of them might have said, "This is a pretty time to bring us up to cross this river! We haven't any boats, or pontoons, or rafts, and how are we to cross the swift and swollen stream?" But, though God keeps them there for three days looking at that great rushing river, we do not hear a word of complaint. God told them to sanctify themselves, and then, on the fourth day, the priests went down to the edge of the water bearing the ark of the Lord, and the water divided and stood up in great heaps on one side and the other, so that the people passed through the river dry shod. There wasn't even a sign of dampness on their shoes.

The ark of God was placed in the bed of the river Jordan. God went down into death—for that is what Jordan means—and held back the waters till the people were all passed over. Then with twelve stones out of the bed of the stream Joshua built a monument to mark the spot where God had brought his people through the river. "Though I walk through the valley of the shadow of death, I will fear no evil: for thou art with me; thy rod and thy staff they comfort me" (Ps. 23:4).

That ark represented the Almighty. He was in the ark, with the ark right there in the midst of death—for Jordan is death and judgment—right in the middle of the stream. He held that stream in the palm of his hand. And now the people pass beyond—three million of them. You can hear their solemn tread. Not a word is said on their march through death and judgment until Joshua led them onto Resurrection Ground.

Circumcision and Passover

As soon as they struck the other shore they kept the law of their God, and circumcised the people, thus putting blood between themselves and their past life in the wilderness. Here is more of blood, you see. They were willing to worship God. They kept the Passover, and after that they started for Jericho (Josh. 5:1–12).

Jericho Captured

Jericho was shut off and surely the hearts of those people were filled with fear. Here the children of Israel had come to their country and their God had brought them through the Red Sea with an outstretched arm. Surely there was a strange God among them. Jericho had no such God as that. He had defended Israel and led them, and had given them light and life after that.

A few days after, Joshua was taking a look at Jericho, when a man with a drawn sword stood suddenly before him. "Art thou for us, or for our adversaries?" asks Joshua.

"Nay; but as captain of the host of the Lord am I come" (Josh. 5:14). I have no doubt but this was the Son of God himself, and that they planned the battle together for the capture of that great city. But what a plan! It was the most absurd battle anyone could imagine. Seven priests with seven trumpets of rams' horns were to march round the city and blow the trumpets, while the ark of the Lord followed, the army going ahead.

Now what an absurd thing that seems to be! Suppose Dr. Gibson and Dr. Goodwin, and Bishop Foley and Bishop Mc'Laren, and some more of our dignitaries, were to march round Chicago in that fashion. Wouldn't they look rather green? Some people would say they ought at least to have silver or golden trumpets instead of those rough looking rams' horns. Round they go, looking at the walls of the great city. "Ha! Did you see that giant lifting his head and shaking his finger at us?"

The next day they go around again, and the next day, and the next, till the people of Jericho began to laugh, and make all manner of sport of them. They have appointed a committee to watch these strange people, and see that they don't undermine the walls; but they seem to be doing nothing but marching round and round and blowing the rams' horns. They haven't any battering rams; there are no cracks in the walls where they can make a rush and get in; there is nothing they can do but to go round. But when God says, "Go round," that is the thing to do.

Well, the seventh day came, and they were up quite early in the morning. Here were these seven men blowing their rams' horns, and the people going around for the seventh time. At the end of the seventh time Joshua says, "Shout, for the Lord has given you the city." They shout, and down tumble the walls of the city. Then they went up and entered Jericho, and every man, woman, and child of that city perished except for Rahab and her family. God had given the order, and his commands were obeyed.

Joshua Is Victorious

The glory of it was all to be the Lord's. God was as good as his promise. No one was able to stand before Joshua all the days of his life. All the kings of the Canaanites, with all their great armies, their giants, their chariots, and their horsemen, were all as grasshoppers before the face of this courageous servant of God. He subdued thirty-one kings, conquered the land of Canaan, and divided it among the tribes of Israel, but for himself he chose only one mountain, which was dear to him because it was near to Shiloh.

Defeat at Ai

We do, indeed, read of one instance in which an army sent out by Joshua failed to stand before its enemies; but Joshua was not with them. After the walls of Jericho had fallen down before them the next place they went to was Ai. Joshua felt so confident that he sent only three thousand men against it; but for some reason or other his little army fled before the men of Ai.

And Joshua rent his clothes, and fell to the earth upon his face before the ark of the LORD until the eventide, he and the elders of Israel, and put dust upon their heads. And Joshua said, Alas, O LORD God, wherefore hast thou at all brought this people over Jordan, to deliver us into the hands of the

Amorites, to destroy us? Would to God we had been content, and dwelt on the other side Jordan! O Lord, what shall I say, when Israel turneth their backs before their enemies! For the Canaanites and all the inhabitants of the land shall hear of it, and shall environ us round, and cut off our name from the earth: and what wilt thou do unto thy great name?

And the Lord said unto Joshua, Get thee up; wherefore liest thou thus upon thy face? Israel hath sinned, and they have also transgressed my covenant which I commanded them: for they have even taken of the accursed thing, and have also stolen, and dissembled also, and they have put it even among their own stuff. Therefore the children of Israel could not stand before their enemies, but turned their backs before their enemies, because they were accursed: neither will I be with you any more, except ye destroy the accursed from among you.

Joshua 7:6–12

That was why they were unsuccessful, that was why they were defeated; and now if there is going to be a defeat in this city, it will be because of the sins of God's people. It is easy enough to talk about unconverted men confessing their sins and turning to God; but if the church does not confess its sins, we cannot expect sinners to do it. Someone says, "A sin unconfessed is like a bullet in a man's body." We cannot expect to be healthy while there is sin in us.

Joshua at Mount Ebal

After leaving Ai, we read that Joshua came to Mount Ebal, and there a wonderful thing took place. On one side, on the slope of Mount Gerizim, were half of the children of Israel, and on the other side, on the slope of Mount Ebal, were the other half. There were three million people gathered there, and the whole law of Moses was read over to them.

It was a solemn sight. Moreover, all the law of God was read—not a part, but the whole. Joshua read the blessings and cursings. He did not stand up there like someone reading a moral essay and say that they must be good for they were going into the Promised Land, that there were blessings for them, and say nothing about the curses. No; he did not do that. He read all.

It says here, in the eighth chapter:

And all Israel, and their elders, and officers, and their judges, stood on this side the ark and on that side before the priests the Levites, which bare the ark of the covenant of the LORD, as well the stranger, as he that was born among them; half of them over against mount Gerizim, and half of them over against mount Ebal; as Moses the servant of the LORD had commanded before, that they should bless the people of Israel. And afterward he read

all the words of the law, the blessings and cursings, according to all that is
written in the book of the law.

Joshua 8:33–34

Now, mark that. "He read all the words of the law, the blessings and
cursings, according to all that is written in the book of the law." If Joshua
had been like many of the present day, he would have said to himself, "I
will read the blessings, but not the cursings. I do not believe God is going
to curse a man if he does wrong, so I will read the blessings and omit the
cursings." But, thank God, he read the whole law—the blessings and the
cursings.

He did not keep back anything. "There was not a word of all that Moses
commanded which Joshua read not" (Josh. 8:35). Thank God for such a
man! That is the kind of men we want nowadays, men who will not cut
the Bible to pieces like the king who took out his penknife and said, "I
don't like that; cut that out. I don't like this. Cut this out." So they cut and
slashed the Bible until very little was left.

The thirty-third verse of the eighth chapter says they were all there—
"as well the stranger, as he that was born among them." You see, Joshua
made no distinction. He read to the stranger as well as to those that were
of the children of Israel. It was all read.

Joshua Defeats the Confederated Kings

And now Joshua is ready to move on. The law had been read, they had
worshipped their God, and they were ready to move on. Undoubtedly the
nations throughout that land had heard how this solemn assembly had
met on the mountainside and the law had been read. They had been there
about three days.

Someone now comes to Joshua with startling news. The messenger
begins with the question, "Joshua, have you heard that there is a confederacy formed to oppose you? Instead of meeting one man you are to
meet five. They are coming down from the mountains with great regi-
ments of giants. Why, the mountains are full of the sons of Anak—full of
giants—and some of them are eight feet high. Why, they are so big that
they would scare our own men to death. Why, one man came out and just
shook his little finger at our men, and scared them out of their lives. There
was not a man who dared to meet them. The whole land is full of giants.
Do you know that they have formed a confederacy? Five kings are coming down against you with hordes of these giants."

I see the old warrior. He does not tremble at all. He had received the
word of God, "Joshua, be of good courage. No man shall be able to stand

against you." He moved on in his godly armor and in the name of his God, and he routed his adversaries. The hour was growing late, and he commanded sun and moon to stand still, and they obeyed him. So there were two days in one. He found the five kings hid away in a cave, and he took them out and hanged them. He took thirty-one kings and kingdoms. He just took that land by faith.

Joshua's Right of Conquest

Now, some people ask, "What right had he to come over and take that land?" If you will read Deuteronomy 9:4, you will see what right he had. "Speak not thou in thine heart, after that the LORD thy God hath cast them out from before thee, saying: For my righteousness the LORD hath brought me in to possess this land: but, for the wickedness of these nations, the LORD doth drive them out from before thee."

That is why he drove them out. Their cup of iniquity was filled, and God just dashed it to pieces. When any nation's cup of iniquity is full, God sweeps them away.

Now, mark the Scripture, "Not for thy righteousness, or for the uprightness of thine heart dost thou go to possess their land; but for the wickedness of these nations the LORD thy God doth drive them out from before thee, and that he may perform the word which the LORD sware unto thy fathers, Abraham, Isaac, and Jacob. Understand therefore, that the LORD thy God giveth thee not this good land to possess it for thy righteousness; for thou art a stiffnecked people" (Deut. 9:5–6).

They were a stiffnecked people. It was not for the righteousness of the children of Israel that the Lord gave them this land. He judged these nations on account of their wickedness.

Joshua's Final Days

Now, Joshua has overcome them and driven them from the face of the earth, and this brings out one noble trait in his character. When he came to divide up the land, Joshua took the poorest treasure himself, that he might be near the ark (Josh. 19:49–50). And there, on Mount Ephraim, he died at the ripe old age of one hundred and ten years. During all those years not a man was able to stand before him. See the contrast between his dying testimony and that of Jacob! Jacob's self-reproach was, "Few and evil have the days of the years of my life been" (Gen. 47:9). He had a stormy voyage.

Look and see this old warrior, Joshua, going to rest. He had tried God forty years. He had heard the crack of the slave driver's whip, down there in Egypt. But probably he had a praying mother, who talked to him about this King of the Hebrews, about the God of Abraham, of Isaac, and of Jacob, and he believed in that God. When Moses came down into Egypt he found this young man just in the prime of his life. Joshua recognized in Moses that he was an instrument of the Almighty, and that the King of the Hebrews had sent him there to deliver his people.

Joshua had tried God forty years in the wilderness and when eighty years old he was called into the Promised Land. He had tried God thirty years in Canaan, and now, at the age of one hundred and ten, the aged and invincible warrior isn't going to die like an infidel. He knows he is about to die, and he calls for all the tribes of Israel and their elders. These come up from the tribe of Benjamin, the tribe of Simeon, the tribe of Zebulon, and so on; and they are gathered at Shiloh, to be there to hear the old prophet and patriarch.

That man of God speaks, and what does he say? What is his dying testimony? How we all linger around the couch of our dying friends! How anxious we are to get their last words!

Well, let us turn back. What are the last words of this man who has tried God and proved God? These are the words: "I am going the way of all the earth: and ye know in your hearts and in all your souls, that not one thing hath failed of all the good things which the LORD your God spake concerning you; all are come to pass unto you, and not one thing hath failed thereof" (Josh. 23:14).

Not one good thing has failed! God has kept his word. God has made his word good. "Not one good thing hath failed." What a dying testimony! How glorious! In the beautiful sunset light the old warrior sank away, like he was going to sleep. In the dusk of a beautiful summer's evening he passed away. There is the old man's dying testimony. He could tell the people of God. He was the only one left. The rest had gone. Moses had sunk into his desert grave, and the other leaders of the tribe of Israel had passed away. But now he was going to die in the Promised Land.

We read that "Israel served the LORD all the days of Joshua, and all the days of the elders that overlived Joshua, and which had known all the works of the LORD, that he had done for Israel" (Josh. 24:31). That is a glorious record. There was courage enough in him to supply a whole nation; and even after he was dead the power of his godly example continued for a generation. May the Lord help us all to be of good courage! We are now at our Kadesh-barnea; the Promised Land is before us. Let us go over and possess it, and may the Lord give us the desire of our hearts in the salvation of multitudes of souls.

Appeal to Faith and Courage

Be of good courage; fear nothing. Believe that God is willing to use you, and then he will use you in such a way that, like Joshua, nothing shall be able to stand before you.

People have been asking me if I don't feel very much encouraged by the great congregations that come to hear me preach. Well, I will tell you what encourages me a great deal more than the crowds. At the noon prayer meeting in Farwell Hall today the Lord was with us. There were a great many who felt their hearts growing tender, and when people begin to have broken hearts before the Lord I always feel greatly encouraged.

It is very gratifying to see so many people here, but we must not depend on numbers. If the people of God are brimful of faith and courage, one shall chase a thousand, and two put ten thousand to flight. If we only had a few hundred people full of the Holy Ghost and of courage, and who meditate upon the word of God, we could lift up the standard of Jesus Christ in this dark city, and the Lord himself would arise and shake terribly the earth.

A great many people are always seeing lions in the way (Prov. 26:13). They are always looking for failure. I think that such people hinder the cause of God more than any other. They are in the way. They are of no use themselves, and they take away the power and courage of others. Look at Elijah at Mount Carmel (1 Kings 18) standing up as bold as a lion in the face of all the priests of Baal. He did a great day's work that day. But the very next thing we hear is that a woman sent him a message threatening to kill him, and the poor man was so scared that he fled for his life into the wilderness, sat down beneath a juniper tree, and began to pray the Lord to take away his life (1 Kings 19:1–4).

Oh, my friends, it is a very bad place for God's people under the juniper tree. What they should do is to come up boldly and face their duty, and not be afraid of men, women, or devils.

27 Judas

Judas felt so badly over the betrayal of his Master, that he went out and hanged himself; but he did not confess—that is, he did not confess to God. He came back and confessed to the priests, saying, "I have sinned in that I have betrayed the innocent blood." It was of no use to confess to them. They would not forgive him. What he should have done was to confess to God; but instead of that, he went right away and hanged himself.

Let us imagine we are living when the Son of God was upon earth—that we were citizens of Jerusalem; that we were at that memorable feast; that late Thursday afternoon we are walking down the street, and we see thirteen men coming down the street. We make inquiries as to who they are, and we are told, "It is Jesus and his disciples. They are going to the guest chamber." They come to a common-looking house. They go upstairs to that guest chamber and sit around the table. Jesus began to be exceedingly sorrowful. He knew that one of his disciples was that night to swear he never knew him; that the Shepherd was to be smitten, and the sheep were to leave him. He was sorrowful unto death.

John was wondering what was making him so sad. He told them that one of them that night should betray him. They all looked startled. At last one says, "Lord, is it I?"

And another says, "Is it I?"

They all began to mistrust themselves, and at last Judas, that awful traitor, who was already plotting with the chief priests to deliver Jesus up, said, "Lord, is it I?"

Jesus gave him to understand that it was, and presently he turned and said, "What thou doest do quickly," and Judas got up and left.

I don't believe you could find a sadder party than they were. Judas had seen him perform mighty miracles; he had been with him when he fed the multitude in the wilderness, when he had wept over Jerusalem. He had been associated with Jesus for three long years, and now he gets up and goes out. It was night, and I hear him as he goes down those stairs. He goes off to the Sanhedrin, to the rulers of the Jews. He asks, "What will you give me?"

He sold Jesus for thirty pieces of silver. How cheaply he sold his birthright. You condemn him, but how many of you are selling him for less? How many would sell him for a night in some drinking saloon?

28 Lame Man of Bethesda

John 5:1–14

The Lame Man's Need

I was going to call this fifth chapter of John the wonderful chapter, but all the chapters of this Gospel are wonderful. Here was a poor lame man, down by the pool of Bethesda, who had suffered an infirmity for thirty-eight years. We think it is bad enough to be sick thirty-eight hours, and if anybody is sick thirty-eight days, that is a terrible thing.

His friends used to carry him about at first, but by and by they got tired of it, and left him to get along the best way he could. There he is down by the pool, among a great number of impotent folks, helpless and friendless. He can't get into the pool himself, and there is no one to put him in. He has quit trying, he has gotten to the end of himself; and this is the very man that Christ is most interested in.

That is always the way with Christ. You'll always find him where he is the most needed. That isn't the way with us. If we were only like the Master we should more often be found in hospitals, prisons, and at the bedside of the sick and dying.

One of the Lord's servants once carried a bouquet to a man in a hospital. The patient took the flowers in his hand, smelled of them, and seemed to be quite delighted with their beauty and fragrance. Then the minister said to the lady who brought them, "If I had only known how much good a bunch of flowers would do a poor sick man, I would have carried a good many more to the hospitals."

I remember reading a story about a man who broke his leg, but was laid up in his own house. One day they brought him the first cluster of grapes that had ripened in his own garden. He took them with great delight, looked at them, smelled them, and then said, "It seems too bad for me to eat these, they are so nice. I want you to take them over to my neighbor, who is sick with the fever. They will do him more good than they will me." When his neighbor got them he was greatly pleased, but he happened to think of a third man who was sicker than he was, so he sent them over to him.

The third man was very grateful, took a good look and a good smell of them, and then said, "Here, take these grapes, with my compliments, and carry them to Neighbor So-and-So. Poor fellow, he has broken his leg and is shut up in his house. I think he needs the grapes more than I."

So the grapes came back to the first man again, and I have no doubt they tasted a great deal sweeter for all the love and gladness they had called forth as they passed round the neighborhood.

Christ Meets the Man's Need

Now, to come back to this chapter. There were three classes of people in this multitude. There were the blind, and the halt, and the withered. I remember during the Civil War down in the army after a battle the surgeons used to take care of the worst cases first. Just so it was with Christ. I suppose this man was the very worst case among them, so the Lord picks him out from all the rest, and says to him, "Wilt thou be made whole?"

"Yes," says the man, "I would like to be made whole, but I have nobody to help me into the pool. No one takes notice of me anymore, and I have about given up all hope of ever being cured. Everybody pushes me back and gets down before me, and I suppose I shall have to be a poor, withered-up man all the days of my life."

Jesus said to him, "Rise! Take up thy bed, and walk." He doesn't tell him to do such and such, and he will get well by degrees, but speaks the word that is to cure him all at once.

It doesn't take God a great while to save a person when he sets about it. But there are a good many people yet who can't believe in sudden conversions.

Now, if he had been a Chicago man he would have argued this way, "What is the use of telling me to rise? I couldn't stand up a minute if I should try. He tells me to walk, and I haven't walked a step for thirty-eight years. What folly to tell me to walk, to say nothing about carrying my bed."

But the man doesn't talk that way. When the Lord tells him to rise he starts to rise, and up he comes. Then he seizes that old couch that he has lain upon so long, swings it over his shoulder—and walks.

My friends, God doesn't tell a man to do a thing that is impossible, and then punish him to all eternity because he didn't do it. With the command always comes the help to obey.

The Sweetest Verse in the Bible

Now I want to read to you what is to me the sweetest verse in the whole Bible. I sometimes call it my platform. I got both feet on it twenty-one years ago, and I have been standing on it ever since. It is John 5:24, "Verily, verily, I say unto you,"—whenever the Lord begins that way you may know something is coming—"He that heareth my word, and believeth on him that sent me, hath everlasting life, and shall not come into condemnation; but is passed from death unto life."

In the verse before it we read about honoring the Son as we do the Father. Don't you know that the best way to please a father is to speak well of his son? Just so the way to please God is to speak well of his Son.

I like that little word "hath." In my Bible it is right in the middle of the verse. There are two lines above it, and two lines below it, and it is right in the middle of the middle line. It doesn't say you shall have everlasting life after awhile, or that God will give it to you when you die; but if you hear the word of the Lord and believe on him that sent him, you have everlasting life in you at this very moment. My friends, get on this text and stand on it. It is a rock. You may tremble sometimes when you stand upon it, but the rock will never tremble.

In John 5:28–29, Christ says, "Marvel not at this: for the hour is coming, in the which all that are in the graves shall hear his voice, and shall come forth; they that have done good, unto the resurrection of life; and they that have done evil, unto the resurrection of damnation." I don't know as this refers to the resurrection of the last day. Perhaps it means that souls are to be raised from the death of sin by hearing and believing the voice of Christ. At any rate it is a greater miracle to convert a soul than it was to raise dead Lazarus.

Now Christ sometimes gives us specimens of his work. When he healed Jairus's daughter, some of those skeptics said the girl never was dead (Mark 5:22; Luke 8:41).

So a little while after, he raises the widow's son from the casket in which they were carrying him out to bury him (Luke 7:11–18). Still some don't believe, and so, after awhile, he comes to the grave of Lazarus, who had been dead so long that the body had begun to decay, and calls to him, "Lazarus, come forth!" (John 11:43).

Someone says there was so much power in the voice of the Lord that if he had not called Lazarus by name all the dead in the graveyard would have come forth to meet him. My friends, you have heard the word of the Lord, accept it, believe it now, and before you leave this hall tonight you may pass from death unto life.

29 Lame Man of Capernaum

Mark 2:1–12

There are four men coming down the streets of Capernaum. I never knew them, but if I met them in the streets of Boston, I should feel like grasping them by the hand. Perhaps one of them was he who was converted not long before. Perhaps the other was the leper who went to Jesus and got cured, and when he came home, his wife didn't know who he was, and couldn't believe it was her husband.

Another had been cured perhaps of blindness, and here was the man with the palsy who had nearly shaken himself into his grave. The doctors of Jerusalem had all given him up as a hopeless case. "Why," they said, "he cannot even get his food to his mouth, he shakes so. We can't do anything with him."

Well, these young converts came along—I suppose they were young. They have more faith than anyone else—and they see this man with the palsy and instantly say that one word from Jesus will put it away.

But they can't get him there; they don't see how they can carry him, and finally one of them goes and gets a neighbor, and says, "Here's a man with the palsy; if we can get him up to where Christ is, he can just heal him at once." I think he would be astonished, and say, "What, save that man; impossible! He can't be cured." But the young convert persists, and tells him of those who had been made to see, and the deaf to hear, and the lame to walk, and so convinced the neighbor that at last he said, "Well, I will help you and go and see this wonderful physician." And away they go and hunt up another young convert, who had been lame for years.

He is not strong enough to help them, however, and they find another man. He has been deaf and dumb for years. And these four young converts take this man with the palsy and put him, I suppose, on what we called during the Civil War, a stretcher, and away they go to Christ. They had faith in what they were about.

I can imagine the young men saying, as they carry him along, "We will not have to carry him back again; the palsy will be gone; it will be cured then." On they go with their load, and when they get to the house, they find it crowded inside and a multitude standing outside.

They say to the people, "Let us pass; we want to take this poor man to Christ."

The people answer, "Why, there is no hope for him; he is past all cure."

"Ah," say the young converts, "that is nothing. Jesus of Nazareth can cure him; all things are possible to him."

But they wouldn't stand aside. They wouldn't allow them to get in. These four men are not going to take this man back home without seeing Jesus. They are determined not to fail. They hesitate a moment, then go to the next house; it is a neighbor's. There were no bells in those days, and so they knock.

When the neighbor comes to the door they say, "We want to get into the next house; let us go through yours."

"Oh, yes," says the man, and they ascend the staircase, and get on the roof, and get over to the next house. There's no entrance through there, and so they dig a hole; they tear up this roof.

A great many people in this city would be opposed to this sort of thing. They would say, "If you want to get into the house, you want things to be done decently; don't tear up the roof in that way."

But, my friends, if we want to go to work for Christ, we must tear up the whole house if it's necessary. We must use vigorous means. These young men had good faith, and that's what we need here. But when they had torn off the roof, they had nothing to let the man down by. So they looked about and made a rope of their own clothing, and down they laid him right among the Pharisees and learned doctors, right at the feet of Jesus.

That is a good place to put a poor sinner. We are not told whether that man with the palsy had any faith. But the Son of God looked up, and saw their faith, the faith of the four men, and it pleased him. It was like a cup of refreshment that satisfied the longings of his soul. He saw the brightness of their faith when he looked upon them. And he said to the sick man, "Son, be of good cheer, thy sins are forgiven thee." The man was healed by the cleansing word of Christ.

30 Leper

Mark 1:40–45

See that poor leper! Do you know what an awful thing leprosy is? A disease so terrible that it separates its victim from all the world, and makes him an outcast, even from his own home. Everyone is afraid of him. His disease is so contagious that to touch him or even to breathe the air near him is dangerous and so these poor, afflicted wretches have to go away and live in a cave or desert all alone.

They sit by the wayside afar off, calling to the passers-by for charity—who sometimes throw them a piece of money and hurry off, lest they also come into that terrible plight.

The Leper Becomes Ill

In the first chapter of Mark there is an account of Christ healing a leper. I can see that man coming home one day, and saying to his wife, "I feel very strange; there is something on my body which looks like leprosy."

This is terrible news. His wife looks at him carefully, and says, "My dear, I am afraid it is leprosy!"

Ah, what a cloud comes over that home. His wife and children are heartbroken all at once. They know very well what the leprosy means. He who is once pronounced a leper becomes a wanderer forever. It is worse than going down to the grave. It is like living in a sepulcher. Banished from home and from society, compelled whenever anyone approaches to cry, "Unclean! Unclean!" with nothing to occupy himself except his own misery. Ah indeed, it is a terrible thing to be a leper!

The Leper Cast Out

The poor man takes his little son in his arms, kisses his wife and all the rest of his heartbroken family, and then he goes to the high priest, who pronounces him a leper and banishes him from amongst mankind. Perhaps someone goes to tell him that his child is sick, or dying, but he cannot go to him. He hears that his son is dead, but he can't go to the funeral. All he can do is to go to the grave when nobody else is near.

The Leper Is Healed by Jesus

By and by the Son of God comes along the road by which the miserable man is begging. He has heard of this Jesus of Nazareth, and when he comes within earshot he cries out to him, "Lord, if thou wilt, thou canst make me clean!"

And Jesus says, "I will; be thou clean!"

All at once a thrill of health and joy goes through the man's body and nerves. He feels himself a new creature. The old leprosy has passed away, and all his life has become new. He can hardly believe it is himself for joy. His flesh is like the flesh of a little child. He begins to pour out his heart in thanks to Jesus, who sends him away to the priests, saying: "Go, show thyself to the priests, and offer the gift that Moses commanded."

The Cleansed Leper Returns Home

I can see him starting at a full run to show himself to the priest, and be pronounced clean, and be permitted to go to his home and his kindred again.

Oh, what joy there is in that house when he comes and tells them he has met the Lord, and the Lord has cleansed him! Very much such kind of joy as there is in many homes these days when wild and wicked souls who were lost in sin, and full of vice and degradation, and have met the Lord at some of these inquiry meetings, have gone to tell their mothers that they have been saved by believing in Jesus.

Ah, my friends, the leprosy of sin is worse than any other leprosy that ever was in this world. It spoiled Lucifer, one of the brightest of the angels in heaven (Isa. 14:12), and yet there are those who cling to their sins, and refuse to let the Savior cleanse them away. Trust yourself to Christ and be made clean.

31 Lot

Genesis 13–14; 19:1–29

The following discourse to parents was preached before an immense congregation in the Chicago Tabernacle. Mr. Sankey sang the solo, "Nothing but Leaves." The Scripture came from Luke 17:28–30 in which Christ is answering the Pharisee who had demanded of him when the kingdom of God should come. "Likewise also as it was in the days of Lot; they did eat, they drank, they bought, they sold, they planted, they builded; but the same day that Lot went out of Sodom it rained fire and brimstone from heaven, and destroyed them all. Even thus shall it be in the day when the Son of man is revealed."

Lot as a Representative Man

I want to speak tonight on the life of Lot. I have chosen him for a subject because he is a representative man. There are hundreds of men like him in Chicago. Where there is one Abraham, or one Daniel, or one Elijah, you may find a thousand Lots.

This man seems to have started out in life well enough, but it wasn't a great while before he got rich, and that was the beginning of all his troubles. He lived with his old uncle, Abraham, until he became possessed of large flocks and herds, so that there was hardly room enough in the country where they lived for his cattle and those of his uncle. After a while there arose a strife among the herdsmen of the two flocks as to what part of the land they should occupy; but, however much the herdsmen might quarrel, he couldn't get up a quarrel with Abraham.

That friend of God didn't want to get into trouble out there among those heathen, who, if they saw him angry over such a matter, would say he

155

was not a whit better than themselves. So he says to Lot, "Is not the whole land before thee? Separate thyself, I pray thee, from me: if thou wilt take the left hand, then I will go to the right; or if thou depart to the right hand, then I will go to the left" (Gen. 13:9).

If Lot had not been so selfish he would have given his old uncle the first choice instead of taking it himself, but he lifted up his eyes and saw the plain of Jordan. It was well-watered and fruitful; so he says, "I will take that." He chose the best for himself, you see, and then pitched his tent toward Sodom. He might have been a pretty good man up to this time, but then he began to backslide.

Perhaps he was ambitious to be richer than Abraham, and so he chose for himself, instead of letting God choose for him. If he had asked God, Lot would not have entered Sodom; no man ever goes into Sodom by God's advice. He determined for himself.

Lot in Sodom

I have no doubt that the Sodomites who got acquainted with him said he was a very shrewd man, a very sharp business man, and predicted that he would sometime be very rich.

How long he stayed in the plain we don't know; but after awhile we find him living in Sodom. What business had Lot to be living in Sodom? He knew what sort of people the Sodomites were, for he had pitched his tent in their neighborhood. He knew they were a wicked, idolatrous, iniquitous people; but, perhaps, he felt that business was pressing. He had a large number of people dependent upon him, and probably he thought he could make money faster by going into Sodom than he could by staying outside and giving his attention to his cattle.

Lot went into Sodom with his eyes open. He knew he was taking his children into bad company, and bringing his household into the midst of the most abominable heathen; but the main question with him seems to have been business, business; money, money! How many of you fathers are doing just the same thing? It was business that took him there.

He might have said, "Well, I've got a large family. I've got a great many dependent upon me, and I must get rich faster; so I will go into Sodom. Business is the first consideration, and it must be attended to."

The next we hear of Lot he is in trouble. They who go to live in Sodom must take the fate of Sodom. The Sodomites were at war with some of their neighbors, who came up with a scouting party, seized some of the people, and carried them away into captivity. Among those captives was Lot; and I suppose he would have spent the rest of his days as a slave if his old uncle Abraham hadn't heard about it, taken a band of three hundred and eighteen of his servants, pursued after the captors, and rescued the captives and spoil.

Now see the difference between these two men. When Abraham comes back from his expedition he meets Melchizedek, a priest of the most high God, and gives him tithes of all the spoils he has taken. Then he meets the king of Sodom, who is very glad to make his acquaintance, and to have his captives brought back again. So he says, "Now, Abraham, you take the goods for your share, and give me back the captives for my share."

"No," says Abraham, "I have made a vow to the Lord, the most high God, that I will not take anything that is thine, lest thou should say, I have made Abraham rich." You see, Abraham didn't want any Sodomite wealth, but Lot was keen to get all he could of it.

Destruction of Sodom

Now you would suppose Lot would say to himself, I have had enough of Sodom; I will get out of the way of these miserable heathen. But perhaps he had lost money in some operation, and he wanted to go back into Sodom and make it up. I have no doubt that after a while Lot became a great man in Sodom—one of the best businessmen in the place. Probably he had a good many corner lots, and some fine business blocks, with his name upon them. Perhaps they admired his talent in money, making so much that they made him mayor of Sodom, or judge—Judge Lot, that sounds very well—or maybe they sent him to Congress, if they had one. Probably Mrs. Lot had a very fine turn-out—the handsomest horses and carriage in all the city; and the Misses Lot were the most fashionable young ladies, and had the handsomest dresses of any young women in all Sodom.

But one evening, while Lot was sitting in the gate of Sodom, he saw two strangers coming, whom he knew were angels, because he had seen them twenty years before at the house of his uncle Abraham. So he bowed himself down at their feet, and begged them to do him the honor of lodging with him. The angels didn't like to go inside the gate and spend the night in Sodom, so they said, "Nay; but we will abide in the street all night."

However, Lot urged them so hard that they entered into the city with him, and went to his house, where he made them a feast.

They hadn't been there a great while before a mob of Sodomites gathered around the house, and made a terrible uproar. Lot must have been very much ashamed of his neighbors, and we learn that he went out and tried to make them behave themselves; but they laughed at him, and abused him. If the angels hadn't struck them blind there is no telling what they might have done.

Poor Lot was dreadfully frightened when he heard the Sodomites trying to break his door down, and was very glad to have the angels there to protect him. Then these strangers inquired if he had any relatives in Sodom besides those that lived in his own house. "For," said they, "we are come down to destroy this city whose cry is waxed great before the face of the Lord."

Then Lot was obliged to confess that he had given some of his daughters to be married to some of those wicked young Sodomites.

"You go and fetch them," said the angels, "for tomorrow morning the Lord will destroy the city."

Poor man! He finds that the way of the world is not the way of the largest profit after all. Those fine buildings of his will all go down in ashes, and up in smoke; all his speculations will come to nothing. But the poor man is so much frightened for his life and the life of his family that he has not much time to think about his real estate.

I can see him groping his way along the streets of Sodom, dodging all the sons of Belial that he sees, until he comes to the house of the man who has married his oldest daughter. He pounds on the door until somebody puts his head out of the window and asks what he wants. It is one of his sons-in-law, and the poor man, trembling from head to foot, tries to tell him about the visit of the angels, and how the Lord is going to destroy the city tomorrow, and that he must take his wife and come over to his house immediately.

But his son-in-law laughs at him. "Ho, ho," says he, "you go home and go to bed. Don't be making a fool of yourself out here in the street, at midnight, waking people up with such a silly story as that! Sodom was never so prosperous in all its history as it is in these days. Don't you imagine that it's going to be destroyed."

Now the poor man is in greater trouble than ever. His son-in-law won't believe him, and he is obliged to leave his daughter to perish with those sinners. He begs and entreats that if he won't come himself, he will at least give him his daughter; but the man abuses him, and shuts the window, and refuses to hear anything more from him. Then the old man goes to the house of another son-in-law, and wakes him up, and tells him the same terrible tale, and he makes fun of it in the same way.

The brokenhearted old man, finding that both his daughters are hopelessly lost, mourns the day he ever came to Sodom. There is nothing for him now but to go home and tell the angels that he cannot make those people believe that the city is to be destroyed.

Oh, you fathers and mothers who have given your children over to wicked, worldly-minded influences, and set them up in life according to the fashion of this world, with people who don't fear God or keep his commandments, what do you suppose that old man thought then about marrying his daughters to wicked men of the world just because they were rich?

As soon as ever it was light the angels hastened Lot, saying, "Arise, take thy wife, and thy two daughters, which are here; lest thou be consumed in the iniquity of the city" (Gen. 19:15). But Lot couldn't bear to go and leave his property to be destroyed, and leave his other daughters to be burned up, and so we find that he lingered until "the men laid hold upon his hand, and upon the hand of his wife, and upon the hand of his two daughters . . . and they brought him forth, and set him without the city" (Gen. 19:16).

Remember Lot's Wife

Poor worldly-minded people! Their hearts were so set upon Sodom that even the angels could hardly get them out of it. Still, I suppose, partly for the sake of his old uncle, Abraham, the Lord wouldn't let Lot be destroyed in Sodom. But there was his wife, whose heart was wholly set upon this world; in spite of all the urging of the angels, she couldn't bear to go away and leave her fine house, and all her elegant furniture, and all her nice dresses to be burned up with fire and brimstone.

When she ought to have been running with all her might to get out of the way of the coming storm, she stopped and looked back, thinking, probably, what a great loss she was suffering—or perhaps she was thinking of her daughters who had been left behind. And the Lord, seeing that her heart was set upon Sodom, let her stay there; and while her husband and daughters escaped to Zoar, she became a pillar of salt. She and Sodom remained together in their destruction.

We are told in the Scriptures that the people were eating, drinking, buying and selling, planning and building until the very moment Lot went out of Sodom. Perhaps not a man in all Sodom took any account of his going out. It might have gotten rumored around that he was going because he believed the city was about to be destroyed, but no man believed it. His sons and daughters did not believe what their father said to them, and the Son of God says they were all destroyed great and small, learned and unlearned, rich and poor. All alike perished.

Bear in mind that if you live in Sodom destruction will come upon you. The world may call you successful, but the only way to test success is to take a man's whole life—not the beginning nor middle, but the whole of it. If a man is in Sodom, he will find at last the fruits of his life to be "nothing but leaves—nothing but leaves."

Avoid Sodom

I have not time this evening to follow this man to the end of his miserable life. We know that it was wretched and disgraceful, and that his fortune, which seemed so favorable while he was with his uncle in the way of righteousness, all turned to ashes and misery when he got into Sodom.

I pray you, businessmen, be warned by the life of this worldly-minded man. If you are a member of the church and are getting rich and increasing in goods, don't forget the word of the Lord, which says, "Seek ye first the kingdom of God, and his righteousness; and all these things shall be added unto you" (Matt. 6:33). Keep out of Sodom for your own sake as well as for the sake of your family.

And you, Christian parents, with a family of daughters, see to it that you don't marry them to wicked men. The wealth of Sodom, and the fashion of Sodom, and the society of Sodom may seem to be very desirable, but the end of all these things is in sorrow, and destruction, and wrath. Oh, ye worldly-minded men and women of the church, keep out of Sodom, lest you perish in its plagues!

32 **Maniac Boy**

Matthew 17:14–21; Mark 9:14–29

Jesus Heals the Maniac Boy

Look at that maniac boy; his father and mother have brought him to the disciples, and asked them to cast the devil out of him. The poor fellow has been tormented with devils all his life. They have tortured and twisted him all out of shape. They have plagued his mind worse than his body. They have wrought all manner of terrible mischief with him—thrown him into the fire, and into the water, so that his father and mother are utterly brokenhearted over him.

But they have heard that Jesus of Nazareth has power to heal the sick and cast out devils, and some of their friends have told them about the man who was in the tombs whom he had saved from his madness. So they bring the boy where they suppose they will find the Savior, but when they come Jesus is not there. He is away on the Mount of Transfiguration.

"Well," says the father, "since the Master is away, I think we might try some of the disciples. Perhaps they can do something for him."

So they bring him to Thomas and ask him if he thinks he can do anything for the poor fellow. Thomas is not quite certain about it. It seems to be a bad case, and he doesn't quite like to undertake it; his faith is not quite up to the point of taking hold of such a devil as that. He has cured some easy cases, but whether he will be able to do any good now is more than he can tell.

He watches the boy in a fit of his terrible agony, and then he musters all the faith and courage he has, and tells the devils to come out.

The devils only laugh at him, and torment the boy worse than ever. Then he calls Matthew, and Bartholomew, and some of the rest of them, and they all try their hands on him, but the devils are stronger than all of them when the Master is away. So the poor boy lies there, wallowing and foaming, all the worse because of the efforts these men are making to drive the devils out.

161

Pretty soon the Master himself comes back, along with Peter, James, and John, and when he hears about it, he looks sorrowfully at those disciples who had failed to cure the lad, and he says, "Bring him to me."

"Mark you," Spurgeon says, "he [the father] was a poor theologian when he came to Christ. He came and said, 'If thou canst do anything,' and the Lord rebuked him right there. He said, 'If thou canst believe.' He put the 'if' in the right place. 'All things are possible to him that believeth; bring him unto me.'"

The devils know their time has come now, and they torture the poor boy, and throw him down, and put him into agony; but the moment the Lord lays eyes upon him, he tells them to depart.

The devils always obey when Christ speaks to them. The father thinks the boy is dead, but the Savior lifts him up, and gives him to him alive, and he goes home happier than words can tell, because Christ has saved his afflicted boy.

Bring Your Children to Christ

My friends, you who are fathers and mothers, you ought to be encouraged by this to bring your children to Christ. Some of your sons are breaking your hearts and rushing down to death and hell. They have not yet lost their reason, but if they were to die as they are now they certainly would lose their souls. Many a father has a worse son than that boy the disciples couldn't cure. I would rather have my son deaf and dumb, and suffering all manner of tortures, than that he should go down to a drunkard's grave!

The parents of this boy carry their son to the disciples, but they can do nothing for him. There is no use of your depending upon any man, or any church, to save the souls of your children. What you must do with them is to bring them to the Master himself.

There is one point in this story that I want you especially to notice. The father, when he came to Christ, said, "If thou canst do anything, have compassion on us and help us." Jesus immediately replies by putting the "if" where it belongs, and says, "If thou canst believe: all things are possible to him that believeth."

There is no lack of power in Christ, but there is a terrible lack of faith in us, and the thing for us to do is just what the father of this boy did. We feel that our faith is too little, but we can pray as he prayed, "Lord, I believe, help thou mine unbelief!" And when the Lord helps our faith, so that we are able to take hold upon him for ourselves and for our children, then comes life, and health, and grace.

33 Martha

Luke 10:38–42; John 11:1–44

There was a woman right in the midst of the darkness, when many of Christ's disciples left him, who came forward and invited him to her home—a woman by the name of Martha of Bethany.

I can imagine Martha coming from Bethany one day, and going into the temple, in Jerusalem, to worship. The great Galilean Prophet came in, who spake as never man spake, and she listened to his words. And as the words came from his lips they fell upon Martha's ears, and she said, "Well, I will invite Jesus to my house."

It must have cost her something to do that. Christ was unpopular. There was a hiss going up in Jerusalem against him. They called him an impostor. All the leading men of the nation were opposed to him. They said he was Beelzebub, the lord of filth. They charged that he was an impostor and a deceiver. And yet Martha invites him to her home. I hope there will always be some Martha to invite Jesus to her home to be her guest. He will make that home a thousand times better than it ever was before.

Martha invited him home with her. We read of his going often to Bethany. The noblest, best, and grandest thing Martha ever did was to make room in her home for Jesus Christ. That one act will live forever. Little did she know, when she invited the Son of God to become her guest, who he was. When we receive Jesus into our hearts little do we know who he is. It will take all eternity to find out who Jesus is.

There was a dark cloud then over that home in Bethany, but Martha didn't know it. Neither did Mary see that cloud. It was fast settling down upon that home. It was soon going to burst upon that little family. The Savior knew all about it. He saw that dark cloud coming across that threshold.

163

But look again, look in that home where Lazarus comes home sick. Some think his occupation was that of a scribe, that he was a writer, and one day he came home weary; perhaps he had a headache, and fever seized him. One of the leading physicians of Jerusalem is sent for, and on the third or fourth day he tells the sisters, "There is no hope for your brother, he is dying, he cannot live."

When all earthly hope had failed, and they had given up, then the sisters sent for Jesus. Those two sisters sent a messenger, perhaps one of the neighbors, off from Bethany; perhaps he would have to go twenty or thirty miles away, on the other side of Jordan, for they heard Jesus was there. They didn't have papers in those days to tell them where he was, and if there had been papers they wouldn't have reported his meetings.

They instructed the messenger to say, "Him whom thou lovest is sick." That was enough. What a title to have to a man's name! What a eulogy to have to a name! And when the messenger came and told the message, he told Jesus that him whom he loved was very sick. The Lord Jesus turned to him and said, "I will go. Take back word to those two sisters. The sickness is not unto death, but I will come."

I can see those two sisters. How eager they are to find out what his success had been. "What did he say?" and the messenger answers, "Why, he said the sickness was not unto death, and he would come and see Lazarus." I can imagine Mary turns to the messenger and says, "I don't understand that. If he were a prophet he would certainly have known that Lazarus is dead, for he was dying when you went away, and he was already dead when he said the sickness is not to death. Are you sure he said that?"

"Yes, that was what he said."

It might have been the second day after his death and he didn't come, and they watch and wait, and the third day they look for him. "Why, it is so strange he treats us in this way."

The fourth day comes, and it is noon, yet he has not come. I can imagine that on the fourth day in the afternoon they receive word that Jesus is just outside of the walls of Bethany with his disciples, and when he comes Martha says to him, "If thou hadst been here my brother had not died." Hear what gracious words fall from the lips of Jesus, "Thy brother shall live again."

Martha said unto him, "I know that he shall rise again in the resurrection at the last day."

Hear the blissful words that fall from the lips of the Son of God, "I am the resurrection, and the life: he that believeth in me, though he were dead, yet shall he live. And whosoever liveth and believeth in me shall never die" (John 11:25–26). Little did Martha think that he who she was entertaining was the Resurrection and the Life, and what a privilege it was to have such a guest!

Then Christ asks, "Where is Mary? Go, call her."

So Martha goes and calls Mary, and says, "Mary, the Master is come, and calleth for thee." Isn't there some Mary today whom he is calling for? Isn't there some unsaved Mary within these walls whom he is calling for? If there is, he wants to bind up your heart—he wants to take away your sin.

And when Mary comes she meets him with the very same words that fell from the lips of Martha, "If thou hadst been here my brother had not died"; and Christ says, "Where have ye laid him?"

Now look at him. These two sisters are standing near him, and perhaps are telling him of the last moments of Lazarus, and how their hearts had been bleeding all these four days. When he saw them weeping, and the Jews also weeping who came with them, the heart of the Son of God was moved with compassion and "Jesus wept." For it says he wept with them that wept, and the tears were streaming down his cheeks. Then said the Jews, "Behold how he loved him."

And they led the way to the tomb. Look at that company moving along toward the graveyard. These two sisters are telling about the last words and last acts of Lazarus. Perhaps Lazarus left a loving message for Jesus. You know what that is. When you go to see friends who are mourning, how they will dwell upon the last words and the last acts of the departed ones! You see Martha and Mary weeping as they went along toward the grave, and the Son of God wept with them.

Jesus said to his disciples, "Take away the stone."

Again the faith of those sisters wavered, and they said, "Lord, by this time he stinketh, for he has been dead four days." They did not know who their Friend was. When the disciples rolled away that stone Christ cried in a loud voice to his old friend, "Lazarus, come forth."

Then Lazarus leaped out of that same sepulcher and came forth. Some old divine has said it was a good thing that Jesus singled out Lazarus, for there is such power in the voice of the Son of God that the dead shall hear his voice, and if he had not called for Lazarus by name all the dead in that graveyard would have come forth. Jesus saith unto them, "Loose him and let him go."

Little did Martha know whom she was entertaining when she invited Christ into her home. The world has been sneering at Martha ever since. But it was by far the grandest, sublimest, and noblest act of her life.

In the little town of Bethany now the sun is just sinking behind one of those Palestine hills, and it is about dusk. You can see the Son of God perhaps, with Lazarus on his arm, and they walk through the street. Ah, that was the happiest home on earth that night. I believe there was no happier home than that in Bethany that night. Isn't it the very best thing that you can do to make room for Jesus?

34 Mary of Bethany

Matthew 26:6–13; Mark 14:1–11; John 12:1–10

In the closing chapters of John's Gospel we have many of the last words and acts of our Lord and Savior, and they ought to be very precious to us. You know when we lose a friend how much we think of his last words. When I went East a few weeks ago, to lay my brother in the grave, the very first thing I wanted to know was, what were his last words, and then I went all over the farm to see the last works he had done.

Jesus at Bethany

I want to call your attention to these words, "Then Jesus six days before the Passover came to Bethany" (John 12:1). He knew that the chief priests had been searching everywhere for him, and had given orders that if any knew where he was they should show it. But no one was able to take him until he gave himself up of his own accord. The officers sent to arrest him went back without him. When the chief priests asked, "Why have ye not brought him?" they said, "Never man spake like this man" (John 7:45–46). Nobody could take him till he gave himself up, and here is another proof of our Lord's divinity.

When he came to Bethany they made him a supper; and while they sat at the table Mary took a pound of ointment of spikenard, very precious, worth forty or fifty dollars, and anointed the feet of Jesus, and wiped his feet with her hair. Judas Iscariot complained of the waste of the ointment. But Jesus said, "Let her alone. Against the day of my burying hath she kept this."

There was a feast at this time in Jerusalem, and people were very much excited over the raising of Lazarus. There is no reason to suppose that anybody, not even the Jews, who were his bitterest enemies, ever disputed that Lazarus had been raised from the dead; but there are a good many people here in Chicago who say they doubt it.

Mary's Action

Now let us look at what Mary did. There are a good many rich men who try to do something to hand down their name to posterity. They give large sums of money to have a library or a town named after them, and in fifty years' time nobody knows whether the town was named after a man or a mountain. But of this act of Mary, Jesus says, "Wheresoever this gospel shall be preached throughout the whole world, this also that she hath done shall be spoken of for a memorial of her" (Mark 14:9). As someone has said, "He chained her name to the gospel chariot, and it has rolled down the ages." My friends, if you want to be immortal go and do something for Christ.

Following Mary's Example

There was a poor widow one day came up to the temple (perhaps she had two or three children clinging to her dress), and she put into the contribution box two mites, which make a farthing (Mark 12:41–44). I suppose the Jerusalem papers, if they had any, came out the next morning with brilliant accounts of the great collection up at the temple, for there were a good many rich men who gave, some a hundred and some a thousand dollars; but the Savior said that the poor widow had given more than they all. There isn't anything on record of what the rich men gave, but the gift of the widow will never be forgotten.

Now I suppose that Mary anointed Jesus out of gratitude to the Savior, who had raised her brother from the dead. Her heart was full of thanksgiving; nothing was too good to show it. Has not the Lord raised up some one of your brothers, a son, or a husband, or a friend, and what have you ever done to prove your gratitude to him on account of it?

Go to the Feet of Jesus

Here is another thing I want to call to your attention. It was his feet and not his head that Mary anointed. There are a great many people who are willing to get to the head of Christ, but are not willing to be at his feet. Young men go to Princeton, Yale, and Harvard to the theological seminaries; but I tell you if a minister doesn't go to the feet of Jesus he can't preach. We have to do just as Mary did—sit at the feet of Jesus and learn of him. That is God's college, and all the other learning in the world will never do you any good unless you learn in that school.

_35_ Mephibosheth

2 Samuel 9

Here is a story in the books of Samuel, away back as far as the time of the kings of Israel, which will help us to understand the gospel. It is about a man by the name of Mephibosheth.

You know what a hard time David had when Saul was hunting him, and trying every way to kill him, and you remember it had been revealed to Jonathan, the son of Saul and heir to the throne, that David was to be the next king instead of himself; but this did not hinder his love for his friend David. Ah, my friends, it must have been a real, true friendship that could stand that sort of thing!

David and Jonathan's Covenant

One day David and Jonathan were taking a walk in the fields together, and Jonathan said to David, "It has been revealed to me that you are to be the king after my father. Now, I want you to promise me one thing: when you come to the throne, if any of the house of Saul are alive I want you to be good to them for my sake."

"I'll do that, of course," said David. So he made a covenant to that effect, and then he went off to the cave of Adullam to get out of the way of Saul (1 Sam. 20:16).

About four years afterward David heard there had been a great battle over by Mount Gilboa, and that the Philistines had beaten the Israelites with great slaughter, and that Saul and Jonathan were both dead. So he got his men together, and went out after the enemies of the Lord and of Israel; and it wasn't a great while before he had turned the tables on them, and set up his kingdom at Hebron, where he reigned seven years and a half.

The Covenant Remembered

It must have been pretty near fourteen years before David remembered his promise to his old friend Jonathan—it is a great deal easier to make promises than to keep them—but one day the king was walking in his palace at Jerusalem, where he had removed his capital, and all at once he happened to think of that promise.

"That's too bad!" says David. "I forgot all about that promise. I have been so busy fighting these Philistines, and fixing things up, that I haven't had time to think of anything else." So he calls a servant in great haste, and says, "Do you know whether there are any of Saul's family living?"

The man said there was an old servant of Saul's by the name of Ziba, and maybe he could tell.

"Go and tell him I want him right away."

When Ziba came, David said, "Ziba, do you know whether there is anybody of the house of Saul in my kingdom?" Ziba said there was one he knew of, a son of Jonathan, by the name of Mephibosheth.

Oh, how that name "Jonathan" must have smitten the heart of David! One of the sons of his old friend living in his kingdom for as much as fourteen years, and he had never known it! What would Jonathan think of him for forgetting his promise that way?

"Go fetch him!" says David, "Go quickly. Tell him I want him. I want to show him the kindness of God."

Mephibosheth Brought to David's Court

Now, my friends, where do you suppose Mephibosheth was all the time? He was down at Lodebar. Did you ever hear of that place? There may be some here who have been round the world; did you ever come across that port? When you have traveled on the railway did any of you ever stop at that station?

Ah! Yes, that is where the whole human race is until they come to Christ for salvation; away down at Lodebar—which means a place of no pasture.

The king is in haste to keep his promise now. His messengers hurry off—maybe they take the king's own chariot—and rattle away to find this son of Jonathan.

When they reached the little out-of-the-way place, I fancy there was a great commotion.

"Where's Mephibosheth? The king wants him."

Poor fellow! When he heard that he hung down his head. He was afraid the king wanted to kill him because he was of the house of Saul, his old enemy. Ah, my friends, that's just the way sinners receive Christ's offer of salvation. They think God hates them and wants to cut their heads off! But that is a great mistake.

"Don't be afraid," said the servants. "The king says he wants to show you the kindness of God. He is in a great hurry to see you; so get ready, and jump right into the chariot. Don't you see the king has sent his own chariot to fetch you?"

It did begin to look as if the king meant no harm to him. But poor Mephibosheth had another difficulty. He was lame in both feet. He was a little fellow when David came to the throne; and an old servant, who was afraid that all the house of Saul were going to be killed, took him up and ran away to hide him (2 Sam. 4:4). Somehow she dropped the lad and lamed him in both feet.

And now I can see poor Mephibosheth looking down at his feet. Maybe the toes turned in, or he was clubfooted. And he says to himself, "I am not fit to go to the king. I am a poor cripple. I am not fit to be seen among the tall, handsome servants of the palace in Jerusalem."

That's just the way with a convicted sinner. He is all the time thinking of his own unworthiness, and saying to himself, I am not fit to be saved.

"Never mind your lame feet, Mephibosheth; so long as the king sends for you it's all right." So they take him up and put him into the chariot, and start for Jerusalem on a run.

As soon as the king sees him, he cries out, "O Mephibosheth, the son of my dear old friend Jonathan! You shall have all that belonged to the house of Saul; and you shall live with me here in my palace and sit at my table."

What a happy man he must have been to hear that! Sinner, that is just what God says to the soul that comes to him. He gives us a great fortune of love and grace; and he promises that we shall live with him in his heavenly palace forever.

That is grace. David didn't say, "Let him come up to Jerusalem when he gets ready," but he sent away to fetch him. "Jerusalem" means the city of peace; and Christ invites you to his Jerusalem.

Some people think that Mephibosheth, like certain low-spirited Christians, must have been all the time worrying over his lame feet there in the palace of the king, but I don't think so. He couldn't help it, and, if David didn't mind it, it was all right. So I think that when he dined with him in state, with the great lords and ladies all around him, he just stuck his clubfeet under the table and looked the king right in the face.

That is just the way with the gospel. We are God's enemies, and the children of his enemies. We are lame, and blind, and wretched, and ragged, and hateful by reason of our sins; but the covenant of grace in Jesus Christ has been made. And now God sends for you, poor sinner, in the name of his Son, to come and eat bread at his table, and be a member of his family, and dwell in his house forever. Will you come? Will you come now?

36 Moses

Exodus 2–4

There is a great deal more room given in Scripture to the call of men to God's work than there is to their end. For instance, we don't know where Isaiah died, or how he died, but we know a great deal about the call God gave him, when he saw God on high and lifted up on his throne. I suppose that it is true today that hundreds of young men and women who are listening for a call and really want to know what their life's mission is, perhaps find it the greatest problem they ever had. Some don't know just what profession or work to take up, and so I should like to take the call of Moses, and see if we cannot draw some lessons from it.

Moses at the Burning Bush

You remember when God met Moses at the burning bush and called him to do as great a work as any man has ever been called to in this world, that he thought the Lord had made a mistake and that he was not the man (Exodus 3). He said, "Who am I?" He was very small in his own estimation. Forty years before he had started out as a good many others have started. He thought he was pretty well equipped for service. He had been in the schools of the Egyptians, he had been in the palaces of Egypt, he had moved in the bon ton society. He had had all the advantages any man could have when he started out, undoubtedly, without calling on the God of Abraham for wisdom and guidance, yet he broke down.

How many men have started out in some profession and made a failure of it! They haven't heard the voice of God, they haven't waited upon God for instruction.

I suppose Moses thought that the children of Israel would be greatly honored to know that a prince of the realm was going to take up their cause, but you remember how he lost his temper and killed the Egyptian, and next day, when he interfered in a quarrel between two Hebrews, they wanted to know who had made him judge and ruler over them (Exod. 2:11–15). He had to flee into the desert, and was there for forty years hidden away. He killed the Egyptian and lost his influence thereby. Murder for liberty; wrong for right; it was a poor way to reform abuses, and Moses needed training.

Moses' Forty Years of Training

It was a long time for God to keep him in his school, a long time for a man to wait in the prime of his life, from forty to eighty. Moses had been brought up with all the luxuries that Egypt could give him, and now he was a shepherd, and in the sight of the Egyptians a shepherd was an abomination. I have an idea that Moses started out with a great deal bigger head than heart. I believe that is the reason so many fail; they have big heads and little hearts. If a man has a shriveled up heart and a big head he is a monster. Perhaps Moses looked down on the Hebrews. There are many people who start out with the idea that they are great and other people are small. They are going to bring them up on the high level with themselves. God never yet used a man of that stamp. Perhaps Moses was a slow scholar in God's school, and so he had to keep him there for forty years.

But now he is ready; he is just the man God wants, and God calls him. Moses said, "Who am I?" He was very small in his own eyes, just small enough so that God could use him. If you had asked the Egyptians who he was, they would have said he was the biggest fool in the world.

"Why," they would say, "look at the opportunity that man had! He might have been commander of the Egyptian army, he might have been on the throne, swaying the scepter over the whole world, if he hadn't identified himself with those poor, miserable Hebrews! Think what an opportunity he has lost, and what a privilege he has thrown away!"

He had dropped out of the public mind for forty years, and they didn't know what had become of him, but God had his eye upon him. He was the very man of all others that God wanted, and when he met God with that question, "Who am I?" it didn't matter who he was but who his God was. When men learn the lesson that they are nothing and God is everything, then there is not a position in which God cannot use them. It was not Moses who accomplished that great work of redemption, for he was only the instrument in God's hand.

God could have spoken to Pharaoh without Moses. He could have spoken in a voice of thunder and broken the heart of Pharaoh with one speech if he had wanted to, but he condescended to take up a human agent, and to use him. He could have sent Gabriel down, but he knew that Moses was the man wanted above all others, so he called him. God uses men to speak to men. He works through mediators. He could have accomplished the exodus of the children of Israel in a flash, but instead he chose to send a lonely and despised shepherd to work out his purpose through pain and disappointment. That was God's way in the Old Testament, and also in the New. He sent his own Son in the likeness of sinful flesh to be the mediator between God and man.

Moses' Excuses

Moses went on making excuses and said, "When I go down there, who shall I say has sent me?" I suppose he remembered how he went before he was sent that other time, and he was afraid of a failure again. A man who has made a failure once is always afraid he will make another. He loses confidence in himself. It is a good thing to lose confidence in ourselves so as to gain confidence in God.

The Lord said, "Say unto them, 'I AM hath sent me.'"

Someone has said that God gave him a blank check, and all he had to do was to fill it out from that time on. When he wanted to bring water out of the rock, all he had to do was to fill out the check. When he wanted bread, all he had to do was to fill out the check and the bread came. He had a rich banker. God had taken him into partnership with himself. God had made him his heir, and all he had to do was to look up to him, and he got all he wanted.

And yet Moses seemed to draw back, and began to make another excuse, and said, "They will not believe me." He was afraid of the Israelites as well as of Pharaoh. He knew how hard it is to get even your friends to believe in you.

Now, if God has sent you and me with a message it is not for us to say whether others will believe it or not. We cannot make men believe. If I have been sent by God to make men believe, he will give me power to make them believe. That power is the work of the Holy Spirit. We can't persuade men and overcome skepticism and infidelity unless we are baptized with the Holy Spirit and with power.

God told Moses that they would believe him, that he would succeed, and bring the children of Israel out of bondage. But Moses seemed to distrust even the God who had spoken to him.

Then the Lord said, "What is that in thy hand?"

He had a rod or staff, a sort of shepherd's crook, which he had cut haphazardly when he had wanted something that would serve him in the desert.

"It is only a rod."

"With that you shall deliver the children of Israel; with that rod you shall make Israel believe that I am with you."

When God Almighty linked himself to that rod, it was worth more than all the armies the world had ever seen. Look and see how that rod did its work. It brought up the plagues of flies, and the thunderstorm, and turned the water into blood. It was not Moses, however, nor Moses' rod that did the work, but it was the God of the rod, the God of Moses. As long as God was with him, he could not fail.

When Seeming Failure Is Success

Sometimes it looks as if God's servants fail. When Herod beheaded John the Baptist, it looked as if John's mission was a failure. But was it? The voice that rang through the valley of the Jordan rings through the whole world today. You can hear its echo upon the mountains and the valleys yet, "He must increase, but I must decrease" (John 3:30). He held up Jesus Christ and introduced him to the world, and Herod had not power to behead him until his lifework had been accomplished.

Stephen never preached but one sermon that we know of, and that was before the Sanhedrin (Acts 7); but how that sermon has been preached again and again all over the world! Out of his death probably came Paul, the greatest preacher the world has seen since Christ left this earth. If a man is sent by Jehovah, there is no such thing as failure.

Was Christ's life a failure? See how his parables are going through the earth today. It looked as if the apostles had made a failure, but see how much has been accomplished.

If you read the book of Acts, you will see that every seeming failure in Acts was turned into a great victory. Moses wasn't going to fail, although Pharaoh said with contempt, "Who is God that I should obey him?" He found out who God was. He found out that there was a God.

But Moses made another excuse, and said, "I am slow of speech, slow of tongue." He said he was not an orator.

My friends, we have too many orators. I am tired and sick of your "silver-tongued orators." I used to mourn because I couldn't be an orator. I thought, oh, if I could only have the gift of speech like some men! I have heard men with a smooth flow of language take the audience captive, but they came and they went. Their voice was like the air, there wasn't any power back of it. They trusted in their eloquence and their fine speeches.

That is what Paul was thinking of when he wrote to the Corinthians, "My speech and my preaching was not with enticing words of man's wisdom, but in demonstration of the Spirit and of power: that your faith should not stand in the wisdom of men, but in the power of God" (1 Cor. 2:4–5).

Take a witness in court and let him try his oratorical powers in the witness box, and see how quickly the judge will rule him out. It is the man who tells the plain, simple truth that has the most influence with the jury.

Suppose that Moses had prepared a speech for Pharaoh, and had gotten his hair all smoothly brushed, and had stood before the mirror or had gone to an elocutionist to be taught how to make an oratorical speech and how to make gestures. Suppose that he had buttoned his coat, put one hand in his chest, had struck an attitude and begun, "The God of our fathers, the God of Abraham, Isaac, and Jacob, has commanded me to come into the presence of the noble king of Egypt."

I think they would have taken his head right off! They had Egyptians who could be as eloquent as Moses. It was not eloquence they needed. When you see a man in the pulpit trying to show off his eloquence, he is making a fool of himself and trying to make a fool of the people. Moses was slow of speech, but he had a message. What God wanted was to have him deliver the message. But he insisted upon having an excuse. He didn't want to go; instead of being eager to act as heaven's messenger, to be God's errand boy, he wanted to excuse himself. The Lord humored him and gave him an interpreter, gave him Aaron.

Now, if there is a stupid thing in the world, it is to talk through an interpreter. I tried it once in Paris. I got up into a little box of a pulpit with the interpreter—there was hardly room enough for one. I said a sentence while he leaned away over to one side, and then I leaned over while he repeated it in French. Can you conceive of a more stupid thing than Moses going before Pharaoh and speaking through Aaron!

But this slow-of-speech man became eloquent. Talk about Gladstone's power to speak! Here is a man one hundred and twenty years old, and he waxed eloquent, as we see in Deuteronomy 32:1–4:

Give ear, O ye heavens, and I will speak; and hear, O earth, the words of my mouth. My doctrine shall drop as the rain, my speech shall distil as the dew, as the small rain upon the tender herb, and as the showers upon the grass: because I will publish the name of the LORD: ascribe ye greatness unto our God. He is the Rock, his work is perfect: for all his ways are judgment: a God of truth and without iniquity, just and right is he.

He turned out to be one of the most eloquent men the world has ever seen. If God sends men and they deliver his message he will be with their mouth. If God has given you a message, go and give it to the people as God has given it to you. It is a stupid thing for a man to try to be eloquent. Make your message, and not yourself, the most prominent thing. Don't be self-conscious. Set your heart on what God has given you to do, and don't be so foolish as to let your own difficulties or your own abilities stand in the way.

It is said that people would go to hear Cicero and would come away and say, "Did you ever hear anything like it? Wasn't it sublime? Wasn't it grand?" But they would go and hear Demosthenes, and he would fire them so with the subject that they would want to go and fight at once. They forgot all about Demosthenes, but were stirred by his message; that was the difference between the two men.

Next Moses said: "O my Lord, send, I pray thee, by the hand of him whom thou wilt send" (Exod. 4:13). Did you ever stop to think what Moses would have lost if God had taken him at his word, and said, "Very well, Moses; you may stay here in the desert, and I will send Aaron, or Joshua, or Caleb!"

Don't seek to be excused if God calls you to some service. What would the twelve disciples have lost if they had declined the call of Jesus! I have always pitied those other disciples of whom we read that they went back, and walked no more with Jesus. Think what Orpah missed and what Ruth gained by cleaving to Naomi's God (Ruth 1:14)! Her story has been told these three thousand years. Father, mother, sisters, brothers, the grave of her husband—she turned her back on them all. Ruth, come back, and tell us if you regret your choice! No, her name shines one of the brightest among all the women that have ever lived. The Messiah was one of her descendants.

Moses, you come back and tell us if you were afterwards sorry that God had called you? I think that, when he stood in glorified body on the Mount of Transfiguration with Jesus and Elijah, he did not regret it.

My dear friends, God is not confined to any one messenger. We are told that he can raise up children out of stones. Someone has said that there are three classes of people, the "wills," the "won'ts," and the "can'ts"; the first accomplish everything, the second oppose everything, and the third fail in everything. If God calls you, consider it a great honor. Consider it a great privilege to have partnership with him in anything. Do it cheerfully, gladly. Do it with all your heart, and he will bless you. Don't let false modesty or insincerity, self-interest, or any personal consideration turn you aside from the path of duty and sacrifice. If we listen for God's voice, we shall hear the call; and if he calls and sends us, there will be no such thing as failure, but success all along the line. Moses had glorious success because he went forward and did what God called him to do.

Moses' Farewell Addresses

Moses was about to leave the children of Israel in the wilderness. He had led them up to the borders of the Promised Land. For forty long years he had been leading them in that wilderness, and now, as they are about to go over, Moses takes his farewell. He said a great many wise and good things on that memorable occasion.

There was not a man on the face of the earth at that time who knew as much about the world and as much about God as did Moses. Therefore, he was a good judge. He had tasted of the pleasures of the world. In the forty years that he was in Egypt he probably sampled everything of that day. He tasted of the world—of its pleasures. He knew all about it. He was brought up in the palace of a king, a prince. Egypt then ruled the known world.

Moses had been forty years in Horeb, where he had heard the voice of God—where he had been taught by God—and for forty years he had been serving God. You might say he was God's right hand man, leading those bondsmen up out of the land of Egypt and out of the house of bondage into the land of liberty, and this is his dying address—you might say, his farewell address. This is the dying testimony of one who could speak with authority and one who could speak intelligently.

If you haven't read that farewell address of Moses, you will find it in the last few chapters of Deuteronomy. I advise you to read it. You are reading a great many printed sermons. Suppose you read that part in Deuteronomy 31:30–32:52. Why, there is as much truth in that farewell address of Moses as there is in fifteen hundred printed sermons at the present time.

Moses in the Promised Land

Moses prayed to enter the Promised Land, but the Lord had something else in store for him. As someone has said, "God kissed away his soul, and took him home to himself." God buried him—the greatest funeral honors ever paid to mortal man. Fifteen hundred years afterward God answered the prayer of Moses, God allowed him to go into the Promised Land, and to get a glimpse of the coming glory. On the Mount of Transfiguration, with Elijah, the great prophet, and with Peter, James, and John, he heard the voice come from the throne of God, "This is my beloved Son; hear him" (Matt. 17:1–9; Mark 9:2–10).

That was better than to have gone over Jordan, as Joshua did, and to sojourn for thirty years in the land of Canaan. So when our prayers for earthly things are not answered, let us submit to the will of God, and know that it is all right.

Murderers Fleeing to Cities of Refuge

31

Numbers 35:6–34; Joshua 20

When the children of Israel came from the land of slavery, and had the visitation of the fiery serpents, and after Moses had been commanded to raise the brazen serpent, he went to Pisgah and died. Joshua led them into the Promised Land. Joshua then received a command from God that he should erect six cities, three on each side of the Jordan, which were to be cities of refuge.

Cities of Refuge Described

These places were to be put far enough apart so as to cover the whole land, that any man no matter where he might be when he should have occasion to seek them, could easily gain access to one of them.

The gates of these cities were to be kept open day and night, and the chief men of each city—the magistrates—were to keep the ways to these places free of all obstacles and stumbling blocks so that no one should be hindered in getting within the walls. And not only should the roads be kept smooth and well in repair, but all the bridges leading over streams and rivers should be kept up and in good condition, and sign posts were also to be placed at intervals along the road, showing the fugitive that he was on the right way—to keep him from straying.

To provide for the contingency of the man who was fleeing not being able to read, there was a red finger put on the posts which pointed the way. Thus a man, even if he could read, was not compelled to stop and thus lose time; he saw the sign and sped on. The cities were also placed on hills, that everyone could see them.

The cities were erected for this purpose. It was considered a great dishonor among the Israelites when a man was killed. The nearest relative at once armed himself and began to seek out the slayer in order to kill him.

Thus a man had no hope, if he had accidentally killed another, of saving his own life from the avenging hand of the brother or other relative except to get within the walls of the nearest city of refuge. It was the law that the moment he entered the city of refuge the relative of the slain man could not touch him.

Flight to a City of Refuge

Suppose I had killed a man unwittingly—that he and I had been out chopping in the woods, and suppose my ax had slipped out of my hand and had crushed in the skull of my companion (Deut. 19:1–6). My only hope would be to get to one of these cities—my only hope would be to escape for my life. I should have no time to loiter, no time to hesitate or argue, no time to consider. I should have to start at once. The brother of my companion who had been killed, though this was truly an accident, was near. He was so incensed or perhaps had some old score to pay off that I should have no chance to stay and plead with him. He had made up his mind to kill me, and there was nothing left for me to do but fly.

I know the young man's hot temper, and I see him on my track. I therefore spring out of the forest into the road. Now it becomes a life and death struggle. I see the city before me. Along the road I speed to the full extent of my strength. Down the hill I go as fast as I can; up the ravine I make my way. Men see me coming. They do not check me, or throw any obstacles in my path. They get out of my way, and as I pass, they wish me God-speed and warn me that the avenger is not far behind. Now I am in full view of the city. The gates are wide open; I know I won't have to stop and knock when I get up to them.

When I get closer, I see the citizens are on the walls. The information has reached them that a poor refugee is coming. Some of them have had to free themselves, and they sympathize with me. They thus await me; but they see I am hard pressed. I am almost on the point of giving out.

But I say to myself, "Courage! Another effort and I shall reach the gates and be safe." Oh, if I can only reach the city!

Ah, my friend, just look at the city; don't let anything take our attention away. Look, look! See what I have to do. If I stop, loiter, or linger I am lost. The avenger will soon be on me. I can almost hear him breathing behind me. I know his sword is ready to hew me down. I get nearer to the walls now. I see the people plainly. They beckon with their hands. I strain every nerve. "Hurry, hurry, he is almost upon you; oh, you will be killed."

I bring every muscle into play. The people crowd around the gate to receive me. "Now, now," they cry. I make one more bound. I pass through the gates. I am safe. That is instantaneous, isn't it? One minute I am under the avenging sword ready to fall upon my head, the next minute I am perfectly secure. The avenger can't enter. The officers see to that. They will not let him come in with his sword.

Christ Is Our Refuge

Can you, my friends, have a better illustration of this life? Don't you know that death is on your track now, and is ready to have you a victim? Don't you know that he may be only a few years, a few months, a few weeks, a few days, or even a few moments from you? Even this very night he may catch up to you. You may think him miles and miles behind on, years and years away. But just as surely as you live death is only a little way behind you now, a great deal nearer than you imagine. Haste, then, to a place of refuge. If you are outside the city you perish; if you come within the walls of salvation you live secure.

God has a city of refuge for you. He shows you by every unmistakable sign where it is, and he gives you warning that if you do not reach its walls you die. Come, then. If you neglect these mercies, how do you expect to save your life? How can you loiter and linger when death is bearing down upon you? A little while and you will be lost, but if you make for the salvation offered to you, you will be safe in Christ. Then you can look back from that safe refuge and challenge death to his face. You can say in triumph, "O death, where is thy sting? O grave, where is thy victory?" (1 Cor. 15:55).

The banner floats from Calvary, and when you come under its folds you are safe. My friends, do you not see it now? Won't you cross the line and be saved? Oh, I have prayed that a thousand may be saved here tonight. Yes, I prayed right now during this sermon. I don't know why you can't be saved. Oh, lift up your hearts in prayer that thousands may leave their sins and their slavery and ruin and come under the protection of the Lord.

Salvation Is Instantaneous

One day I was walking through the streets of York in England. I saw a little way ahead a soldier coming toward me. He had the red uniform on of the infantry—the dress of the army. I knew at once when I saw him that he was a soldier. When he came near me I stopped him. I said, "My good man, if you have no objection I would like to ask you a few questions."

"Certainly, sir," said he.

"Well, then, I would like to know how you first became a soldier."

"Yes, sir, I will tell you. You see, sir, I wanted to become a soldier, and the recruiting officer was in our town, and I went up to him and told him that I wanted to enlist. Well, sir, he said, 'All right,' and the first thing he did, sir, he took an English shilling out of his pocket, sir, and put it into my hand. The very moment, sir, a recruiting-sergeant puts a shilling into your hand, sir, you are a soldier."

I said to myself, "That is the very illustration I want." That man was a free man one time—he could go here and there, do just what he liked; but the moment the shilling was put into his hand he was subject to the rules of war, and Queen Victoria could send him anywhere and make him obey the rules and regulations of the army. He is a soldier the very minute he takes the shilling. He has not got to wait to put on the uniform.

And when you ask me how a man may become converted at once, I answer, just the same as that man became a soldier. The citizen becomes a soldier in a minute, and from being a free man becomes subject to the commands of others. The moment you take Christ into your heart, that moment your name is written in the roll of heaven. You are enlisted a soldier of Christ, and you cannot then do as you choose, but you must do what he lays down. Don't you see then how you can become a Christian at once, my friends? It is very plain. Don't go out of this hall today, then, and say you can't see it. I don't see how I can make it any more plain. Though you accept Christ, yet you are a sinner still, but a saved sinner.

There is a great deal of difference between the two—between a saved and an unsaved sinner. I have been a saved sinner myself for twenty-one years. You ask me if I don't sin. Yes, I do, but I hate sin. For twenty-one years I have been a soldier—a poor and unworthy soldier, but still a soldier. Twenty-one years ago this month I took, as I may say, the English shilling; I enlisted in the army of Christ, and he has been ever since my life, my Lord, my all. Now, dear friends, won't you have Christ? "But as many as received him, to them gave he power to become the sons of God, even to them that believe on his name" (John 1:12). Oh, just say you will receive him now.

38 Naaman

2 Kings 5

Our subject tonight is Naaman. We are told that he was a great man—but he was a leper. He was a great general—but he was a leper. He had been very successful in war, and his king had greatly honored him—but he was a leper. Day and night this terrible fact tortured him, and I suppose he thought he had to go down to his grave with that loathsome disease upon him.

Hope for Naaman

But among the Hebrew captives in his land was a little girl who waited on Mrs. Naaman, and who, I doubt not, had been brought up by her praying mother to trust in the God of Israel. She wasn't ashamed to confess her faith, and there is no doubt but she was a good and truthful girl, or else no one would have believed her strange words.

One day she said to her mistress, "Would to God my lord were with the prophet that is in Samaria! For then he would recover him of his leprosy."

Her mistress looked at her with amazement. "What! What is that you say? Cure my husband of his leprosy? Did you ever hear of this prophet curing a leper?"

"No," says the little girl, "I didn't; but I have heard of his doing greater things than that would be." And then, perhaps, she told how the prophet had taken the mantle of Elijah and smote the River Jordan with it, and it opened and let him through dry shod; and how he had saved the two sons of that widow from being sold into slavery by means of that little bit of oil; and how he had raised to life the dead son of another woman. Naaman hears it and believes the little girl, so he goes to the king about it.

This girl must have had something about her to make those people listen to her. She must have shown her religion in her life. Her life must have been consistent with her religion to make them believe her.

"I'll tell you what I'll do," says the king, "I'll write you a letter of introduction to the king of Israel, and you go down and try it."

So he gives him a letter to the king, thinking if the thing is possible the king will know all about it. Off the man goes, about one hundred and fifty miles, to see the king of Israel. He took along a pretty good payment for the doctor's bill, too. I don't just know how to figure it, but it was over a hundred thousand dollars, and with the letter to the king, no doubt he thought everything was all right.

I can see him and his escort sweeping out of the gates of Damascus, and coming up, in due time, to the palace of the king of Israel in grand style. He sends in the letter, and when the king reads it he turns round and says, "What does this mean? Am I God, to kill and to make alive? Here is the king of Syria sending me a letter saying, 'Now, when this letter is come unto thee, behold, I have therewith sent Naaman my servant to thee that thou mayest recover him of his leprosy.' This means war. The king of Syria is trying to get up a quarrel with me." Then the king of Israel rent his mantle from top to bottom.

Naaman Comes to Elisha

It is not long before the news of it goes through the whole city, and at last it comes to the ears of Elisha that the king has rent his clothes on account of a letter which a Syrian general has brought him, asking him to cure his leprosy. So he sends word to the king, saying, "Wherefore hast thou rent thy clothes? Let him come now to me, and he shall know that there is a prophet in Israel" (1 Kings 5:8).

So the man goes down to the house of the prophet, a very plain house it might have been, and sends in word that Major-General Naaman, of Syria, is outside. No doubt he thought the prophet would feel very much honored by the presence of such a great man, but the prophet doesn't even go out to see him. He merely sends out his servant to say to him, "Go and wash in Jordan seven times, and thy flesh shall come again to thee, and thou shalt be clean" (1 Kings 5:10).

And now Naaman is as mad as he can be. "The idea! Go and wash in Jordan! That ditch! We wouldn't call it a river at all in Damascus. Does he mean to insult me? Does he mean to insinuate that I don't keep my body clean? I thought—"

Ah, that is just the trouble. He had marked out a way of his own for the prophet to heal him, and was mad because he didn't follow his plan. That is just the trouble with a great many people who come to God to be saved. They think God ought to come in this way, and he comes in that way. No matter what way you have marked out for God, he will take some other way. You will never get into God's kingdom till you are ready to come in God's way.

"I thought, he will surely come out to me, and stand, and call on the name of the LORD his God, and strike his hand over the place, and recover the leper" (1 Kings 5:11).

What he probably thought was, "I thought he would come out, and bow, and scrape, and be very much honored at receiving a call from the distinguished Major-General Naaman, and instead of that he pays me no attention at all!"

That is just the way with some seekers of religion; they don't want to be converted in this way, but in that way. Sometimes they won't be converted in such revival meetings as these, but must be converted at some regular church. Sometimes they say, "I won't be converted at a Methodist church, even if I ain't converted at all." Or, "I won't be converted in a Baptist church, anyhow." But the very way they won't go is often the way they must go, for God sees it is necessary to break their stubborn wills and mortify their pride.

When we were in Glasgow we had an employer converted, and he wanted to get a man in his employ to come to our meetings, but he wouldn't come. If he was going to be converted, he wouldn't be converted by those meetings. You know, when a Scotchman gets an idea into his head he is the most stubborn man you can find. He was determined not to be converted by Moody and Sankey. The employer argued and pleaded with this man, but he couldn't get him to come to the meetings then being held.

Well, we left Glasgow, and got away up to the north of Scotland—in Inverness—and the employer sent his stubborn friend up there on business thinking he might be induced to go into the meetings. One night we were singing "On the Banks of That Beautiful River," and he happened to be passing. He wondered where the sweet sounds were coming from. He came into the meeting, and I happened to be preaching that evening on the very text: "I Thought."

The stubborn man from Glasgow listened attentively, and soon did not know exactly where he was. He was convicted—he was converted—and he became a Christian. Verily, a man must yield his own way to the way of the Lord.

Now, you can see all along that Naaman's thoughts were altogether different from those of God. He was going to get the grace of God by showing favors—just as many men now believe they can buy their way into the kingdom of God. But we can't purchase the favor of heaven with money. If you get a seat in heaven, you must accept salvation as a gift.

Naaman had another thought. He believed he could get what he wanted by taking letters to the king—not to the prophet. The little maid told him of the prophet, yet he was going to pass the prophet by. He was too proud to go to the prophet. But pride, if you will allow me the expression, got a knock on the head on this important occasion.

It was a terrible thing for him to think of obeying by going down to the Jordan and dipping seven times. He had better rivers in Damascus, in his own wisdom, and he queries: "Can't I wash there, and be clean?" Naaman was angry, but when he got over it he listened to his servants.

Naaman Surrenders His Pride

I tell you I had a thousand times rather a man should get mad under a sermon than go to sleep under it. If he gets mad and goes out he will come back again when he gets over it; but if he is asleep it is all lost time trying to save him. When a man is asleep there is no chance of reaching him, but if he is angry we may get at him. It is a good thing for a man to get angry sometimes, for when he cools off he generally listens to reason.

"Now," said the servants, "if he had told you to do some great thing wouldn't you have done it? Suppose he had told you to take cod-liver oil three times a day for ten years, wouldn't you have done it? If he had prescribed some awful bitter drug wouldn't you have swallowed it? If he had told you to go and bring him twice as much money wouldn't you have thought the cure cheap enough at that price? And now, when he says, 'Go wash in the Jordan seven times,' hadn't you better do it?"

He was influenced by the servant, and he went. That was one good point in Naaman's character—he was influenced by a humble messenger. A good many people will not accept a messenger unless he is refined and cultured and educated. But it is the message you want—not the messenger. It would be the message I would want. And so it was with Naaman. It was a little Hebrew girl who first told him to go to Samaria, and now he was told to wash by his servant. So Naaman goes down to dip himself in the waters of the Jordan River.

Down to Jordan he goes, and dips himself once in the water, saying to himself, "They will laugh at me terribly when I get back if I don't get cured of my leprosy, so I may as well try it." But when he comes up and looks to see if his leprosy is one-seventh gone, and finds no change at all, he begins to be discouraged. But he is in the way of obedience. God's prophet has told him to dip seven times, and he is going to do it.

"Behold, to obey is better than sacrifice" (1 Sam. 15:22). If ever you get out of the pit of Adam you must get out just where he got in. He got in by disobeying God, and the way out again is by obedience. Down he goes the second time.

Now, if there had been some of these Chicago Christians there they would have said, "Well, Naaman, how do you feel now?" but he didn't feel any better. Down he goes the third time, and again, and again; still no change. The sixth time he comes out and shakes himself, and rubs the water off him, and looks at his flesh.

Still no improvement! Once more; and now, as he comes up, he feels a thrill of health. As quickly as he can get the water out of his eyes he sees that he is cured! His leprosy has floated away in the waters of Jordan, the waters of death and judgment, and now he comes out in a new body—a resurrected body!

He lost his temper; then he lost his pride; then he lost his leprosy. That is generally the order in which proud, rebellious sinners are converted.

And now how happy he is. Hear him shout, "This is the happiest day of my life. I am cleansed; I am cleansed; I am a leper no more!"

God's Cleansing Is Free

Away he goes to the prophet's house and offers him the gifts he has brought, but the prophet won't have anything at all.

It would have spoiled this beautiful story if he had taken anything for his work. "The gift of God is eternal life" (Rom. 6:23). You cannot buy anything of God. So far as God and his prophet are concerned Naaman takes back to Syria with him everything he brought—except his leprosy.

And that is the way with you, sinner. When you come to Christ you haven't anything that Christ wants to take from you except it be your sins. Naaman might have taken his leprosy back with him if he hadn't obeyed the prophet and dipped seven times in Jordan. You will take your sins down to death with you unless you submit your will to Christ. The battle has to be fought out on the line of your will. Who will obey Christ tonight? Who will trust him tonight? May God open your eyes and show you how to be saved!

39 Nehemiah

I should like to call your attention to the prophet Nehemiah. We may gain some help from that distinguished man who accomplished a great work. He was one of the last of the prophets and was supposed to be contemporary with Malachi. His book was one of the last of the Old Testament books that was written. He might have known Daniel, or he was a young man in the declining years of that very eminent and godly statesman. We are sure of one thing at least—he was a man of sterling worth. Although he was brought up in the Persian court among idolaters, yet he had a character that has stood all these centuries.

Nehemiah's Prayer

Notice his prayer (Neh. 1:5–11) in which he made confession of Israel's apostasy from God. There may be some confessions we need to make to be brought into close fellowship with God. I have no doubt that numbers of Christians are hungering and thirsting for a personal blessing, and have a great desire to get closer to God. If that is the desire of your heart, keep in mind that if there is some obstacle in the way which you can remove, you will not get a blessing until you remove it.

We must cooperate with God. If there is any sin in my heart that I am not willing to give up then I need not pray. You may take a bottle and cork it up tight, and put it under Niagara, and not a drop of that mighty volume of water will get into the bottle. If there is any sin in my heart that I am not willing to give up, I need not expect a blessing. The men who have had power with God in prayer have always begun by confessing their sins. Take the prayers of Jeremiah and Daniel. You find Daniel confessing his sin, when there isn't a single sin recorded against him; but he confesses his sin and the sins of the people. Notice how David confessed his sins and what power he had with God. So it is a good thing for us to begin as Nehemiah did.

Nehemiah Learns Jerusalem's Need

It seems that some men had come down from his country to the Persian court, perhaps to see the king on business. This man, who was in high favor with the king, met them, and finding that they had come from Jerusalem he began to inquire about his country (Neh. 1:1–2). He not only loved his God, but he loved his country.

I like to see a patriotic man. He began to inquire about his people and about the city that was very near to his heart, Jerusalem. He had never seen the city. He had no relatives back there in Jerusalem of which he knew. Nehemiah was not a Jewish prince, although it is supposed he had royal blood in his veins. He was born in captivity. It was about one hundred years after Jerusalem was taken that he appeared upon the horizon. He was in the court of Artaxerxes, a cupbearer to the king, and held a high position.

Yet he longed to hear from his native land. When these men told him the condition of the city, that the people were in great need, distress, and degradation, that the walls of the city were still down, and that the gates had been burned and never restored, his patriotic heart began to burn. We are told he fasted and prayed and wept (Neh. 1:3–4), and not only did he pray for one week, or one month, but he kept on praying. He prayed "day and night."

Having many duties to perform, of course, he was not always on his knees, but in his heart he was ever before the throne of grace. It was not hard for him to understand and obey the precept, "Pray without ceasing" (1 Thess. 5:17). He began the work in prayer, continued in prayer, and the last recorded words of Nehemiah are a prayer.

It was in November or December when those men arrived at that court, and this man prayed on until March or April before he spoke to the king. If a blessing doesn't come tonight, pray harder tomorrow, and if it doesn't come tomorrow, pray harder. Then, if it doesn't come keep right on, and you will not be disappointed. God in heaven will hear your prayers and will answer them. He has never failed a person who has been honest in his petitions and honest in his confessions. Let your faith beget patience. "God is never in a hurry," said St. Augustine, "because he has all eternity to work." When he began to pray I have no idea that he thought he was to be the instrument in God's hand of building the walls of Jerusalem. But when a man gets into sympathy and harmony with God, then God prepares him for the work he has for him. No doubt he thought the Persian king might send one of his great warriors and accomplish the work with a great army of men. But after he had been praying for months, it may be the thought flashed into his mind, "Why shouldn't I go to Jerusalem myself and build those walls?" Prayer for the work will soon arouse your own sympathy and result in your effort.

Nehemiah Goes to Jerusalem

It meant a good deal for Nehemiah to give up the palace of Shushan and his high office, and identify himself with the despised and captive Jews. He was among the highest in the whole realm. Not only that, but he was a man of wealth, lived in ease and luxury, and had great influence at court. For him to go to Jerusalem and lose caste was like Moses turning his back on the palace of Pharaoh and identifying himself with the Hebrew slaves. Yet we might never have heard of either of them if they had not done this. They stooped to conquer.

When you get ready to stoop God will bless you. Plato, Socrates, and other Greek philosophers lived in the same century as Nehemiah. How few have heard of them and read their words compared with the hundreds of thousands who have heard and read of Nehemiah during the last two thousand years! If you and I are to be blessed in this world, we must be willing to take any position into which God puts us. So, after Nehemiah had prayed a while, he began to pray God to send him, and that he might be the man to rebuild the walls of Jerusalem.

After he had been praying some time, he was one day in the banqueting hall, and the king noticed that his countenance was sad. We might not have called the face sad; but much prayer and fasting change the very countenance of a man. I know some godly men and women, and they seem to have the stamp of heaven on them. The king noticed a strange look about this cupbearer, and he began to question him.

Then the thought came to Nehemiah that he would tell the king what caused his sorrow, how his own nation was degraded, and how his heart was going out for his own country. After he had told the king, the king said, "What is your request?"

Now, some people tell us they don't have time to pray, but I tell you if anyone has God's work lying deep in the heart, time will be found to pray. Nehemiah shot up a prayer to heaven right there in the king's dining hall that the Lord would help him to make his request in the right way. He first looked beyond Artaxerxes to the King of Kings. You need not make a long prayer. A man who prays much in private will make short prayers in public.

The Lord told Nehemiah what to ask for, that he might be sent to his own country, that some men might go with him, and that the king would give him letters to the governors through whose provinces he would pass so that he might have a profitable journey and be able to rebuild the walls of his city (Neh. 2:1–10). God had been preparing the king, for the king at once granted the request, and before long this young prince was on his way to Jerusalem.

When he reached the city he didn't have a lot of men go before him blowing trumpets and saying that the cupbearer of the great Persian king, the converted cupbearer, had arrived from the Persian court, and was going to build the walls of Jerusalem. There are some men who are always telling what they are going to do. Man, let the work speak for itself. You needn't blow any horns; go and do the work, and it will advertise itself. Nehemiah didn't have any newspapers writing about him, or any placards.

However, there was no small stir. No doubt everyone in town was talking about it, saying that a very important personage had arrived from the Persian court; but he was there three days and three nights without telling anyone why he had come.

One night he went out to survey the city (Neh. 2:11–16). He couldn't ride around; even now you can't ride a beast around the walls of Jerusalem. He tried to ride around, but he couldn't, so he walked. It was a difficult task which he had before him, but he was not discouraged. That is what makes character. Men who can go into a hard field and succeed, they are the men we want. Any quantity of men are looking for easy places, but the world will never hear of them. We want men who are looking for hard places, who are willing to go into the darkest corners of the earth, and make those dark places bloom like gardens. They can do it if the Lord is with them.

Nehemiah Begins the Work

Everything looked dark before Nehemiah. The walls were broken down. There was not a man of influence among the people, not a man of culture or a man of wealth. The nations all around were looking down upon these weak, feeble Jews. So it is in many churches today; the walls are down, and people say it is no use, and their hands drop down by their sides. Everything seemed against Nehemiah, but he was a man who had the fire of God in his soul. He had come to build the walls of Jerusalem.

If you could have bored a hole into his head, you would have found "Jerusalem" stamped on his brain. If you could have looked into his heart you would have found "Jerusalem" there. He was a fanatic; he was terribly in earnest; he was an enthusiast. I like to see a man take up some one thing and say, "I will do it; I live for this thing; this one thing I am bound to do." We spread out so much, and try to do so many things, that we are spread so thin the world never hears of us.

After he had been in the city three days and nights, he called the elders of Israel together, and told them the reason he had come. God had been preparing them, for the moment he told them they said, "Let us rise up and build."

Nehemiah Encounters Opposition

But there has not been a work undertaken for God since Adam fell which has not met with opposition. If Satan allows us to work unhindered, it is because our work is of no consequence. The first thing we read after the decision had been made to rebuild the walls is, "When Sanballat the Horonite, and Tobiah the servant, the Ammonite, and Geshem the Arabian, heard it, they laughed us to scorn, and despised us, and said, What is this thing that ye do? Will ye rebel against the king?" (Neh. 2:19).

These men were very indignant. They didn't care for the welfare of Jerusalem. Who were they? A mixed multitude who had no portion nor right nor memorial in Jerusalem. They didn't like to see the restoration of the ruins, just as people nowadays do not like to see the cause of Christ prospering. The offense of the cross has not ceased.

It doesn't take long to build the walls of a city if you can only get the whole of the people at it. If the Christians of this country would only rise up, we could evangelize America in twelve months. All the Jews had a hand in repairing the walls of Jerusalem. Each built near his own house, priest and merchant, goldsmith and apothecary, including the women. The men of Jericho and other cities came to help. The walls began to rise.

This stirred up Nehemiah's enemies, and they began to ridicule. Ridicule is a mighty weapon. "What do these feeble Jews try to accomplish?" said Sanballat. "Will they fortify themselves? Will they sacrifice? Will they make an end in a day? Will they revive the stones out of the heaps of the rubbish which are burned?"

"Even that which they build, if a fox go up, he shall even break down their stone wall," said Tobiah the Ammonite (Neh. 4:3).

But Nehemiah was wise. He paid no attention to them. He just looked to God for grace and comfort: "Hear, O our God; for we are despised: and turn their reproach upon their own head, and give them for a prey in the land of captivity: and cover not their iniquity, and let not their sin be blotted out from before thee: for they have provoked thee to anger before the builders" (Neh. 4:4–5).

Young man, if you wish to be successful in this world, don't mind Sanballat or Tobiah. Don't be kept out of the kingdom of God or out of active Christian work by the scorn and laughter and ridicule of your godless neighbors and companions.

Next, these enemies conspired to come and fight against Jerusalem. Nehemiah was warned, and took steps to guard against them. Half of the people were on the watch, and the other half held a sword in one hand and a trowel in the other. There was no eight-hour working day then. They were on duty from the rising of the sun till the stars appeared. They did not take off their clothes except to wash them.

Fancy this man who came from the Persian court with all its luxury, living and sleeping in his clothes for those fifty-two days! But he was in earnest. Ah, that is what we need! People who will set themselves to do one thing, and keep at it day and night.

All the people were bidden to lodge within the city, so that they should always be on hand to work and fight. Would to God that we could get all who belong inside the church to come in and do their share. "Happy is the church," says one, "whose workers are well skilled in the use of the Scripture, so that while strenuously building the Gospel Wall, they can fight too, if occasion require it." We ought all be ready to use the sword of the Spirit.

Opposition by Deception

By and by the enemies wrote a friendly letter, and wanted Nehemiah to go down on the plain of Ono and have a friendly discussion. It is a masterpiece of the devil to get men into friendly discussions. I don't know whether Nehemiah had a typewriter in those days or not. I don't know whether he had a printed form of letters, but he always sent back the same reply, "I am doing a great work, so that I cannot come down."

How many a church has turned aside for years to discuss "questions of the day," and has neglected the salvation of the world because they must go down to the "plain of Ono" and have a friendly discussion! Nehemiah struck a good keynote—"I am doing a great work, so that I cannot come down." If God has sent you to build the walls of Jerusalem, you go and do it.

They sent him another letter, and again he sent word back, "I am doing a great work, so that I cannot come down." He did not believe in "coming down." They sent him another, and he sent back the same word. They sent him a fourth letter, with the same result. They could not get him down. They wanted to slay him on the way.

I have seen many Christian men on the plain of Ono, men who were doing a splendid work but had been switched off. Think how much work has been neglected by temperance advocates in this country because they have gone into politics. How many times the Young Men's Christian Association has been switched off by discussing some other subject instead of holding up Christ before a lost world!

If the church would only keep right on and build the walls of Jerusalem they would soon be built. Oh, it is a wily devil that we have to contend with! Do you know it? If he can only get the church to stop to discuss these questions, he has accomplished his desire.

Nehemiah's enemies wrote him one more letter, an open letter, in which they said that they had heard he was going to set up a kingdom in opposition to the Persians, and that they were going to report him to the king. Treason has an ugly sound, but Nehemiah committed himself to the Lord, and went on building.

Then his enemies hired a prophet, one of his friends. A hundred enemies outside are not half so hard to deal with as one inside—a false friend. When the devil gets possession of a child of God, he will do the work better than the devil himself. Temptations are never so dangerous as when they come to us in a religious garb. So Tobiah and Sanballat bought up one of the prophets, and hired him to try to induce Nehemiah to go into the temple, that they might put him to death there.

"Now, Nehemiah, there is a plan to kill you; come into the temple. Let's go in and stay for the night."

He came near being deceived, but he said, "Shall I, such a man as I, be afraid of my life, and do that to save my life?"

After he had refused their invitation he saw that this man was a false prophet. By his standing his ground he succeeded in fifty-two days in building the walls of Jerusalem. Then the gates were set up and the work was finished.

Nehemiah's Lasting Influence

Now during all these centuries that story has been told, if Nehemiah had remained at court, he might have died a millionaire, but he never would have been heard of twenty years after his death. Do you know the names of any of Nineveh's millionaires? This man stepped out of that high position and took a low position, one that the world looked down upon and frowned upon, and his name has been associated with the walls of Jerusalem all these centuries.

Young person, if you want to be immortal, become identified with God's work, and pay no attention to what men outside say. Nehemiah and his associates began at sunrise and worked until it grew so dark they couldn't see. A man who will take up God's work, and work summer and winter right through the year, will have a harvest before the year is over, and the record of it will shine after he enters the other world.

Nehemiah Encourages Revival

The next thing we learn of Nehemiah is that he got up a great open-air meeting for the reading of the law of Moses in the hearing of the people. A pulpit of wood, large enough to hold Ezra the scribe and thirteen others, was built. The people wept when they heard the words of the law, but Nehemiah said, "Mourn not, nor weep. . . . Go your way, eat the fat, and drink the sweet, and send portions unto them for whom nothing is prepared: for this day is holy unto our Lord: neither be ye sorry; for the joy of the Lord is your strength" (Neh. 8:9–10).

He did not forget the poor. Reading the Bible and remembering the poor—a combination of faith and works—will always bring joy.

Nehemiah Governs Jerusalem

Nehemiah then began to govern the city and correct the abuses he found existing. He gathered about fifty priests and scribes together and made them sign and seal a written covenant. There were five things in that covenant I want to call attention to.

First, they were not to give their daughters to unbelievers. They had been violating the law of God, and had been marrying their daughters to the ungodly. God had forbidden them to intermarry with the nations in the land of Canaan; "for they will turn away thy son from following me, that they may serve other gods: so will the anger of the Lord be kindled against you, and destroy thee suddenly" (Deut. 7:4).

I have known many a man who has lost his power by being identified with the ungodly. If you want to have the blessing of God rest upon you, you must be very careful about your alliances. The Jews always got into trouble when they married with the nations round about. The houses of Ahab and of Solomon lost their kingdom by that sin. That was the cause of the overthrow of David's kingdom. Families who marry for wealth, and marry the godly to the ungodly, always bring distress into the family.

Then he made them sign a covenant that they would keep the Sabbath, that they would not buy upon the Sabbath. Think of a man going from a heathen court where they had no Sabbath, a man brought up in that atmosphere, coming up to Jerusalem and enforcing the law of Moses! It is recorded that they brought up fish, and he would not let them into the city on the Sabbath, and the fish spoiled. After they had tried that a few times, they gave it up. If you will take your stand for God, even if you stand alone, it will not be very long before you will get other men to stand with you. God stood with this man, and he carried everything before him.

I don't believe we shall have the right atmosphere in this country until we can get men who have backbone enough to stand up against the thing they believe is wrong. If it is a custom rooted and grounded for a hundred years never mind; you take your stand against it if you believe it is wrong. If you have gatherings, and it is fashionable to have wine and champagne, and you are a teetotaler; if they ask you anywhere and you know that they are to have drink, tell them you are not going.

A man said to me some years ago, "Mr. Moody, now that I am converted, must I give up the world?"

I said, "No, you needn't give up the world. If you give a good ringing testimony for the Son of God, the world will give you up pretty quick; they won't want you around."

Nehemiah said, "We will not have desecration of the Sabbath." Men break the Sabbath and wonder why it is they have not spiritual power. The trouble nowadays is that it doesn't mean anything to some people to be a Christian. What we must have is a higher type of Christianity in this country. We must have a Christianity that has in it the principle of self-denial. We must deny ourselves. If we want power, we must be separate.

The next thing they were to do—and bear in mind this was a thing they had to sign—was to give their land rest.

For four hundred and ninety years they had not let their land rest, so God took them away to Babylon for seventy years, and let the land rest. A man that works seven days in the week right along is cut off about five or ten years earlier. You cannot rob God. Why is it that so many railroad superintendents and physicians die early? It is because they work seven days in the week. So Nehemiah made them covenant to keep the law of Moses. If the nations of the earth had kept that law, the truth would have gone to the four corners of the earth before this time.

Then he made them sign a covenant that they would not charge usury. They were just grinding the poor down. I believe that the reason we are in such a wretched state in this country today is on account of crowding the poor, and getting such a large amount of money for usury. People evade the law, and pay the interest, and then they give a few hundred dollars to negotiate the loan. There is a great amount of usury, and see where we are today! See what a wretched state of things we are having, not only in this country, but all over the world!

The fifth thing he made them do was to bring their firstfruits to the sons of Levi. They were to give God a tenth, the first and best. As long as Israel did that they prospered, and when they turned away from that law they did not prosper. You can look through history and look around you and see the same thing today. As long as men keep God's law and respect God's testimony, they are going to prosper, but when they turn aside, like Samson, they lose their strength; they have no power.

If you take these five things and carry them out, you will have prosperity. Let us all do it personally. If it was good for those men it is good for us. The moment we begin to rob God of time or talents then darkness and misery and wretchedness will come.

40 Nicodemus

John 3:1–21

Nicodemus stood very high. He was one of the church dignitaries. He stood as high as any man in Jerusalem, except the high priest himself. He belonged to the seventy rulers of the Jews. He was a doctor of divinity and taught the law. There isn't one word of Scripture against him. He was a man that stood out before the whole nation as of pure and spotless character. If he lived now he would be called the Rev. Dr. Nicodemus, and we would make him president of some theological seminary, perhaps give him a chair at Andover.

He was a man who stood high, and yet this very man Christ said must be born again. I am glad this was said to Nicodemus and not to the poor woman at the well, because then the moral men in Boston would have said, "I hope the revival will reach all the harlots and drunkards in Boston, but we respectable people don't need it. Oh, no!" But if Nicodemus, that moral man in Jerusalem, needed to be born again, so does every man in Boston. This idea that you who are born in Boston don't need to be born of the Spirit comes from the devil; it doesn't come from the Bible.

When I was born in 1837, I was born after the flesh, with a wicked nature which I had inherited all the way back from fallen Adam; but when I was born again in 1856 then I became a child of God.

41 Noah

Genesis 6:5–7:16

I wonder how many of these people here this evening would like to be saved? I am not going to ask those who would to rise. I don't know whether anyone would have courage enough to rise, and by that act say, "I would like to be saved." Perhaps you say to yourselves, "If that man will just tell me the way I can be saved this evening, I will be saved." I believe one reason why so few are saved is because they don't come out to the meetings expecting to be saved. They don't come for that purpose.

There was a lady who came to our meeting in Philadelphia—to the noon meeting at 11 o'clock; she came early so as to get a good seat. After the meeting was over we had another meeting for women, and she stayed at that. In the afternoon we had another meeting, and she stayed at that. She had made up her mind not to leave the meetings until she had found Christ. She did not find him at that meeting, but she might have found him. He was offered freely to everyone at all of them. So she stayed at the afternoon meeting, and still no light came.

She stayed at the evening meeting, and went into the inquiry meeting afterward. Between 11 and 12 o'clock she took me by the hand and said, "I will trust him." And she rejoiced in the Savior's love. I met her afterward. There was not a face that shone more than hers did. There was a woman who came determined to find Christ. When we search for God with all our hearts we are sure to find him.

I am not going to preach so much of a sermon tonight, as I am going to try to tell you the Way of Life. I had a long talk with a man yesterday who I really believe was honestly seeking the kingdom of God; but the trouble was, he was determined to try to seek him in his own way, and trying to work the thing out himself, instead of just trusting to Jesus for it. I hope he is here tonight, and that the Lord may bless this little talk to his soul, and that he may tonight sleep safely in the arms of Jesus Christ. It is supremely important to every soul here this day to trust in Christ and be saved.

When I was in Manchester, in one of the inquiry meetings, I went up into the balcony to talk with a few men who were standing together, and who were inquirers of the Way of Life. And while they were standing in a little group around me there came up another man who got on the outside of the group. I thought by the expression of his face that he was skeptical. I didn't think he had come to find Christ. But as I went on talking I noticed the tears trickling down his cheeks. I said, "My friend, are you anxious about your soul's salvation?"

He said, "Yes, very." I asked him what was the trouble, and I kept on talking to that one man, thinking that if he could understand me perhaps the others would. He said he wanted to feel right about it. I explained it to him by means of an illustration, and asked him, "Do you see it?"

He said, "No."

I used another, and asked him, "Do you see it yet?"

He said, "No," again.

I gave still another and still he said he did not see. I then said, "Was it Noah's feelings that saved him, or was it his ark? Was it Noah's righteousness that saved him? Was it his life, was it his prayers, was it his tears, was it his feelings, or was it the ark?"

He came immediately and grasped me by the hand, and said, "I see it now; it is all right now. I've got to go away on the next train, and I'm in a hurry, but you have made it plain to me; good-by."

And he went off. I thought it was so sudden that he could not have understood it. But the next Sunday afternoon he came and tapped me on the shoulder, and smiled, and asked me if I remembered him. I said, "No, I remember your face but can't tell who you are or where I've seen you before."

He said, "Do you remember a man that came up to you the other day, and you explained to him how it was Noah's ark that saved him? I did not see any illustration until you used that one, and then I saw it all."

I remembered him then and asked him how he was. He said he had been all right ever since, and that the ark of Christ's mercy had saved him. I afterward learned that he was one of the best businessmen of Manchester, England. His feelings didn't save him. The ark of Christ's salvation saved him.

New Birth Is Instantaneous

I want to prove to you that salvation is instantaneous. It is just as sudden as a man walking through a doorway. One minute he is on this side, the next he is on that side. There was one minute when Noah was exposed to the wrath that was to come over the whole world; but when he went through the doorway of the ark, that moment he was safe. There are many who are trying to make an ark for themselves out of their feelings, out of their own good deeds. But God has provided an ark.

If Noah had had to build himself an ark when the flood came, he would have been lost like the rest. A good many of those men who perished when that flood came tried to make arks for themselves, but they all perished helplessly. They tried to make boats, and tried every way they could to save themselves, but they perished because they were not in the ark that God had appointed. So, today, every man and every woman must perish that is not in the ark which God has appointed for their salvation.

A knowledge about the ark is not going to help you. A great many persons flatter themselves that they are going to be saved because they know a great deal about Jesus Christ. But your knowledge of him will not save you. Noah's carpenters probably knew as much about the ark as Noah did, and perhaps more. They knew that the ark was strong. They knew it was built to stand the deluge. They knew it was made to float upon the waters. They had helped to build it. But they were just as helpless when the flood came as men who lived thousands of miles away. Men who lived right in sight of the ark, that knew all about it, perished like the rest because they were not in the ark.

I know something about the different lines of steamers, and I have crossed the Atlantic. Here is another man that has never heard there was such a line of steamers. We both want to go to Europe. My knowledge of a line of steamers does not help me a bit if I do not take the means to go there. You may hear about Christ, but if you don't believe in Christ you cannot be saved. Your knowledge is not going to help you to your salvation. What you want to do is just to make Christ your ark, and then to step into that ark and be saved.

I want to call your attention to Genesis 7:1, "And the LORD said unto Noah, Come thou and all thy house into the ark."

We meet that little word "come" very often in the Scriptures. This is the first time it is used as an invitation. It is the voice of grace, mercy, and love. One hundred and twenty years before the time of the text Noah received the most awful communication that ever came from heaven to earth. God told him that he was going to destroy the world on account of the great increase of wickedness.

Sin came into the world full grown; the first man born of woman was a murderer. The fact is, man has always been bad; there is nothing good in him—he is bad by nature. We don't need to go to the Bible to prove that. You can look around you and find plenty of proofs. Leave man alone and see how quickly he will go to ruin! See how the nations of the earth have gone to ruin when they have been left alone. It was their own sin that drove them to ruin, and it is just the same with individuals. But wickedness had increased in those days. If possible men were worse then than they are now; and so God told Noah to build an ark for the saving of his house, for he was about to destroy the world by a flood. Noah, having faith in God, obeyed the command.

Building the Ark

Noah was instructed to warn the people of their coming doom, but they didn't pay any attention to him. They asked where the sign was that the world was to be destroyed, and scoffed, just as men now do, at the idea. When Noah was told to build the ark he knew he would be the laughingstock of the city. But the old man toiled on despite the jeers of his fellows. Thank God! There was one man in that age who dared to go against public sentiment and obey the voice of the Lord.

It was one of the wonders of the world; but he worked away on his ark, and what was more, he got his children to believe and help him. While the ark was being built perhaps the people came to look at it, and considered its builder a lunatic for wasting his time and money on this apparently useless undertaking. Men undoubtedly talked then as they do now. You talk with the scoffers of Chicago and you will see that men put up their little puny reason against the Almighty. I have heard some men say that God can't destroy this world and others declare that there is no God. Undoubtedly the antediluvians, the people before the flood, thought in the same way, and some would probably say that if there was a God he couldn't destroy his world.

I can imagine that business was brisk, and that the warning gave them little trouble. Their saloons were full every night, and Noah and his ark were the standing joke among them. One hundred years rolled away, and yet no sign of a flood. There were probably astronomers in those days who tried to read the heavens, but who could see no change. There were geologists, no doubt, who dug down into the bowels of the earth to bring up some dead carcass to prove that there was no God. I don't know but some of them believed that men were descended from the monkeys, and some subscribed to the evolution theory we hear so much about. At any rate, whatever notions they had, none of them believed in the coming of the flood.

There were Noah's carpenters. You might see them, a gang of men going into the saloons at night, loafing and drinking and making sport of the foolish old fellow, as they called their master, and excusing themselves for working for him on the grounds that his money was as good as anyone else's. Poor Noah, what a discouraging time he must have had!

I remember once when I felt very much discouraged. I suppose I got under the juniper tree, where Elijah went. It seemed to me as if I was not accomplishing anything, and all my work went for nothing. While I was feeling very glum and sorrowful, one of the Sunday school teachers came in and asked me how the work had been on the Sunday previous.

"Oh, very poor, very dull," said I. "How was it with you?"

"Very good, indeed," said he. "We had a very profitable time studying the character of Noah."

I thought I knew all about Noah, but I inquired what new thing they had found out about him.

"Oh, nothing new; but just study him, and you will find very much that will help you."

So when he was gone away I took down the Bible and began to study Noah; and I found, among other things, that he had preached a hundred and twenty years without making a single convert; but still he kept at it, preaching and working on the ark, and holding on to his faith for more than a hundred years.

We might suppose Noah would get discouraged after working at the ark a hundred years. I suppose by that time some of the timbers had gotten rotten that were put in at first, and had to be replaced with new ones. Still he worked away. God had said a flood was coming and told him to prepare the ark, and it didn't make any difference about the time. It was his business to preach and to build.

That day I went down to the Farwell Hall prayer meeting, and a man rose up and asked us to pray for the salvation of his soul.

Well, I thought, how much good that would have done Noah, to have had somebody rise for prayers. But there wasn't anybody who wanted to be saved. How ashamed I ought to be to complain of my want of success!

Noah's Ark

One hundred and twenty years before, God had come to Noah and told him to build this ark, and now he called him into it. It was a great boat. If you should put it into one story and one floor, it would be fifteen hundred feet long and two hundred and forty feet wide. This room is about two hundred feet wide, and the ark was seven times as long as this building and a great deal wider, and about sixteen feet high.

Some infidels and skeptics have tried to make out that the ark was not large enough to hold all that is said to have gone into it, but there is no trouble about that. Undoubtedly in those days they thought it was too large. I can imagine that they complained of Noah for building such a large ark when there was nobody who agreed with him, and none to go into it but his own family. He certainly did not confer with flesh and blood, or he would never have undertaken to build the ark at all. The people jeered and scoffed at him, called him a lunatic, and if they had had insane asylums, I have no doubt they would have shut him up in one of them.

But Noah, in the face of all obstacles, still goes on with the work which has been assigned him. I can imagine that after one hundred years have rolled away the people become more skeptical. They laugh, and mock, and say, "We don't believe there is any danger. There is no sign of a flood. The light shines the same; the sun is as bright as it has been the last thousand years. It is a very strange thing if this world is to be destroyed, for we are getting on so well and are so prosperous." And so they went on scoffing, drinking, marrying, and giving in marriage, feeling perfectly safe (Matt. 24:38).

Some people excuse them because their consciences were not touched and awakened. So it may be said of you, but that only made their fate worse. It is a good deal better for you to heed the voice of God.

Well, twenty years more have rolled away, and that is the time God has set. The people had been looking into the heavens but could see no sign. The geologists scoffed, and the astronomers predicted fine weather. The philosophers, and the astrologers, and the scientific men, and the wise men, and the great men, all united to testify that Noah was wrong—that God could not drown the world.

But God, who created this world out of nothing, certainly can destroy it. Don't flatter yourselves, my friends, that God can't destroy the world. Don't go on thinking that God isn't going to call this world to judgment. He is a God of mercy, but there is one thing we must keep in mind, he is also a God of justice. We are taught that if a man won't have grace, he shall have judgment. You can have grace, mercy, and love, or you can have judgment and the curse of God.

I can imagine that Noah's contract is finished, and everything is ready. It is spring, and all the people are busy planting their crops. But Noah plants nothing.

"Look," they say, "he plants nothing. He will surely starve." They are very much startled at his course.

At length God tells Noah to occupy the ark he had built. When he moves in they all say, "Why doesn't he wait till a storm comes? The sun is shining brightly without any sign of rain. The flocks and herds are grazing on the hillsides, and everything moves on as it has for the last two thousand years."

Noah Enters the Ark

But Noah goes into the ark. The people who had ridiculed the old man are alarmed as they see the beasts coming up from the fields and forests; the tiger out of its den, the bear out of its cave, the lion and the lamb going in together. All kinds of birds are flying to the ark, and even the little insects are creeping toward it.

After they had all gone in, we are told that God shut the door. In another place in the Bible, we are told that what God shuts no man opens (Jer. 13:19). Still the flood didn't come. There were seven days grace, as it were. If those people had cried for mercy then I believe God would have saved them. They didn't believe that he would destroy the world—but did that change the decrees of heaven?

The Flood Begins

At last the storm began, and we are told that the fountains of the great deep were broken up. Not only did the waters come out of the heavens and pour upon them, but it seems that they burst up from the earth; and the ocean broke from its banks. After the storm had raged for perhaps forty-eight hours the scoffers began to change their tune. They pray to God for mercy. They go to the door of the ark and cry, "Noah, let us in! Noah, let us in!"

But there comes a voice from within, "I cannot; God has shut the door." My friends, the door that shuts God's people in will shut the scoffer out.

Are You in the Ark?

I would like to have you ask yourselves the question now, before I go on any further, "Am I in the ark of Christ's salvation?" If you can't answer the question—if you are not able to say you are in the ark—won't you just lift up your hearts in prayer, if you never prayed before, and ask the Lord to give you light on the question today?

Now if these scriptures are true, and I have no doubt about it, it is an awful thing for a man or woman to die outside of the ark.

So, today, God has provided an ark for every soul in this house. He says he doesn't want any of us to perish (John 3:16). He doesn't want any of us to die outside of the ark. He wants us all to come to Christ. O hear his loving call today, "Come thou and all thy house into the ark!"

O you who are parents—I am speaking to a good many parents here today—you come in first. Noah went in first, and his wife and children followed him. He had lived such a life as to give his children confidence in him. If you, parents, do not go into the ark yourselves, how can you expect your children to go in? God calls you today. Will you come?

But one more thought. Men cavil now and say, "We don't believe in the deluge at all; we believe in the teachings of the New Testament, but not in the Old. We can't believe that God would destroy so many people at once."

My dear friends, do you know that every thirty years more people die now than were destroyed then? The deluge was simply their destruction a few years sooner—that was all. Not only that, but the Son of God has said, "As it was in the days of Noe, so shall it be also in the days of the Son of man" (Luke 17:26). Don't let the devil make you think God is not coming to destroy the world by fire, for he is going to do it.

The first two or three hours of the Chicago fire men were on the streets laughing, and saying it would soon be over. But the fire continued to rage until nearly the whole city was destroyed, and their laughing was soon turned to weeping. It seemed to me that on that memorable night I got a glimpse of what the judgment day will be.

What is your refuge? Is it some false hope? May the God of mercy sweep it away today! Thank God, we don't have to wait a hundred and twenty years for the building of the ark! God has brought it right to the door of every man's heart. All we have to do is to hide in Jesus, and we are saved for time and eternity.

Noah and Joy

There is a difference between mirth and cheerfulness. Mirth flashes and is gone. Cheerfulness is calm and steady. It comes from God, and is closely allied with the spirit of praise. Some people keep their houses shut up and dark. Everything is in perfect order, but the atmosphere is that of gloom— of death. So, many keep their hearts. They exclude the sunlight of God's love. We read that there were three stories in the ark. But Noah and his family did not stay down in the lowest one, below the waterline, where all was dark. Many Christians, however, live spiritually down in the cellar.

We ought to go into the highest story, and get as near to God as we can. Joy is deeper and more abiding than happiness. Joy sings in the dark like the nightingale. The Christian can have joy, even in adversity. We ought to rejoice always. Unless we are joyful, we cannot be useful. We read in Nehemiah 8:10, "The joy of the LORD is your strength."

A joyful Christian will have power. If we are occupied with ourselves and our own burdens, we can't help others. But if we cast our burdens on the Lord, then we are ready to work for him. We get joy by trying to make others joyful. A farmer who kept all his grain and would not sell any or sow any wouldn't do any good or get any good. There is nothing on earth so powerful as a church full of joy. Such was the apostolic church.

42 **Paul**

Acts 9:1–31; 16:6–40

To my mind the case of Saul of Tarsus is a great deal harder than that of the prodigal son. It didn't take long to convince the prodigal of his duty after he had spent all and began to be in want. Down there among the swine he was at the bottom of the ladder, but up among the Pharisees in Jerusalem, Saul of Tarsus was at the top. There couldn't be a more hopeless case. Even Caiaphas or Pilate might be converted to Christ easier than Saul. He was a mad persecutor of the Christians; he helped in the murder of Stephen (Acts 8:1–3). He was full of zeal and fury, and also full of religion. If anyone had told him that he would become a Christian at Damascus how he would have raved about it!

Saul's Anger

One reason he was so mad was that when the disciples had been scattered from Jerusalem they went everywhere preaching the gospel of the Son of God. Now the news had come that some of them had gone down to Damascus and were preaching the gospel there. Then Saul, breathing out threats and slaughter, goes to the chief priests and gets the necessary documents so that he may bring these heretics, bound, to Jerusalem.

Now Saul of Tarsus was an upright man. He prayed as long as any other man; he knew all about the law, and kept it; he was blameless as touching the law; and, according to some people in Chicago, he didn't need to be converted at all. He was good enough already. True, he hated Jesus Christ, but so do a great many other men who are honest and pay their debts and are thought to be good enough without conversion.

I don't think he was a stranger to Christ. It was but three years since Christ's ascension, and Saul must have seen him and known all about his miracles, his death, and his resurrection. He was probably well acquainted with Nicodemus, a member of the Sanhedrin, and with Joseph of Arimathea, who was a prominent man, both of whom were friends of Christ. But he hated Christ, and all who believed in him.

Saul's Conversion

I can see him as he rides out of the city starting for Damascus, one hundred and thirty-six miles distant. He rides through Samaria, but the Jews have no dealings with the Samaritans, and so he doesn't speak a word to one of them. Now he comes in sight of the beautiful city, so beautiful, it is said, that Mohammed, when he saw it, wouldn't look at it a second time, lest it should win his heart from the city of the prophet. It is noon; the sun shines in meridian splendor; but just then there is a blinding light above the brightness of the sun, and the whole company, in amazement, fall from their frightened horses and lie with their faces to the dust.

The Son of God just drew back the cloud and gave one look, and the brightness of his face was so dazzling that they could not bear the sight for an instant. Saul caught one glimpse of it and it made him blind.

Then a voice, "Saul, Saul!" The Son of God knew him by name. He knows every sinner by name, knows where he lives just as well as he knew where Saul was when he sent Ananias to his lodging in Damascus. I hope the Son of God will call sinners here by their names, and that they will hear his voice and be converted, like Saul.

And now this question, "Why persecutest thou me?" What reason could Paul give for persecuting the Son of God?

Some people may think it was hard for the Christians in Damascus to have Saul come down to arrest them, and to bring them bound to Jerusalem. But it was a great deal harder for Saul than for anyone else. Christ says to him, "It is hard for thee to kick against the pricks."

In that country they used a long stick, with a bit of steel in the end of it, for driving cattle; and sometimes, when the ox was contrary, he would kick back against the piece of steel, striking it into himself. This was the illustration which Christ used to show the stubborn Pharisee that his way was a hard one.

A lady in the inquiry room the other night said to me, "It is so easy to sin, and so hard to do right."

Now that is the same as saying that the service of the devil is an easy service, and that God's service is a hard one. But Christ says, "My yoke is easy, and my burden is light" (Matt. 11:30).

It is "the way of the transgressor" that is hard.

Let us take some of the different classes of the devil's servants. Take a harlot: is her life an easy one? It is a short one; only an average of seven years, with shame and sorrow all the time. What memories of the old home, and of mother and sisters, come up to haunt the poor fallen one. Those who flatter her do not love her, and at last she dies in loneliness, and perhaps in want, and is laid in a nameless grave.

Take the drunkard: is his life an easy one? I have a man in my mind whom I tried to warn from the beginning of his evil ways before I went to England. He was only a moderate drinker then, but now he is a sot. His wife has died of a broken heart; his children have been taken from him and placed where he may never see them again. He is wandering about the streets of Chicago a lost and ruined man.

Take the rum seller. He laughs at these meetings, laughs at the Bible, and says there is no hell. I have a man in my mind whose place of business was the curse of a whole community. Fathers and mothers used to beg of him not to sell liquor to their sons, but he only laughed at them. He had a son of his own, of whom he fairly made an idol, and that wretched young man, after coming to be a miserable drunkard, at last found life so hateful that he took a pistol and blew out his own brains.

O rum seller, you who ruin other men's sons, there is a time coming when you will reap what you have sowed! You think you are safe from the law of man, but God, the God of equity, has a law from which you cannot escape. You ruin the sons of other men, and your sons will be ruined, and you, like this rum seller, will have a miserable end.

Take the fashionable smooth-tongued libertine: your time is coming by and by. If a woman fails she is thrust out of society, while these oily-tongued villainous men are praised and flattered. But there is a God who will judge you, and you will find out soon enough that "the way of the transgressor is hard."

The other night I read a letter from a brokenhearted woman asking me to pray for her husband, who had committed a forgery and had fled from his home for fear of the penalty of the law. Up in the balcony he sat while I read that sorrowful letter, and after the meeting was over he came to me and confessed his sin. I never pitied a man so in all my life.

We prayed together, and the next night he came again, saying, "I feel as if Jesus had forgiven my sin; but I am not my own; I belong to the law. I have made up my mind to go home and give myself up to the officers of justice, and I suppose they will send me to prison for ten years. And now won't you pray for my poor family whose hearts I have broken, and from whom I must be separated by my punishment and disgrace?"

Ah, my friends, that man didn't find it easy to fight against God. It is a thousand times harder to serve the devil than to serve the Lord.

Now all at once we find a great change coming over this man Saul. A few minutes before he was breathing out threats and slaughter, and pushing on to Damascus to hunt out and punish the followers of the Galilean prophet. But now, after this great light has shined round about him, he falls down to the ground; and with a very humble voice he says, "Lord, what wilt thou have me to do?"

Any of you who don't believe in sudden conversions had better read this ninth chapter of the Acts of the Apostles and find out how long it took to convert Saul of Tarsus.

Paul Begins His New Life

Now he rises from the earth and goes on his journey, but for an altogether different purpose. I suppose that Ananias was one of the very men whom he was going to hunt out and bring to punishment. Now, by the commandment of the Lord, whom he had so terribly hated but half an hour ago, he pushes on for Damascus, and that same Ananias is sent to open his eyes. It may be Ananias was rather doubtful about going to this man—perhaps he didn't believe in sudden conversions either—but the Lord had told him to go, and when he went he found Saul had become an inquirer.

What a curious experience it must have been for that raging persecutor, Saul of Tarsus, to go staggering along in his blindness, led like a little child to Damascus. Now Ananias speaks to this terrible man and says, "Brother Saul, the Lord, even Jesus, that appeared unto thee in the way as thou camest, hath sent me, that thou mightest receive thy sight, and be filled with the Holy Ghost" (Acts 9:17). And immediately there fell from his eyes as it had been scales, and he received sight forthwith; and straightway, the account goes on to tell us, he preached Christ in the synagogues, that he is the Son of God.

How amazed those Damascus Christians must have been to hear this man preaching the gospel of Christ and confounding the Jews who didn't believe in Jesus. I suppose they had received letters from their brethren in Jerusalem telling them to look out, for the terrible Saul of Tarsus was coming down to make trouble for them. Perhaps they had some prayer meetings while he was on the road to ask the Lord to save them from the hands of this terrible persecutor of the church; and when he comes, behold he is on their side!

Some time afterward Saul goes up to Jerusalem. At first the brethren there didn't have any faith in him, but after awhile Barnabas takes him and introduces him, and tells them all about how he has been converted. After awhile they receive him as one of their company, and from this time he is one of the very foremost men in defending the church he used to despise.

Paul's Church-Planting Ministry

Before long we hear of him suffering persecution for the sake of the Lord Jesus. He starts out on a preaching tour, and pretty soon we hear of him in the Philippian jail.

Satan got a match when he got Paul. He tried to get him away from God, but Paul never switched off. Look how they tortured him. Look how they stripped and beat him. Not only did the Romans do this, but the Jews also. How the Jews tried to drag him from his high calling. How they stripped him and laid upon the back of the apostle blow after blow. And you know that the scourge in those days was no light thing. Sometimes men died under that punishment.

If one of us got one of the stripes that Paul got, how the papers would talk about it. But it was nothing to Paul. He just looked at it as if it were a trivial thing as if it were a light affliction. When he was stripped and scourged by his persecutors you might have gone and asked him, "Well, Paul, what are you going to do now?"

"Press toward the mark for the prize of the high calling of God in Christ Jesus" (Phil. 3:14).

Take your stand before him and ask him as they bring the rod down upon his head, "What are you going to do now, Paul?"

"Do? I am going to press toward the mark of the high calling of God in Christ Jesus." He had one idea, and that was it.

Look at him as they stoned him. The Jews took up great stones to throw upon the great apostle. They left him for dead, and I suppose he was dead, but God raised him up. Come up and look at him all bruised and bleeding as he lies. "Well, Paul, you've had a narrow escape this time. Don't you think you had better give up? Go off into Arabia and rest for six weeks. What will you do if you remain here? They mean to kill you."

"Do?" he cries as he raises himself like a mighty giant, "I am going to press toward the mark of the high calling of God."

And he goes forth and preaches the gospel. I am ashamed of Christianity in the nineteenth century when I think of those early Christians. Why, it would take all the Christians in the Northwest to make one Paul. Look at his heroism everywhere he went. Talk about your Alexanders; why, the mighty power of God rested upon Paul. "Why," said he, "thrice was I shipwrecked while going off to preach the gospel." What did he care about that?

Cold churches wouldn't trouble him, although they trouble us. What would lying elders and false deacons be to him? That wouldn't stop him. He had but one idea, and over all obstacles he triumphed for that one idea. Look at him as he comes back from his punishment. He goes up some side street and gets lodgings. He works during the day and preaches at night on the street. He had no building like this, no committee to wait on him, no carriage to carry him from the meeting, no one to be waiting to pay his board bills.

There he was toiling and preaching, and, after preaching for eighteen months, they say, "We'll have to pay you for all this preaching, Paul," and they take him to the corner of the street and pay him with thirty-nine lashes! That is the way they paid him.

Oh, my friends, when you look at the lives of such men doesn't it make you feel ashamed of yourselves? I confess I feel like hanging my head. Go to him in the Philippian jail and ask him what he is going to do now.

"Do? Press forward for the mark of my high calling." And so he went on looking toward one point, and no man could stand before him.

There is a man for you! Stoning, and scourging, and prisons were all the same to him, so that he might win Christ.

Paul Finishes Well

The last we see of him is in that prison at Rome. In a few days he is to be led out to execution. Nero has condemned him to death. So he takes a piece of paper and writes a letter to his son Timothy.

"Good-by, Timothy. Keep on preaching; preach the word; hold fast that whereunto thou hast attained. As for me, I have finished my course; I have kept the faith henceforth there is laid up for me a crown of righteousness, which the Lord shall give me in that day."

In a few days they take him out to the place of execution; the ax falls on his neck, and his head rolls down into the dust. But there is one of the Lord's chariots waiting for his soul; and now that he is delivered from his poor little aching body, he leaps into it and sweeps upward through the sky, and into the gates of the New Jerusalem.

There are a great many people who know him there, and through all these eighteen hundred years there are souls coming up to glory and giving him new joy over the work which he did for Christ.

"Paul, I thank you for that Epistle to the Romans," says one. "It was the means of bringing me to Christ."

"Paul, I thank you for that sermon on Mars Hill," says another, "that saved me from my worship of the unknown God."

"Paul, I thank you for that Epistle to the Corinthians. It gave me victory over the grave."

"Paul, I thank you for that Epistle to the Thessalonians; it showed me that the Lord who was gone away would sometime come back again."

Ah, this Saul of Tarsus, this preacher of righteousness, so often rejected, is a great man in heaven now. Talk about Alexander shaking the world with his armies: this little tentmaker of Tarsus shook the world without any armies.

It was a wise thing for him to count all things but loss for the excellency of Christ Jesus his Lord. Didn't he say that chastening afterward yieldeth the peaceable fruits of righteousness unto them that are exercised thereby? Didn't he tell us to rejoice evermore, and, like David, do you not think he was satisfied when he awoke in the likeness of his Lord?

43 Penitent Thief

Luke 23:39–43

The cross of Christ divides all mankind. There are only two sides, those for Christ, and those against him. Think of the two thieves; from the side of Christ one went down to death cursing God, and the other went to glory.

From Curses to Singing Hallelujahs

This thief was saved at the very last. Christ found him on the very borders of hell. Not only was he a thief, but he was the worst kind. He had been tried, found guilty, sentenced, scourged, and now they nailed him to the cross. When the world was mocking and deriding Jesus these two thieves joined in it (Matt. 27:44); but all at once one of them changed his cry and began to rebuke the other, saying, "Dost thou not fear God, seeing thou art in the same condemnation?" (Luke 23:40).

Now Solomon tells us that this very fear of the Lord is the beginning of wisdom (Prov. 9:10). What convinced him that Jesus was different from those about him we are not told, but I think we have a right to use our imagination, and right here I tell you what I think convinced him that Christ was more than man. While the crowd was mocking and the soldiers casting lots for his garments, instead of Christ calling down fire from heaven to consume them, he sent up that piercing cry, "Father, forgive them; for they know not what they do" (Luke 23:34).

I can imagine the thought flashing into his soul that this can't be a man like himself. I can imagine him saying to himself, "I wouldn't ask for mercy on my enemies."

I seem to hear this thief talking to himself in this way. "What a strange man this must be! He says he is the Son of God. Why doesn't God send his angels and destroy all this crowd of people who are torturing his Son? If he has power now, as he used to have when he worked those miracles they talk about, why doesn't he sweep all these wretches to destruction? I would do it in a minute if I had the power. But this man prays God to forgive them. Strange! Strange! I am sorry I said a word against him when they hung him up here. What a difference there is between him and his accusers.

"Here we are on two crosses, side by side; but the rest of our lives we have been far enough apart. I have been robbing and murdering, and he has been visiting the hungry, healing the sick, and raising the dead. I won't rail at him anymore. Indeed, I begin to believe he must truly be the Son of God; for surely no son of man could forgive his enemies this way."

This poor man had been scourged, beaten, nailed to the cross, and hung up there for the world to gaze upon; and he wasn't sorry for his sins one single bit—but when he heard the Savior praying for his murderers, that broke his heart.

The Thief's Outstanding Faith

But now that he is convicted just see what he does. The very first thing, he rebukes that other thief; then the next step is, he confesses his sin, "We suffer justly, this is what we deserve."

So if man wants to be saved he will want to confess his sins; but instead of this, most people try to justify themselves. This thief confessed his sin right there, and the moment he did so he was in a position that the God of all grace could deal with him. Then help came.

The next thing we notice is that he confesses Christ. The two go together. First he confesses his own sin, and then he says, "But this man has done nothing amiss," thereby confessing Christ. To me it is the most extraordinary confession, and the most extraordinary faith on record. I think this faith ought to entitle him to take his place at the head of all those who lived before him.

Talk about the faith of Moses, and of Abraham and Elijah, and the faith of these disciples. Why, the disciples had been with him three years, and had seen him raise the dead and perform all his other great miracles, but this thief perhaps had never even seen Christ before. Yet right there in that dark hour, when there was no eye to pity, when there was no one to help Christ, when the world was mocking him and putting him to death, this thief had faith.

That very night one of his foremost disciples had betrayed him. That very night one of his foremost disciples had denied him. The other disciples had forsaken him and fled, yet right there that poor thief had faith. It must have been like a refreshing cup to our Lord, when there was no one in the wide, wide world to own him, that that poor thief should confess him. He took his place as a sinner, and cried for mercy, and you know Jesus has come to deal with mercy and to bless; and although he was nailed to the cross, he was in a position to help the poor sinner.

And what did Jesus say in answer to his prayer? He looks kindly upon him and says, "Today shalt thou be with me in paradise" (Luke 23:43).

He got more than he asked for. He only asked to be remembered, but Christ says to him, "I will take you right into my kingdom today."

No doubt Satan said to himself, "I will have the soul of that thief pretty soon down here in the caverns of the lost. He belongs to me." But Christ snapped the fetters of his soul and set him at liberty. Satan lost his prey.

What a contrast! In the morning he is led out a condemned criminal; in the evening he is saved from his sins. In the morning he is cursing— Matthew and Mark both tell us that those two thieves came out cursing— and in the evening the repentant thief is singing hallelujahs with a choir of angels. In the morning he is condemned by men as not fit to live on earth; in the evening he is reckoned good enough for heaven. In the morning nailed to the cross; in the evening in the paradise of God, crowned with a crown he should wear through all the ages. In the morning not an eye to pity; in the evening washed and made clean in the blood of the Lamb. In the morning in the society of thieves and outcasts; in the evening Christ is not ashamed to walk arm in arm with him down the golden pavements of the eternal city.

Jesus had died before his very eyes, and hastened before him to get a place ready for this first soul brought from the world after he had died.

You have heard of the child who didn't want to die and go to heaven because he did not know anybody there. But the thief had one acquaintance, even the Master of the place himself.

Jesus calls to Gabriel and says, "Prepare a chariot; there is a friend of mine upon that cross. They are breaking his legs now. He soon will be ready to come. Make haste and bring him to me."

And the angel in the chariot swoops down the sky, takes up the soul of the poor penitent thief, and hastens back again to glory; while the gates of the city swing wide open, and the angels shout their welcome to this poor sinner "washed . . . in the blood of the Lamb" (Rev. 7:14).

Call on Jesus Now!

Men say now they haven't faith, after living with an open Bible for these hundreds of years. Although, if we look around us, and see men lifted up from the very gutter, drunkards become reformed, gamblers turned away from sin, we see everywhere monuments of grace. People say the fact is we haven't got faith. Why do you not have faith? If the thief had faith in that dark hour, why don't you have faith? Sinner, why not call upon him now?

You say you don't know how to pray. Could you not make the same prayer as this thief? It was very short, wasn't it? "Lord, remember me when thou comest into thy kingdom" (Luke 23:42).

Don't you see this man was saved, you might say, in the twinkling of an eye. He was saved by grace, and grace alone. He couldn't use his hands for the Lord, for they were nailed to the cross. He couldn't run an errand for the Lord, for his feet were nailed to the cross.

Some people say, "Well, but, Mr. Moody, you must not preach salvation distinct from the ordinances."

I don't know how many abusive letters I have gotten about this. God forbid that I should speak against the ordinances. I would let my right hand forget its cunning before I would do it. The Bible teaches baptism and coming to the Lord's table to break bread, but when I preach regeneration I don't preach baptism. Now, if that thief couldn't be saved without baptism there would be no hope for him, for there wasn't anyone to baptize him, and if there were he wouldn't be allowed off the cross for that purpose. I think this story is given just to teach us this one lesson, that all these ordinances are distinct from salvation. Salvation is by grace alone.

44 Peter

One of the first glimpses we have of this man Simon, whom Jesus surnamed Cephas, or Peter (that is, a stone), was when he and his brother Andrew, who were two poor men making their living by fishing in the Sea of Galilee, were called by Christ to follow him.

Peter's Call

I want you all to notice that Peter was first called to be a disciple and then to be an apostle. He didn't leave his work until he was called the second time. I think it is well for us to notice this, because there are a good many young converts these days who are looking to the work of the ministry, and it is questionable whether they have ever been called to the ministry. It is one thing to be called to be a disciple, and quite another to be called to be a minister.

John Wesley used to say to the young candidates for the ministry after they had preached their trial sermons, "Did you make anyone mad? Did you convert anybody?"

And if to both of these questions they answered, "No," he would say, "Then that is very good evidence you are not called to the ministry."

Now, we find, in the fifth chapter of Luke (vv. 1–11), and also in the fourth chapter of Matthew (vv. 18–22), where Peter got his calling. He was out with his partners and others, fishing, when Jesus came along and told them to cast their net, or to launch out into the deep and cast their net into the sea.

"But," said Peter, "we have toiled all night and caught nothing."

"Nevertheless," commanded Jesus, "let down your nets."

At the word of God they did so and were successful, and when they got ashore they found Jesus had called them to be his disciples. Christ just said to them, "Follow me, and I will make you fishers of men" (Matt. 4:19). No one was more successful in the world, in catching men, than Peter. If you will just follow the Lord and believe in him, he will make you fishers of men.

Now, some may wonder why it was that God did not call them when they had their nets empty. It seems to me that he did so because he wanted them to leave something. There are a good many of us willing to be disciples of the Lord if it does not cost anything.

We find in another place that Peter says to the Lord, "We have left all, and followed thee" (Mark 10:28; Luke 18:28); but the "all" was not a great deal—a few old boats and broken nets and one great haul of fish. What was all that in comparison to what he gained by becoming a disciple of the Lord? He left his boats and his nets and his fish, and he gained the friendship of Christ, which was worth more than all the world.

Peter Called to Walk on Water

The next time we get a glimpse of Peter is in the fourteenth chapter of Matthew (vv. 22–33), where the Lord called him to walk to him on the water. Here we find Peter in doubt. He got on well enough so long as he kept his eye on Christ, but we find by the account that he turned away his eyes from the Lord and began to look at the water. When he saw the waves and heard the boisterous wind, he began to be afraid. Ah, my friends, that is the way it is with all of us; when we get our eye off from Christ, the troubles and dangers of this life look very terrible.

Now let me call your attention to Peter's prayer on this occasion. It was a short prayer, and right to the point: "Lord, save me." It didn't begin with a long preamble, as a great many prayers do. If it had taken him as long to come to what he wanted to say as it does some people in our prayer meetings, he would have been forty feet under water before he would have reached it.

"Lord, save me." That was a good prayer, and the Lord immediately answered it.

Peter's Confession

Again, in the sixteenth chapter of Matthew (vv. 13–20) we find that Christ is asking his disciples, "Whom do men say that I am?" And when they answer, "Some say, John the Baptist, and some say, Elias, and some say, one of the old prophets," he turns to Peter and says, "Whom say ye that I am?"

And Peter answered, "Thou art the Christ, the Son of the living God." So, you see, Peter was a Trinitarian. He believed in Jesus Christ as the Son of God, and made his confession accordingly.

And Jesus answered and said unto him: "Blessed art thou, Simon Barjona: for flesh and blood hath not revealed it unto thee, but my Father which is in heaven" (Matt. 16:17).

See! Jesus blessed Peter right there, and I have yet to find the first man and the first woman who are willing to confess Christ who will not say that God has blessed their souls after they have confessed him.

Now, let me call your attention to another scene in the life of Peter. He got to be a sort of a—well, I may say a sort of "high church" man. He belonged to the "high church." He was a sort of a ritualist. He had gotten this idea that Christ was the same as any other saint; that he was to be put on a level with some of the rest of the saints. He did not make any distinction.

Peter on the Mount of Transfiguration

When Jesus goes up to the Mount of Transfiguration Peter is one of the men he takes with him. On this occasion Peter seems to have been confused in his ideas of worship, and he proposes to make three tabernacles, one for Moses, and another for Elijah, and another for the Son of God.

But God is not pleased with this idea, so he just snatches away Moses and Elijah, and leaves them Jesus only. God caught them right away. God would not have them placing Moses and Elijah on a level with his Son.

He is above the angels of heaven and we find over here, in the last chapter of the Bible, and in almost the last verse in it, that John was guilty of the same thing—of worshipping angels. It says over here in Revelation 22:8–9, "And I John saw these things, and heard them. And when I had heard and seen, I fell down to worship before the feet of the angel which showed me these things. Then saith he unto me: See thou do it not: for I am thy fellowservant, and of thy brethren the prophets, and of them which keep the sayings of this book: worship God."

It seems to me there is a great deal too much minister-worship and church-worship in the present day. What we want is the worship of Jesus.

Peter's Fall

In the twenty-sixth chapter of Matthew (vv. 31–35, 69–75) we find an account of Peter's fall. He became self-confident and proud, and the Lord couldn't use him any more till he had been humbled.

I want you to notice the fact that some of the greatest characters in the Bible failed at that point in their character where they seemed to be the strongest. Men who have stood the highest, in Scripture, have often fallen on their strongest point.

Moses was noted for his humility. Right there he fell. He got angry instead of being humble, and fell through lack of humility.

Elijah was noted for his boldness. Right there he fell. Why, he stood on Mount Carmel and defied the whole nation. He stood there alone. He seemed to be the boldest man in the whole nation. But after a while he got word that Jezebel was going to take his life, and then he lost all his boldness and got scared at the threat of a woman.

There was Samson, who was noted for his strength. He lost his hair, wherein his strength consisted, but he recovered it. They cut off his hair, but they did not remove the roots, and it grew out again.

Abraham was noted for his faith. But he got into Egypt, and denied his wife.

There was only one time, I am told, that Edinburgh Castle was ever taken by the enemy, and that as done by climbing on the back rocks. The rocks were so steep the besieged did not believe the enemy could get in that way, but that was just where they got in.

I used to think when I had been a Christian ten or twelve years I should be so strong that there would be no danger of my ever being tempted, but I find that I was blind. I have more temptations now than I ever had before, and it takes twenty times as much grace to keep me now as at first. Let every man take heed, lest he fall. We can't tell how quickly we may fall if we are not kept by the grace of God.

Peter had said, "I will never be offended because of thee"; but Christ, who could see the future as well as the present, said, "This night, before the cock crow, thou shalt deny me thrice" (Matt. 26:34). Here was the beginning of Peter's downfall. He was too self-confident. The Christian who begins to boast is on the very brink of destruction.

But, in spite of the words of Christ, Peter did not take warning. "What! I deny the Lord? Impossible! Though all should deny thee, yet will not I."

It is not very long before we find Peter guilty of disobedience. When Christ took him with him into the garden of Gethsemane he told him to watch and pray; but instead of that Peter fell asleep. Some people say this sleep was supernatural, but that is all nonsense. There are plenty of sleepy

Christians and sleepy churches to be found in all ages of the world; and wherever a church goes to sleep something always goes wrong. Those who expect to follow Christ must keep awake.

The next downward step of Peter was when the crowd came out to arrest his Master, and he drew his sword and cut off the ear of the high priest's servant. That wasn't the way to confess his Lord. If Jesus Christ was indeed the Son of God, as he had professed to believe him, he needed no help from Peter's sword. Christ rebuked him, and told him to put up his sword again into its place, and afterward he replaced the servant's ear, and made it as good as ever. Perhaps Peter was mortified at this. At any rate, he seems to have gone down very rapidly from this point to the time—a few hours later—when we find him denying his Master.

Poor Peter! This man, who is so strong and zealous, who is going to stand by the Lord when everybody else forsakes him. This man, who slashes about with his sword in order to defend him—is frightened almost out of his wits by a servant girl!

Peter is now guilty of lying. He has told one lie, and that always needs a hundred to keep it up. Again and again he declares that he doesn't know the Savior, and the last time he adds the terrible sins of cursing and swearing.

"Thy speech betrayeth thee," said one of those who recognized Peter as one of Christ's disciples.

It is a good thing for us to be known as Christians by our speech. I suppose Peter's speech was simply a dialect spoken by the people among whom he lived. Perhaps the dialect of Galilee was different from that of Judea, and so the servants in the hall of the high priest knew him for one of Christ's disciples, because he spoke in the Galilean dialect. There is a lesson for us here: If by any sign in our words people can know that we are the disciples of the Lord Jesus, it is nothing for us to be ashamed of.

But, in spite of his wicked denial, Christ did not cast him off. He just gave him one look, and that won him back forever. Oh! How ready the Savior is to forgive those who wander away from him if they will only come back as Peter did. I suppose poor Peter would have been altogether heartbroken and so ashamed of himself that he never would have ventured to appear among the disciples again, if it hadn't been for that token of Christ's continued love.

Peter Restored

We read in the account of the resurrection that Jesus sent a special message to Peter through an angel, "Go . . . tell his disciples and Peter" (Mark 16:7). Don't leave out Peter, though he was the one who denied me.

But when he appeared unto them at the Sea of Galilee, he reminded Peter of the boast he had made, and said unto him, "Simon, son of Jonas, lovest thou me more than these?" (John 21:15).

Peter was the only man who had boasted that he was better than his brethren, and he was the only man, except Judas, who denied his Lord. And now, instead of repeating that boastful speech, "Though all should forsake thee, yet will not I," he does not venture to compare himself anymore with his brethren, but modestly answers, "Yes, Lord, thou knowest that I love thee."

Peter has learned a lesson of humility, and now, though not before, Christ can make him his chief apostle.

45 The Pharisee and the Publican

Luke 18:9–14

In this parable we are told that men ought to pray always and everywhere, that prayer should not be left to a few in the churches, but all men ought to pray. Jesus gives us a picture so that we may understand in what spirit we ought to pray.

Two Representative Men

Two men went up to the temple—one to pray to himself and the other to pray to God. Here are two representative men; and I suppose you might divide this audience into the two classes they stand for. One of them trusts in his own righteousness; the other doesn't have any righteousness to trust in, and so he goes to the Lord.

I think this whole community might be divided into Pharisees and publicans. One of them trusted in his own righteousness and the other did not have any trust in it, and I say I think all men will come under these two heads. They have either given up all their self-righteousness—renounced it all and turned their backs upon it—or else they are clinging to their own righteousness. You will find that these self-righteous men that are ever clinging to their own righteousness are continually measuring themselves by their neighbors.

The Pharisee's Prayer

Now let us take a look at this Pharisee, whose picture Christ has painted for us. His spirit is very common among certain types of people. He is proud and conceited—thinks he is not like other men. Ah, my friends, pride is a plant which grows in all sorts of climates and all sorts of soils. It is one of the greatest enemies to the kingdom of Christ. Nebuchadnezzar lost his throne and reason by it; by it Lucifer fell from heaven, for even up among the angels he raised the flag of revolt close by the throne of God. How many people there are who, like this Pharisee, are just living on the forms of religion! If you will only give them the show, they don't care anything for the substance; just give them the husk, and they don't care for the wheat.

How many men there are that have become drunkards, who are all broken up—will gone, health gone—and yet are just as full of pride as the sun is of light! It will not let them come to Christ and be saved. How many men are today just living on empty forms! They say their prayers, but they do not mean anything.

Why, this Pharisee said plenty of prayers. How did he pray? He prayed to himself. He might as well have prayed to a post. He did not pray to God, who knew his heart a thousand times better than he himself. He forgot that he was a sepulcher, full of dead men's bones, forgot that his heart was rotten, corrupt, and vile. He comes and spreads out his hands and looks up to heaven.

We read that this man stood and prayed "with himself." That is a queer way to pray. He stood up there and stretched himself, and said, "God, I thank thee that I am not as other men"; and this, too, while the angels in heaven were veiling their faces, and crying, "Holy, holy, holy is the Lord!" But this man is full of himself. He goes on to tell God all about his goodness, as if God didn't know him better than he knew himself. Just listen to him. "I fast twice in the week." His church only told him to fast once, so, you see, he is laying God under obligation to him by fasting twice as much as is necessary. "I give tithes of all that I possess." Oh, yes, he thought a great deal of himself for that! Just as some people think a great deal of themselves for their gifts to the cause of religion in these days. I have no doubt there are some people who say, "Oh, yes, I will give something toward that Tabernacle and those meetings. They are very good things for common people, but then, of course, they are not of any use to me."

"Oh, yes, I will give you fifty dollars for your church if you will be sure to put my name in the newspapers." Many a man gives his money patronizingly, and thinks he is doing something for God; but God doesn't know anything about such gifts. He never writes down any such credits in the book of life.

There is another curious thing about this man's prayer. There isn't any confession of sin in it, because the man doesn't think he has any sins to confess. Still more, the man doesn't ask for anything. He is so well satisfied with himself that he is wholly taken up with talking to the Lord about his righteousness. He has everything he wants.

There was not a petition in his prayer. It seems to me that was a very prayerless prayer. He said a prayer, but he didn't pray at all. But how many men have just gotten into that cradle and been rocked to sleep by the devil!

Now take a good look at this Pharisee, and see who he is like. His prayer has thirty-four words in it, and there are nine great capital I's. If he prayed as long as some people do, and put in "I's" in proportion, the printer would have to go and borrow some capital "I's" if he wanted to set it up. If you have such a man in your churches you find him always ready to pray when the minister asks him, but it is always a cold, prayerless prayer that puts everybody to sleep. There is many a man in your churches who, if they got a look at themselves in God's mirror, would find themselves very much like this Pharisee.

Prayerless Prayer

A short time ago I put this question to a man, "Are you a Christian?"

"Of course I am; I say my prayers every night."

"But do you ever pray?"

"Didn't I tell you I prayed?"

"But do you ever pray?"

"Why, of course I do; haven't I said so?"

I found that he thought he prayed, but he only went through the form, and, after a little, I found that he had been in the habit of swearing.

"How is this?" I asked. "Swearing and praying! Do your prayers ever go any higher than your head?"

"Well, I have sometimes thought that they did not."

My friends, if you are not in communion with God your prayers are but forms; you are living in formalism, and your prayers will go no higher than your head. How many people just go through the form! They can't rest unless they say their prayers. How many are there with whom it is only a matter of education?

A great many people have a rule of their own, by which they measure themselves, and by that rule they are perfectly ready and willing to forgive themselves. So it was with this Pharisee. The idea of coming to God and asking his forgiveness never enters his mind. While talking to a man—one of those Pharisees—some time ago about God and the need of Christ, he said to me, "I can do without Christ. I do not want him. I am ready to stand before God anytime." That man was trusting in his own righteousness.

Salvation by God Alone

Now, take a another good look at this Pharisee. You know, I have an idea that the Bible is like an album. I go into a man's house, and, while waiting for him, I take up an album from a table and open it. I look at a picture. "Why, that looks like a man I know." I turn over and look at another. "Well, I know that man." By and by, I come upon another. "Why, that man looks like my brother." I am getting pretty near home.

I keep turning over the leaves. "Well, I declare! Here is a man who lives on the same street I do. Why, he is my next-door neighbor." Then I come upon another, and I see—myself. My friends, if you read your Bibles, you will find your own pictures there. It will just describe you.

Now, it may be there is some Pharisee here tonight. If there is, let him turn to the third chapter of John, and see what Christ said to the Pharisee, "Except a man be born again, he cannot see the kingdom of God" (v. 3). Nicodemus, no doubt, was one of the fairest specimens of a man in Jerusalem in those days, yet he had to be born again, else he could not enter into the kingdom of God.

"But," you may say, "I am not a Pharisee. I am a poor and miserable sinner—too bad to come to him." Well, turn to the woman of Samaria, and see what our Lord said to her. See what a difference there was between that publican and that Pharisee. There was as great a distance between them as between the sun and the moon.

One was in the very highest station, and the other occupied the very worst station. One had only himself and his sins to bring to God, and the other was trying to bring in his position and his aristocracy.

I tell you, when a man gets a true sight of himself, all his position and station and excellencies drop. See this prayer: "I thank God." "I am not." "I fast." "I give." "I possess."

When a man prays—not with himself, but to God—he does not exalt himself; he does not pass a eulogy on himself. He falls flat down in the dust before God. In that prayer you do not find him thanking God for what he had done for him. It was a heartless and prayerless prayer—merely a form.

I hope the day will come when formal prayer will be a thing of the past. I think the reason why we cannot get more people out to the meetings is because we have too many formal prayers in the churches. These formal Christians get up, like this Pharisee, and thank God that they are better than other men, but when a man gets a look at himself he comes in the spirit of the publican.

You see this Pharisee standing and praying with himself, but God could not give him anything. He was too full of egotism—too full of himself. There was no religion in it. God could not bless him.

The Publican's Prayer

Now take a look at the other man. His prayer is short; there isn't a capital "I" in it. "God be merciful to"—some other sinner? "God be merciful to"—that church member who has wronged me? "God be merciful to"—that hypocrite over there? No. "God be merciful to me a sinner." He wouldn't so much as lift up his eyes to heaven, but that didn't hinder his lifting up his heart to God. He smites his breast and says he is a sinner.

Mr. Spurgeon says that the publican was the sounder theologian of the two. He was like David, who prayed, "Have mercy upon me, O God, according to thy lovingkindness . . . wash me thoroughly from mine iniquity" (Ps. 51:1–2). If God washes away our iniquities the devil can't find one spot in us.

A great many people are trying to wash away their own iniquities, but it never does any good. Take the case of Elijah. He was in great trouble there under the juniper tree, and the Lord comes to him, and says, "Elijah, what's the matter?"

"Oh," says he, "I have been very jealous for thy name; now everything is going wrong, and I wish I might die."

Now you can see he was not so jealous for his God's name as he was for his own name, for, when the Lord asks him what is the matter, he goes right to talking about himself. Ah, my friends, what we need is to get these capital "I's" out of the way.

We have been praying that God will search us and try us and see if there be any wicked way in us. Now let us be honest. Are we willing to know the sin that is in us, and when God shows it to us are we ready to put it away? These are solemn times. We begin to see the secret things in our hearts. The Holy Spirit reveals them, and we begin to have a conscience on matters that were out of sight before.

You remember the temple of Jerusalem. There was the outer court, the court of the Gentiles. Anyone might go there, but if he wished to go further he had to go as one of God's people. There were sacrifices and sin offerings to be made, and purifyings with water, and white robes. Then there was the holy of holies, into which only the high priest might enter, and he but once a year. We are praying God to take us into the holy place, but first we have need to be purified by the sin offering which Christ has made for us.

Search Your Heart

This heart-searching is a tender thing. The flesh shrinks from it. If there is covetousness in us, or pride, or if we have evil habits; if we are guilty of light and trifling conduct or foolish conversation and jesting; if there be any evil way in us, let the Holy Spirit show it to us, even though it prostrates us in the dust before him.

There is a leaky ship at sea. The captain finds her settling down deeper in the water and laboring heavily, and he sends a man down into the hold to look for the leak; but he doesn't find it, and reports that everything is all right. But it isn't all right, and if the leak cannot be found there is nothing to be done but to take her into port, put her into the dry dock, and give her a thorough overhauling.

So with men. You who have secret sins, who are worldly-minded, who neglect family and secret prayer, who are settling down deeper and deeper into the life of sin, whose family and business partners do not recognize your Christian character, and who dare not speak of Christ to your neighbors for fear of being called a hypocrite, you want a thorough overhauling by the power of the Holy Spirit.

We read that our God is a consuming fire. This day is the anniversary of the great Chicago fire. Five years ago tonight the fire swept across the river at the place where this Tabernacle stands, and burned up the wood and the stone, and melted the iron of these rows of great buildings—burned everything that could be burned. So let the fire of God sweep across our souls and burn up all the dross of our natures and cleanse us from all our sins!

In one of our meetings a man got up to speak whom I didn't know at first. When I lived here he used to be a rum seller, but he afterward broke up his business and went to the mountains and I lost track of him. He and his partners opened a grand billiard hall, and, of course, there was a bar in it. It was one of the most magnificent billiard halls on the West Side, all elegantly gilded and frescoed.

When they got ready to open it they sent me an invitation to be present. So the day before they opened I went around and saw them, and asked them if they were willing to allow me to bring a friend with me. They inquired who it was. I told them it was the friend who always went with me everywhere. Then they began to mistrust me, and tried to make me tell who my friend was, and I told them it was the Lord, and that if I saw anything wrong on that occasion I should want to speak to him of it.

"See here now, Moody," said they, "we ain't going to have any praying."

"But," said I, "you gave me an invitation to your opening, and I am coming, and am going to bring my friend with me."

"But we don't want you to come now, anyhow."

"Ah! But I am coming," said I.

Well, after I found we couldn't agree upon it, I said, "I'll tell you what I'll do. We will compromise this matter, if you will kneel down here now while I pray for both of you." So I kneeled down, with a rum seller on each side of me, and prayed for them. It turned out that one of them had a praying mother, and the prayer touched his heart. I asked God to bless the souls of these men, and to spoil their business; and in a few months, sure enough, their business failed, and one of these men went away to the Rocky Mountains.

When he came back he stood up in that meeting and gave me an account of himself something like this. Life had become a burden to him out there in the mountains. He had lost all his money, and made up his mind to kill himself. With this terrible thought in view he went to a lonely place in the mountains, took out his knife, and was just going to plunge it into his heart when he heard a voice—it seemed to him it was the voice of his dead mother—saying to him over again the words which he had heard her say when she was dying, "John, if ever you get into trouble, pray to God."

The knife dropped from his hand. He didn't know how to pray, but this publican's prayer came into his head. So he kneeled there upon the ground, with his heart broken over his sin and sorrow, and cried out in the bitterness of his soul, "God be merciful to me a sinner!"

The Lord heard his prayer and blessed him. Just the moment he cried for mercy he got it. What a glorious thing it would be if every soul here would lift up this publican's prayer, "God be merciful to me a sinner!"

46 Philip

John 6:1–14

"For the Son of Man is as a man taking a far journey, who left his house and gave authority to his servants, and to every man his work, and commanded the porter to watch."

Mark 13:34

Now, by reading that verse carefully it doesn't read, "to every man some work," or "to every man a work," but "to every man his work." And I believe if the truth was known that every man and woman in this assembly has a work laid out for them to do; that every man's life is a plan of the Almighty, and way back in the councils of eternity God laid out a work for each one of us. There is no man living that can do the work that God has for me to do. No one can do it but myself.

Faithfulness in Service

If the work isn't done, we will have to answer for it when we stand before God's bar. For the Bible says that every man shall be brought unto judgment, and everyone shall give an account of the deeds done in the body (2 Cor. 5:10).

It seems to me that every one of us ought to take this question home tonight, "Am I doing the work that God has for me to do?" God has a work for every one of us to do. Now in the parable of the talents (Matt. 25:14–30) the man who had two talents had the same reward as the man who had five talents. He heard the same words as the man who had five talents.

"Well done, thou good and faithful servant, enter thou into the joy of thy Lord."

The people that take good care of the talents that God has loaned them will find he always gives them more. Just as if we take the talent that God has given us and lay it away carefully in a napkin and bury it away, God will take even that from us. God doesn't want a man that has one talent to do the work of a man that has five talents. All a man has got to answer for is the one that God has given each man. If we were all of us doing the work that God has for us to do, don't you see how the work of the Lord would advance? I believe in what John Wesley used to say, "All at it, and always at it," and that is what the church ought to say.

But men say, "I don't believe in these revivals; it's only temporary, it only lasts a few minutes."

Yes, if I thought it was only to last a few minutes, I would say "Amen" to everything they say. My prayer has been for years that God will let me die when the spirit of revival dies out in my heart. I don't want to live any longer if I can't be used to some purpose. For what purpose are we all down in this world of sickness and sorrow unless it is to work for the Son of God, and improve the talents he has given us.

Some people are not satisfied with the talents they have, but are always wishing for someone else's talent. Now, that is all wrong. It is contrary to the Spirit of Christ. Instead of wishing for someone else's talent, let us make the best use of the talents God has given us. Now, there isn't a father or mother here but would think it a great misfortune if their children shouldn't grow any for the next ten or fifteen years. That little boy there, if he shouldn't grow any for ten or fifteen years, his mother would say, "It is a great calamity."

I know some men of my acquaintance who make the same prayers they made fifteen or twenty years ago. They are like a horse in a treadmill—it is always the same old story of their experiences when they were converted, and going round and round.

Philip's Talent

Oh, the joy there is in bringing people to Christ! This is what we all can do if we will. If God has not given us but half a talent, let us make good use of that. When God told the people to take their seats by fifties, he told Philip to get food for them. "What," says Philip, "feed them with this little loaf? Why, there is not more than enough for the first man."

"Yes, go and feed them with that." Philip thought that was a very small amount for such a multitude of hungry men. He broke off a piece for the first man, and didn't miss it; a piece for the second man, and didn't miss it. He was making good use of the loaf, and God kept increasing it. This is what the Lord wants do with us. He will give us just as many talents as we can take care of.

There are many of us that are willing to do great things for the Lord, but few of us willing to do little things. The mighty sermon on regeneration was preached to one man. There are many who are willing to preach to thousands, but are not willing to take their seat beside one soul, and lead that soul to the blessed Jesus. We must get down to personal effort— bringing one by one to the Son of God. We can find no better example of this than in the life of Christ himself.

47 Prodigal Son

Luke 15:11–32

We have for our text tonight the man Mr. Sankey was singing about in the song he has just sung, "The Ninety and Nine." The trouble with this son was the same as with nine-tenths of the men in this city who are away from God tonight. He started out wrong. If anyone had told the young man that he needed the grace of God to keep him when he was starting out to make his fortune he might have laughed at it, but we see how poorly he got along without it.

The Son Leaves Home

I don't know why he wanted to go away from home. Perhaps he thought his father was too strict because he wouldn't let him stay out late at night. Perhaps he couldn't get along well with his elder brother. Maybe his mother had died and left him to the care of someone who didn't love him. Perhaps she had died praying for her wayward son, and he wanted to get away from the place, so as to be able to forget her prayers that troubled him every time he thought of them.

So he goes to his father and says, "Father, I think I could get along better if you would divide your estate and give me my share now, and let me go and begin a life for myself." I suppose the old gentleman was rich, and perhaps, weakminded; at any rate he made a very great mistake. There is nothing worse for a young man than to give him plenty of money and send him out into the world alone.

People talk a great deal about self-made men, and about poor men's sons who have to struggle for their places in the world; but I tell you, I have a great deal more respect for the rich man's son who turns out well than for the poor boy who has to work his way in the world. There is nothing that puts so many temptations in a young man's way as having plenty of money.

The boy gets his money, and away he goes. He feels very independent. He can take care of himself; he can work his own way. I don't know where he went. Perhaps he went away down to Memphis in Egypt. And having plenty of money I have no doubt he was very well received, and became very popular. He was well educated and agreeable; perhaps he was able to sing and could entertain his friends with comic songs. He used to go to the opera four nights in the week, and the other three nights he spent at the theater and billiard rooms.

The Son Runs out of Money

He was certain to have plenty of friends as long as his money lasted, but after awhile he got to the end of his rope, and then his friends all deserted him. Just as they did a poor fellow whom I once knew, who had plenty of friends and money, but after awhile he broke down, and got into jail, and not one of his sporting friends ever came near him. Some Christian people who were visiting at the jail went to see him in the name of the Lord, and that woke him up to understand who his real friends were.

The Son Works Feeding Swine

We read that after awhile this prodigal began to be in want. His friends were gone, and he had gotten down very low, but I am happy to say, he didn't get down low enough to beg.

There was no meaner thing a Jew could do than to take care of swine; but it is very much to his credit that he chose to do this rather than lie around the streets loafing and begging. I had a thousand times rather be a swineherder than a beggar.

I can see him there among the swine troughs, ragged and hungry, the tears standing in his eyes as he thinks of his father's well-filled table—a long table with a good many people around it, but not long enough to reach to him in that faraway country.

No one gave him anything to eat. If he had been a pig they might have fed him, but being nothing but a man he was left to take care of himself.

Oh, my friends, that is just the way with the devil. He will lead you away from home, and off into a far country, and into pleasure and vice; and then, when you have lost everything in his service, he will push you down, down, down; and when he gets you into the ditch, or into the pit of ruin, instead of giving you anything to help you, he will laugh at you, and mock you for your folly.

There was another thing which the prodigal lost besides his money, and that was his testimony. Some of those old friends of his, if they chanced to see him out there among the swine, would doubtless laugh at him, and he, perhaps, would straighten himself up and say, "You laugh at me, and call me a fool and a vagabond because I am poor, and all in rags, but you needn't be so proud. I belong to a respectable family; my father has plenty of money; he lives in a fine house, and even his servants dress better than you do." How those young fellows would laugh at that! "Your father rich! You look like it, don't you? Your father have servants! Your father have clothes!" And then the poor fellow, thinking of himself, couldn't answer them a word. He had lost his testimony: nobody would believe that he was the son of a great rich man up there in Judea.

Just so every backslider from God loses his testimony when he falls into temptation, and gets away from the favor of his Lord; and if he does sometimes stand up in meeting and talk to the people about that way of life they laugh at him, and say, "You don't look or act as if you were a child of God."

The Son Returns Home

Sin took this young man away from home, just as it takes us all away from God. Now the question is, how did he come to get back again?

The parable tells us, that after awhile he came to himself; that is, he woke up to the fact that he was miserable because he was away from his father. There was one thing that the prodigal never lost. He lost his home; he lost his money; he lost his clothes; he lost his good name; he lost his respectability; he lost his testimony; but he never lost his father's love. That was his right through it all.

I find a good many men who are living in sin, who wonder why it is that God does not answer their prayers. I will tell you why it is. God loves them too much to answer their prayers while they stay away from him. Suppose the prodigal son had written his father a letter, saying, "Father, I am in want; please send me some money." Do you suppose his father would have sent it? If he had it would have been the worst thing he could have done for the boy.

The proper thing for the prodigal to do was to go home; and just as long as his father kept him supplied with money off there in that foreign country there was no reason to expect him to come back. If you have gone off into sin, if you have gotten away from God, you must never expect him to feed you, and clothe you, and to supply all your wants, the same as if you were in his house sitting down with him and the other children at his table. What God wants of his "prodigal sons" is for them to come home, and when he gets them with him he will supply their wants and answer their prayers.

Well, I can imagine that one day a neighbor from his native town inquired after the young man, and, at last, found him down there among the swine. Of course he was greatly surprised.

"Why don't you go home to your father?" says the neighbor.

"I don't know," says the prodigal. "I am not quite sure that my father would receive me. I am such a miserable vagabond."

"Your father loves you as much as ever," says the neighbor.

"My father! Did you see him? How do you know he loves me? Does he ever speak of me?"

"Ever speak of you! He talks of you by day and dreams of you by night. I was over at his house the other day, and when I told him I was coming into this country, the old man, with tears in his eyes, begged me to look up his lost boy, and tell him to come right home, for his father was breaking his heart because he stayed so long away."

Oh, if there is a poor prodigal here tonight, don't go on in that terrible delusion that your heavenly Father has forgotten you! There isn't one of God's children that is ever out of his memory.

One of the chief things in the way of this young man was his pride. I suppose he would have gone home long before he did if it hadn't been for his pride; but he said to himself, "I came away with abundance, and now I don't like to go back in rags."

But at last he comes to himself, and when he finds out that his father loves him and wants to have him back again, he makes up his mind to return. You can see him out there in the field, as he gets down on his knees and buries his face in his hands, like Elijah upon Mount Carmel, saying to himself, "I think I had better go home; there is no one in the world that loves me as much as my father. I am surprised that he is not altogether ashamed of me, for well he might be. But I have been here as long as I can stand it, and now I will arise and go to my father!"

Then the memories of the old home come back to him. He calls to mind his childhood, and how his mother used to sing to him and pray with him, and how kind and good his father was, and how carefully they watched over him, and kept him away from harm and evil. He thinks of the tears of his mother, and remembers the day they buried her—I can't help thinking that he had lost his mother, for there isn't anything said about her in the story—he remembers the morning he left home, and how his old father wept over him, and how he prayed at the family altar that the Lord God of heaven would save his boy from sin, and how he asked the Lord to send his angel to watch over him.

Then the prodigal opened his eyes and looked at himself: shoeless, coatless, hatless—just covered with miserable rags. "Why," he says to himself, "the very servants in my father's house are better off than I; there is bread enough and to spare in my father's house, and I am so starved that my bones almost prick through my skin. I will arise and go to my father!"

Oh, that thousands here tonight would say with this prodigal, "I will arise and go to my Father." Nine-tenths of the battle was won when he said those words.

The Father Receives the Son with Joy

And now I see him starting on his way. He goes to the man that owns the pigs and tells him he isn't going to take care of them any longer. He says he has heard from his father, who is a great and good man up there in Judea, and he is going back to him. He has been away too long already.

There is joy up in heaven now. I see the guardian angel who watches over him smiling and happy. I hear them ringing the bells of heaven because the lost one has come to himself and started for home.

I can see him now. He has resolved. His old associates laugh at him, but what does he care for public opinion? "I have made up my mind," he says. He doesn't stay to get a new suit of clothes, as some men do in coming to Christ. They want to do some good deeds before they come. He just started as he was.

I see him walking on through dusty roads and over hills, and fording brooks and rivers. It didn't take him long to go home when he made up his mind. Then the prodigal is nearing the homestead; see him? I remember going home after being away for a few months. How I longed to catch a glimpse of that old place. As I neared it I remembered the sweet hours I had spent with my brother, and the pleasant days of childhood.

Here is the prodigal as he comes near his old home; all his days of happy childhood come before him. He wonders if the old man is still alive, and as he comes near the home he says, "It may be that the old man is dead." Ah! What a sad thing it would have been if on returning he had found that his father had gone down to his grave mourning for him. Is there anyone here who has a father and mother whose love he is scorning and to whom he has not written for years?

I said to a prodigal the other night, "How long is it since you have written to your mother?"

"Four years and a half."

"Don't you believe your mother loves you?"

"Yes," he replied, "it is because she does love me that I don't write to her. If I was telling her the life I've been leading, it would break her heart."

"If you love her," I said, "go and write her tonight and tell her all."

I got his promise, and I am happy. I can't tell how glad I feel when I get those young prodigals to turn to their fathers and mothers, because I know what joy will be in the hearts of those parents when they hear from their prodigal sons.

It is a long journey and a hard one, but he never looks behind him: he has had too much of that far away country already, and his only thought is of his home. I can imagine his feelings as he comes to his native land. The sky is brighter and the fields are greener than the fields and skies in that strange country. Sometimes, as he trudges along his weary way, he wonders if his father is still living, or if he has died with a broken heart because of his waywardness.

As he nears home, he wonders again if his father's heart has turned against him, or if he will receive a welcome. Ah, he doesn't know his father's heart. I can see the old man up there on that flat roof, in the cool of the day, waiting for his boy. Every day he has been there, every day straining his eyes over the country to catch the first glimpse of his son should he return.

This evening he is there, still hoping to see the wanderer come back. By and by he sees a form in the distance coming toward the house. As he comes nearer and nearer he can tell it is the form of a young man. He can't tell who it is by his dress. His robe is gone, his ring is gone, his shoes are gone, but the old man catches sight of the face.

I see him as he comes running down, as if the spirit of youth has come upon him. See his long white hair floating in the wind as he leaps over the highway; the spirit of youth has come back to him. The servants look at him and wonder what has come over him. It is the only time God is represented as running, and that is to meet a poor returning prodigal soul.

"But when he was yet a great way off his father saw him, and had compassion" on him. He didn't say, "He went away without cause, I will not go to meet him"; but, rushing out, he falls upon his neck, and kisses him; and the servants come running out to see what is the matter.

And now the boy begins to make his speech, "Father, I have sinned against heaven, and in thy sight, and am no more worthy to be called thy son"—and just as he is going to say, "Make me as one of thy hired servants," the father interrupts him, and says to one servant, "Go bring the best robe and put it on him!" To another he says, "Go to my jewel box and get a ring and put it on his finger!" And to another one, "Go and get him a pair of shoes!" And to another, "Go and kill the fatted calf!" What joy there was in that home!

Welcome Home, Prodigals

My friend, don't you know that since that time this story has been repeated nearly every day—prodigals coming home—and I never yet heard of anyone but what had a warm welcome.

I have got a letter here. I think it is one of the last letters I received from England. The letter goes on to state that a son and husband had left his father's house—left his wife and children—without a cause; and now, in closing up the letter, the sister says, "He need not fear reproach, only love awaits him at home." That man may be here tonight. My words may reach him, and if so I beg him to return from his erring ways. Listen! Your sister says that no reproach or harsh words will meet you on your return home; only love will welcome you when you enter the door.

The father of the prodigal did not reproach his boy; and so God does not reproach the sinner. He knows what human nature is—how liable a mortal is to go astray. He is always ready to forgive and take you back. Christ says he will forgive; he is full of love, and compassion, and tenderness. If a poor sinner comes and confesses, God is willing and ready to forgive him.

There was a lady who came down to Liverpool to see us privately. It was just before we were about to leave the city to go up to London to preach. With tears and sobs she told a very pitiful story. It was this: She said she had a boy nineteen years of age who had left her. She gave me his photograph, and said, "You stand before many and large assemblies, Mr. Moody. You may see my dear boy before you. If you do see him, tell him to come back to me. Oh, implore him to come to his sorrowing mother, to his deserted home! He may be in trouble or he may be suffering; tell him for his loving mother that all will be forgiven and forgotten, and that he will find comfort and peace at home." That young man may be in this hall tonight. If he is, I want to tell him that his mother loves him still.

My oldest brother was a prodigal who left home and was gone for many years without ever a message home to us. We loved to sit around the fire on the stormy winter nights and listen to the stories that mother used to tell us about our father who had died when I was little, about what he said, how he looked, how he was kind to a friend and lost a great deal of money by him so our little home was mortgaged and we were poor. But if anybody happened to speak the name of that lost boy a great silence would fall upon us, the tears would come into my mother's eyes, and then we would all steal away softly to bed, whispering our good-nights, because we felt that the mention of that name was like a sword thrust to the heart of our mother.

After we got to bed we would lie awake and listen to the roaring of the wind among the mountains, thinking perhaps he was out in the cold somewhere. Maybe he had gone to sea, and while we were snug in bed he might be keeping watch on the wave-beaten deck, perhaps climbing the mast in just such darkness and storm.

Now and then, between the gusts, a sound would be heard like the wail of the summer wind when it used to make harpstrings of the leaves and branches of the great maple trees in the door-yard: now, soft and gentle, then, rising louder and louder. How we would hold our breath and listen! Mother was sitting up to pray for her lost boy. Next morning, perhaps, she would send one of us down to the post office to ask for a letter—a letter from him, though she never said so. But no letter ever came.

Long years afterward, when our mother was growing old and her hair was turning gray, one summer afternoon a dark sunburned man, with a heavy black beard, was seen coming in at the gate.

He came up under the window first and looked in as if he were afraid there might be strangers living in the house. He had stopped at the church yard, on his way through the village, to see whether there were two graves instead of one where our father had been laid so many years ago, but there was only one grave there. Surely his mother was not dead. But still she might have moved away. Then he went around and knocked at the door, and his mother came to open it.

Years of hardship and exposure to sun and storm had made him strange even to his mother. She invited him to come in, but he did not move or speak; he stood there humbly and penitently; and, as a sense of his ingratitude began to overwhelm him, the big tears found their way over his weather-beaten cheeks.

By those tears the mother recognized her long-lost son. He had come at last. There was so much of the old home in him that he couldn't always stay away. But he would not cross its threshold until he confessed his sin against it, and heard from the same lips which had prayed so often and so long for him the sweet assurance that he was forgiven. "No, no," said he, "I cannot come in until you forgive me."

Do you suppose that mother kept her boy out there in the porch until he had gone through with a long list of apologies, done a long list of penances, and said ever so many prayers? Not a bit of it. She took him to her heart at once; she made him come right in; she forgave him all; and she rejoiced over his coming more than over all the other children that hadn't ran away.

And that is just the way God forgives all the prodigal souls who come back to him. O wanderer, come home! Come home!

48 Rich Man in Hell

Luke 16:19–31

The rich man in hell had a missionary spirit when he got there. He said, "Send someone to my father's house, and warn my five brothers not to come to this place of torment." It would have been better if he had had a missionary spirit before he got there. It would be better that you should wake up and come to the Lord Jesus Christ and go to work to save your friends while you are on praying ground, and in this world.

Your missionary spirit won't help you when you are in hell; it won't help you when you are in the lost world.

49 Shepherd

Ezekiel 34; John 10

I want to call your attention to the work of the shepherd. The work of a shepherd is to feed and to care for his flock. Someone asked a young convert how he knew Christ was divine. He said, "Because he has saved me and because he keeps me." A pretty good proof, it seems to me. I see a person in the house that is troubled about the divinity of Jesus Christ.

I was once talking with an atheist in my town, and I got him to read the New Testament. He came back in a few days and said, "Mr. Moody, I have taken your advice and read the life of Jesus Christ, and I have come to the conclusion that John the Baptist was a greater character than Jesus Christ. Why don't you preach John the Baptist?"

"Well," I said, "you go through the country and preach in the name of John the Baptist, and I will follow and preach in the name of Jesus Christ, and I venture to say that I will have more followers than you."

"Oh, well," he said, "of course you would, because people are very superstitious."

"No, when they buried John the Baptist they buried him and he hasn't gotten up yet. But when they buried the Son of God they couldn't hold him. He rose again. We don't worship a dead Christ. He is a glorified Christ." If Christ hadn't risen do you believe this audience would be here this afternoon? Never! Gathered around a dead Jew, who was buried in the sepulcher at Jerusalem! Do you believe his name would give power and quicken?

243

Shepherd Ministry

Now, I want to get your attention. Let's come to the work of the shepherd. In the thirty-fourth chapter of Ezekiel there are several things that he tells us the shepherd will do. I haven't got time to take them all up, but will just read a few things that the shepherd has promised to do.

I will seek them out (v. 11). Christ when he came said he had come to seek and save that which was lost. That is his work. It is the work of the shepherd to seek the lost. Who ever heard of a sheep seeking out a lost shepherd? A great many people say they cannot find Christ. He is seeking you out to find you. And not only does he find you, but he keeps you. That is what he came from heaven to do, to seek and save the lost.

I remember when we were in London, they found one old woman who was eighty-five years old and not a Christian. After the worker had prayed, she made a prayer herself, "Oh, Lord, I thank thee for going out of thy way to find me." He is all the time going out of his way to find the lost. At one time he went way up to the coast of Tyre. There was a poor woman groping in the darkness and the Shepherd went and found her.

I will feed them in a good pasture (v. 14). Now I tell you he has a good many lean sheep, but some old divine says he has none in his pasture; they have gotten out. If they will go into forbidden places they will get lean. You get your leanness by going after the world and worldly things. But he feeds them in a good pasture.

I will deliver them (v. 12). That is his work. Now, he not only saved the children of Israel but he delivered them. He not only saves us but he delivers us. I thank Jesus Christ that he is a deliverer. I don't believe he saves us and then leaves us in prison. "I will deliver them."

I will gather them from the people (v. 13). Separate them. That is what we need, separation. And if we are going to have real Holy Ghost power here, we must be separated. There must be a separation. That is when God's people have power, not when they are in sympathy with the ungodly. Remember, we are his witnesses. We want to keep that in mind.

I will bring them to their land (v. 13). That is what he wants, to bring them out of the world to his own land.

I will bind up that which was broken (v. 16). Yes, every broken heart, every bleeding heart he will bind up. That is what God sent him into the world to do. There is not a broken, bleeding heart here today but that Christ can heal it.

I will strengthen (v. 16). People say that they haven't any strength. That is all right. We don't need any of our own strength, we need his strength. He has plenty of strength. All that you need. The weaker we are the better for us, for then we lay hold of God's strength. He will put strength into every one of his sheep if they will let him.

I will save my flock (v. 22). I want to tell you, my dear friends, if your religion isn't saving you from sin and keeping you day by day from it, it is a sham, it is not the religion of Jesus Christ. "Thou shalt call his name Jesus, for he shall save his people from their sins" (Matt. 1:21). He comes to us in our sins, but saves us from our sins. That is the only test that is worth having; that Christ is saving you from sin.

I will set up one shepherd over them (v. 23). You may have your different churches, but we have only one Christ after all. Do you know that? All these miserable sectarian walls have been built up by men. The Catholics have the same Christ as the Protestants—one Shepherd, one Christ. The quicker we recognize that fact the better. We must get nearer and nearer together if we are going to have power. If we are going to get nearer the Shepherd we have got to get nearer together.

I will make them a covenant of peace (v. 25). He brought peace. People are trying to make it. He made it by the blood of the cross, and all we have to do is enter into it.

I will cause evil beasts to cease out of the land (v. 25). When a man is at peace with God, he is at peace with everyone. He can have a beautiful, peaceful, joyful Christian life if he will only walk with God. That is what we want, is just to have this victorious life.

I will cause the showers to come down (v. 26). That is just what we need here. Isn't it? If you want the real fruit, just pray. He is able and willing and anxious to do it, and it will bring great honor and glory to his Son if the tide comes in here and a wave goes out from this city that will go away across this continent. Why not? Let us expect great things and we shall not be disappointed.

I will raise them up a plant of renown (v. 29). Thank God he has been raised up. Christ has come since that was prophesied.

I will satisfy them (v. 29). I want to say that there is only one thing that will satisfy a longing heart, and that is Jesus Christ. The world will not satisfy. A proof of that is that the man who has the most of this world's goods gets the least out of it. Isn't it so? You never saw a millionaire in your life that was satisfied. When he gets one million he wants three; and when he gets three, he wants ten, and so on. Why, I remember myself when a millionaire was considered quite a rich man; but he is nothing now. He must have a hundred million. I pity him, don't you? I do. I just pity them because they are not satisfied.

The fact is when God made your heart and mine he made them a little too big for this world. That is just what Christ undertakes to do, to satisfy. You know sheep never lie down until they get enough to eat and drink. And so it says, "I will make them rest." He will just satisfy them so that they rest. That is just what we want. We want rest for ourselves before we can work for others. If we are restless and agitated and don't get rest for our own soul, we are the last ones to help anyone else. He instructed us and kept us as the apple of his eye. He keeps. Wonderful Shepherd. He is able to keep every one of his sheep. People are always talking about not being able to keep Christ. Man, let Christ keep you.

Support the Sheep

I remember when my little girl was about four years old she was always teasing for one of those black and white muffs, and she kept on teasing and teasing, and one day her mother brought her home a black and white muff. She came to my room and said, "Come, papa, let's go and take a walk." I was very busy and said I couldn't go. But you know when you have an only daughter she can do about as she wants to with you. She knew she would get me.

And we went out. It was icy, and I said, "Emma, you had better let me take your hand." But she wouldn't let me, and she strutted down the street. She wanted to walk as her mother did and show off her new muff. We went along and finally she fell and hurt herself a little. I said, "Now, Emma, you better let me take your hand."

"No, no," she wouldn't. Very independent!

But by and by down she went again, and she said, "Papa, I wish you would let me take your little finger."

"You better let me take your hand." But she wouldn't, she only wanted my little finger. So I gave her my little finger.

Down she went again, and she hurt herself that time. "Papa, just take my hand, please."

I put my big hand around her little wrist, and when her feet went from under her again, she didn't go down. That is the way the Shepherd does. He keeps. Give the whole self-effort thing up. Your trying doesn't amount to anything. Trust him to hold and keep you. The Shepherd will keep all that commit themselves to him. Just say, "Lord, I cannot stand without your help. The temptations are so numerous that I cannot help myself, but I have put my hand into the hand of the Eternal God and I believe he will hold me."

Thank God for the promise that he will keep us. Let that sink down into your soul. He will keep all who commit themselves to him. Just trust him now to keep you. Remember that it is his work to keep you, and if you go astray it is his work to bring you back. The Shepherd goes and gets the sheep and puts it on his shoulder and brings it back.

That man who had the hundred sheep didn't say he would let the sheep find its way back. He went out to find it. He went out and searched until he found it, and when he found it he didn't beat or maul or kick it, but just kindly put it on his shoulder and carried it home.

Don't Beat the Sheep

There was a young minister I heard about some time ago, who went to take charge of a church that had been under the care of an old pastor; and he went to scolding the people, and he kept that up for six months. One day one of the old deacons asked him home to dinner with him. After dinner the old deacon asked him if he had read the twenty-first chapter of John.

"Read it! I hope I have read every chapter in the Bible. Read it! Why, of course I have."

So the old deacon got his Bible and began to read it. He got down to where the Lord is sifting Peter and testing him (John 21:15–17). "Peter, lovest thou me more than these? Beat my sheep." "Peter, lovest thou me more than these? Maul my sheep." "Lovest thou me more than these? Wallop my sheep."

"Why," said the minister to the deacon, "that isn't there."

"Well, I thought I would read it to you as you have been at us for the last six months and see how it sounded."

You never make sheep fat by scolding and beating them. Feed them well if you want them to work and grow fat. I tell you I honestly believe we have too much preaching in the exhorting line. Exhort! Exhort! Exhort! I believe that the church needs to be fed; and where there is one sermon preached to the unconverted, I wish we had one hundred preached to the church members. They watch the church members and say, "Look at that man and woman, they are members of the church. If that is religion, I don't want any of it." And I don't blame them. Do you? Now, what we want is to keep that in mind. Feed them. That is what the Good Shepherd will do. Why, a man said he would take a fat sheep and make it lean in a week. There was a bet on that statement, and they put up the money. They took a sheep and put it in a cage, and then they went and got a dog. That dog kept barking at the sheep and worried it so that it was quite poor in a week. There are lots of sheep that are scared.

Preserving the Sheep

"And I give unto them eternal life; and they shall never perish, neither shall anyone pluck them out of my hand" (John 10:28). Never. Twenty-eight times in this chapter (John 10) he uses the pronoun to tell what he will do for his sheep. Some old divine has said that all of God's sheep have three marks. You know in California and some of those places where they have a great many sheep they have their mark and register them just as some businessmen register their trademark.

First, they hear his voice; second, they know his voice; and third, they follow the Shepherd. That is the way you can tell a true sheep. They know God's voice and they don't try to follow, but they do follow. You can tell a sheep from a goat in that way. Now, if you want life to your soul, just listen to the word of God; let the word of God sink down into your soul. "Verily, verily, I say unto you"—put your name in there. "He that heareth my word, and believeth on him that sent me, hath everlasting life, and shall not come into condemnation; but is passed from death unto life" (John 5:24). You can come into the open fold through that door this very hour if you will. There is not an unsaved one here who may not enter the fold of God now if he will.

They know his voice. A great many people cannot tell the voice of God from the voice of a false shepherd. I got up in Scotland once and quoted a passage of Scripture a little different from what it was in the Bible, and an old woman crept up and said, "Mr. Moody, you said—." I might make forty misquotations here and no one would tell me about them. Like two lawyers, one said in court that the other didn't know the Lord's prayer. The other said he did. "Now I lay me down to sleep." "Well," he said, "I give it up. You do know it." Didn't either one of them know it, you see.

Now, they do follow. Mark you. They don't try to follow, I wish we could abolish that word "try." I really believe I have had more than twenty-five people here tell me they were going to "try real hard to be Christians." My friends, that doesn't amount to anything. That is a very slippery rock to get on. Try, try, try. I have heard persons say, "You know the Bible says try, try, try again." They thought that was in the Bible. You can't find a place in the Bible where you are told to try. Just follow him. Let that word "try" be banished, and put in the word "trust."

God will always help a man or a woman that wants to follow his Son. Now, people are looking for happiness, peace, and joy, after the fruits of the spirit. My dear friends, you get done looking after these things and look to Christ, and you will have them. You don't have to look for these things. I remember when I was a boy I used to try to jump over the shadow of my head, but I never succeeded in getting over it. Then I would try to outrun it, but I never could. I remember coming down the mountainside one night and a boy was trying to catch me. I looked around and saw my shadow running after me.

Well, the sweetest lesson I have learned since I have been in Christ's school is just to face the great Shepherd and the shadow follows. Look for Christ and you will not be in the dark. Now if there is a man or woman here that is in the dark today, I will tell you why. It is because you have gotten away from the Shepherd, because you are afraid of him. Just get near the Shepherd if you want food, light, peace, and joy. Don't try to follow, but just follow.

When you were a boy and went to school it wasn't a matter of feeling, but obedience. What you want is will. The thing we are told to do is just to follow, and if we do we are not going to be allowed to walk in the dark. Tenth chapter of John, third verse: "He calleth his own sheep by name." I get a good deal of comfort out of that fact—that the Shepherd knows me by my name. Why! He knew all about Saul of Tarsus. He knew little Samuel. See! The Shepherd knows us by name.

A friend of mine was in Syria, and he found a shepherd that kept up the old custom of naming his sheep. This friend of mine said he wouldn't believe that the sheep knew him when he called them by name. So he asked the shepherd if the sheep were all named and if they all knew their names. "I wish you would just call one or two."

The shepherd said, "Carl." The sheep stopped eating and looked up. The shepherd called out, "Come here." The sheep came and stood looking up into his face. He called another and another, he called about a dozen sheep and there they stood looking up at the shepherd. "How can you tell them apart?"

"Oh, there are no two alike. See, that sheep toes in a little; this sheep is a little bit squint-eyed; that sheep has a black spot on its nose."

My friend found that he knew every one of his sheep by their failings. He didn't have a perfect one in his flock. I suppose that is the way the Lord knows you and me. There is a man that is covetous; he wants to grasp the whole world. He wants a shepherd to keep down that spirit. There is a woman down there who has an awful tongue; she keeps the whole neighborhood stirred up. There is a woman over there who is deceitful, terribly so. She needs the care of a shepherd to keep her from deceit, for she will ruin all her children. They will all turn out just like their mother.

There is a father over there who wouldn't swear for all the world before his children, but sometimes he gets provoked in his business and swears before he knows it. Doesn't he need a shepherd's care? I would like to know if there is a man or woman here who doesn't need the care of a shepherd. Haven't we all got failings? If you really want to know what your failings are, you can find someone who can point them out. God would never have sent Christ into the world if we didn't need his care. We are as weak and foolish as sheep.

The Tenderness of the Shepherd

I wish I had time to dwell on the tenderness of the Shepherd. I find that Satan takes the advantage of some people in this way. A child dies, is taken from a home, and Satan says, "Ministers tell about the tenderness and kindness and love of the Shepherd, don't you see how he has wounded you?" My dear friend, don't let Satan get the best of you.

A friend of mine in New York sat right by me and worked as no other minister did. He had four beautiful children, and scarlet fever just came in and swept them all away. The poor man tried to get comfort. He couldn't find it, and he went off to Europe, traveled all through Great Britain, couldn't get rest, and finally went off to Syria. One day he and his wife went down to the stream; they saw a shepherd come down with a flock of sheep. The shepherd went into the stream and called the sheep after him. They looked down at him very wistfully but couldn't follow because they had little lambs.

Finally the shepherd came out of the water and picked up a little lamb and put it into his bosom. The two old sheep that had lost their little ones, instead of looking at the water in fear began to look up to the shepherd and bleat. They followed him close into the stream because their loved ones were there.

By and by he got them all over into a greener pasture, into a better place, and when he got them safely over, he took the little lambs out of his bosom. The father and mother stood there and watched, and they said, "That is what the great Palestine Shepherd has done with our little ones. He has taken them across the stream into greener pasture, home to a better place." They are back in New York at work for other children.

My friends, don't let Satan get the advantage of you. A titled lady was telling me some time ago when I was in England that one day she was out riding and she saw a shepherd who had some dogs driving sheep. If the sheep stopped to drink out of the pools in the streets he would have the dogs after them. She kept saying, "Oh, you cruel man!" But by and by he came to a beautiful park, opened the great iron gate, and let all the sheep in there where there was knee-high, beautiful, sweet, fresh grass, and a beautiful river running right through the park; and she said he wasn't so cruel after all. He was only trying to get them to a better place. My dear friends, our loved ones are passing away, but they are going to a better field.

There is a passage here I would just like to read to you. Hebrews 12:5–6: "And ye have forgotten the exhortation which speaketh unto you as unto children, my son, despise not thou the chastening of the Lord, nor faint when thou art rebuked of him, for whom the Lord loveth he chasteneth, and scourgeth every son whom he receiveth."

50 Simon the Pharisee

Luke 7:36–50

The Lord was one day at Jerusalem, and a banquet was given him by Simon the leper. There was a banquet table in the house, arranged according to the fashion of that day. Instead of chairs for the guests, the guests sat reclining on lounges.

The Woman Who Washed Jesus' Feet

Well, it was just one of these repasts that our Lord sat down to, along with the wealthy Simon and his many guests. But no sooner had he entered than a certain woman followed him into the house. She fell down at his feet, and began to wash them with her tears.

It was the custom in those days to wash one's feet on entering a house. Sandals were worn, and the practice was necessary. This woman had gotten into the house by some means, and, once inside, had quietly stolen up to the feet of the Savior. In her hand was a box; but her heart, too, was just as full of ointment as the box she carried. And there was the sweetest perfume as she stole to his feet.

Her tears started to fall down on those sacred feet—hot, scalding tears, that gushed out like water. She said nothing while the tears fell, and then she took down her long black hair and wiped his feet with the hair of her head. And after that she poured out the ointment on his feet.

At once the Pharisees began to talk together. How, all through the New Testament, these Pharisees kept whispering and talking tougher! They said, shaking their heads, "This man receiveth sinners. Were he a prophet, he would know who and what manner of woman this is that touches him,

251

for she is a sinner." No prophet, they insisted, would allow that kind of a woman near him, but would push her away from him.

But Jesus read their thoughts, and quickly rebuked them. He said: "Simon, I have something to say to thee."

Simon answered, "Master, say on."

"Seest thou this woman? I entered into thine house, thou gavest me no water to wash my feet; but she has washed my feet with tears, and wiped them with the hairs of her head. Thou gavest me no kiss, but this woman, since I came in, hath not ceased to kiss my feet. My head with ointment thou didst not anoint, but this woman hath anointed my feet with ointment."

Simon was like many Pharisees nowadays, who say, "Oh, well! We will entertain that minister if we must. We don't want to, for he is a dreadful nuisance; but we will have to put up with him. It is our duty to be patronizing."

The Grateful and Ungrateful Debtors

Well, the Master said more to his entertainer, as follows, "There was a certain creditor which had two debtors. The one owed five hundred pence, and the other fifty. And when they had nothing to pay . . ." (Luke 7:41–42).

Mark that, sinner; the debtor had nothing to pay. There is no sinner in the world who can pay anything to cancel his debt to God. The great trouble is that sinners think they can pay—some of them seventy-five cents on the dollar, some even feel able to pay ninety-nine cents on the dollar, and the one cent that they are short they believe can be made up in some manner. That is not the correct way; it is all wrong. You must throw all the debt on God. Some few, very likely, will only claim to pay twenty-five cents on the dollar, but they are not humble enough, either; they can't begin to carry out their bargain. Why, sinner, you couldn't pay one-tenth part of a single mill of the debt you are under to God.

Now, it is said in this parable the debtors couldn't pay their creditor anything. They had nothing to give, and their creditor frankly forgave them both.

"Now, Simon," the Master asked, "which should love that man the more?"

"I suppose," was the reply, "he that was forgiven the more."

"You have rightly judged. This woman loves much because she has been forgiven much." And Jesus went on to tell Simon all about her. I suppose he wanted to make it plainer to Simon, and he turned to the poor woman and said, "Thy sins are forgiven; go in peace."

All her sins were forgiven—not simply part of them; not half of them, but every sin from the cradle up. Every impurity is blotted out for time and eternity. Yes, truly, she went out in peace, for she went out in the light of heaven. With what brightness the light must have come down to her from those eternal hills! With what beauty it must have flashed on her soul! Yes, she came to the feet of the Master for a blessing, and she received it.

51 **Sower**

Matthew 13:1–23; Mark 4:1–20;
Luke 8:1–15

Our Savior, as he sat by the seaside, saw a man go forth to sow his field and pointed to him. He gave his hearers a lesson about preaching the gospel.

This parable classifies the hearers of the gospel. It is true now as it was then and will be to the end of time. I am glad that Christ spoke this parable, for it keeps me from being discouraged when I see so many go back after they have been interested in the truth. Christ himself explains the parable, and we have only to apply it.

The Wayside Hearers

The first class are wayside hearers. They are impressed by the truth but the impression is transient. They like the meetings, the singing, and the crowd. They are sympathetically interested. But if they don't go further and become converted, they will get more harm than good. If the gospel doesn't soften, it hardens. The wayside was not in the condition to receive the seed because it was trampled hard. And so if a man's heart is full of business or amusements, if he only comes to the meetings now and then, with a preoccupied mind, they will do him no good. Things not wrong in themselves may so engross the thoughts that the good seed can't take root.

254

The Stony Ground Hearers

The second class are the stony ground hearers. Here the seed springs up quickly and grows well for a time, but soon it withers and dies. These hearers are like trees that blossom but fail to perfect their fruit. There are a good many Christians of this class. They want to be religious, but they don't count the cost. They go with the crowd when it shouts "hosanna" to the Son of David today, and they will go with it when it cries "crucify him" tomorrow.

A little opposition discourages them. Sunshine is good. It makes the tree grow that is well rooted. But it withers the tree that has no root. Storms that will develop the vigor of trees in a deep soil will blow down those that are in a shallow soil. And so it is in churches. When all is calm and the minister is popular, the shallow professor gets along pretty well. But when trials come he falls away. How easily some people are offended! If we are truly converted—if we are united to God and not merely to a church or a minister—we won't let any ill treatment or neglect drive us away. We will cling to him, whatever others may do or fail to do. What we want is a personal Savior. If we have him, all trials will only drive us nearer to him.

The Unfruitful Hearers

The third class presented in the parable are the unfruitful. Alas! How many such are in all the churches. Stunted, useless, good for nothing, choked with worldly cares. It is not enough to plant good seed in a good soil. There must be cultivation. The weeds must be kept down. The richer the soil, the ranker will be the growth of weeds. This person will take no personal interest in the work of the church or in the cause of missions. And so the God of this world will keep him from bearing fruit.

The Fruitful Hearers

The fourth class, those whose hearts are good ground in the parable, do three things: hear the Word, receive it, and respond to it. The good seed in the good soil brought forth some thirty-, some sixty-, and some a hundredfold. We don't have to make the fruit, but only to receive and cultivate the seed. Christ says, "Let your light shine." You don't have to make the light. You don't have to shine. You are to let God shine in and through you. If I am a good hearer of the Word my life will be a success. I will grow and be useful.

There is a great difference between receiving a man's word and God's. There is power in the words of God. They are spirit, and they are life. Hence the sower must not scatter his opinions. Even if they were precious as gems, they would not grow. There is no life in them. They can produce no spiritual harvest. The sower must sow the Word. And if that seed falls into a good and honest heart it will grow and bear fruit. By a good heart is not meant a perfect one, but one that welcomes the truth. The gospel is not for the righteous, but for sinners.

52 Stephen

Acts 6:5–7:60

When Stephen was being stoned he lifted up his eyes, and it seemed as if God just rolled back the curtain of time and allowed him to look into the eternal city and see Christ standing at the right hand of God. When Jesus Christ went on high he led captivity captive and took his seat, for his work was finished. But when Stephen saw Jesus he was standing up.

I can imagine Jesus saw that martyr fighting, as it were, single-handed and alone, the first martyr, though many were to come after him. You can hear the tramp of the millions coming after him to lay down their lives for the Son of God. But Stephen led the van; he was the first martyr, and as he was dying for the Lord Jesus Christ he looked up; Christ was standing to give him a welcome, and the Holy Ghost came down to bear witness that Christ was there. How then can we doubt it?

53 Syrophenician Woman

Matthew 15:21–28; Mark 7:24–29

And from thence he arose, and went into the boarders of Tyre and Sidon, and entered into an house, and would have no man known it: but he could not be hid. For a certain woman, whose young daughter had an unclean spirit, heard of him, and came and fell at his feet. The woman was a Greek, a Syrophenician by nation; and she besought him that he would cast forth the devil out of her daughter. But Jesus said unto her, Let the children first be filled: for it is not meet to take the children's bread, and cast it unto the dogs. And she answered and said unto him, Yes, Lord: yet the dogs under the table eat of the children's crumbs. And he said unto her, For this saying go thy way; the devil is gone out of thy daughter.

Mark 7:24–29

Now, just see how Christ dealt with that woman—a Syrophenician, a Gentile. She didn't belong to the seed of Abraham at all. He came to save his own, but his own received him not. Christ was willing to give to the Jews grace. He dealt in grace with a liberal hand, but those that he was desirous to shower grace upon wouldn't take it. But this woman belonged to a different people—and just hear her story.

I wonder what would happen if Christ should come and speak that way now? Suppose he should come into this assembly and take any woman here and call her a dog. Why, that Syrophenician woman might have said, "Call me a dog! Talk to me like that! Why I know a woman who belongs to the seed of Abraham who lives down near me, and she is the worst and meanest woman in the neighborhood. I am as good as she is any day."

She might have gone away without a blessing if she had not felt her utter destitution and lost condition. But Jesus only said that to her just to try her, and after calling her a dog, she only broke forth into a despairing cry, "Yes, Lord—yes, Lord." She was satisfied to be given only a crumb, as long as he heard her petition. So, instead of giving her a crumb, she got a whole loaf. And so will you get the fullest beneficence of Christ if you lift your heart up to him.

54 Widow of Nain

Luke 7:11–16

The Death of the Son

Think of that poor widow at Nain! She is an old woman now; and her only son, who is the staff of her life, is sick. How she watches him: sits up all night to see that he has his medicine at the right time; sits by his bedside all day, fanning him, keeping away the flies, and moistening his parched lips with water! Everything he asks for she brings. The very best doctor in Nain is sent for, and when he comes and feels the pulse of the young man, and looks at his tongue, he shakes his head; and then the poor woman knows there is no hope.

I can hear her say, "My son, my only son, must die! What will become of me, then?"

Sure enough, the doctor is right; in a little while the fever comes to its crisis, and the poor boy dies, with his head upon his mother's bosom. The people come in to try to comfort the poor woman, but it is of no use. Her heart is broken. She wishes she were dead too. Some of you know what it is to look your last upon the faces of those you love. Some of you mothers have wept hot tears upon the cold faces of your sons.

Jesus Raises the Son

They make him ready for burial, and when the time comes they put him on the bier to carry him away to the grave. Just as they come out of the city gates they see a little company of thirteen dusty-looking travel-

260

ers coming up the road. There is one among them tall and fair, fairer than the sons of men.

He is moved with compassion when he sees this little funeral procession, and it doesn't take him long to find out that the woman who walks next the bier is a poor widow, whose only son she is following to his grave. So he tells the bearers to put down the casket and while the mother wonders what is to be done he bends tenderly over the dead man and speaks to him in a low, sweet voice—"Arise!"

The dead man hears him.

He is struggling with his grave clothes! They unbind them and set him free. He leaps off the bier, remembers that he had been dead, catches a sight of his mother, takes her in his arms, and kisses her again and again; and then he turns to look at the stranger who has wrought this miracle upon him. He is ready to do anything for that man—ready to follow him to the death. But Jesus does not ask that of him. He knows his mother needs him, and so he doesn't take him away to be one of his disciples, but gives him back to his old mother.

I would have liked to see that young man reentering the city of Nain arm in arm with his mother. What do you suppose he said to the people who looked at him with wonder? Wouldn't he confess that Jesus of Nazareth had raised him from the dead? Wouldn't he go everywhere declaring what the Lord had done for his dead body?

Oh, how I love to preach Christ, who can stand over all the graves, and say to all the dead bodies, "Arise!" How I pity the poor infidel who has no Christ, and so goes down to a hopeless grave!

Woman with the Issue of Blood

Matthew 9:20–22; Mark 5:25–34;
Luke 8:43–48

The next case is of a poor woman who has spent all her living on physicians, and none of them have done her any good. She has been up to the Jerusalem doctors, and, perhaps, she has been down to Memphis, in Egypt, to see the doctors there. They have gotten all her money, and they haven't done her any good, but rather have made her worse. She has given up all hope long ago.

But one day a neighbor comes in to see her, and says, "Have you heard of Jesus of Nazareth, who is curing so many sick people just with a word?"

"No," says the sick woman, "I haven't."

"Why, they say he cured a man at the pool of Bethesda the other day who had been sick for thirty-eight years. Another man was sick of the palsy at Capernaum, and they let him down through the roof into the midst of the crowd, right before Jesus; and as soon as he saw it he told the man to rise, and sure enough he got right up, slung his bed over his shoulder, and started off for home, sound and well. He is the greatest physician that ever was seen in this country."

"What does he charge?" asks the woman. That is an important point with her, for she has spent all her money long ago.

"Nothing at all. He cures for nothing; the poor as well as the rich."

"Well he surely won't heal a woman!"

"Oh, yes! I have heard many stories of his healing of women. He will heal anyone."

"Well," says the sick woman, "if he ever comes into these parts, I will try to go and see him."

A few days after, she hears that Jesus is in the neighborhood. Did you know that Jesus is in your neighborhood today? She puts on her old shawl and an old sunbonnet—she is so poor that she hasn't any good clothes—and starts to go and see Jesus.

"Now, mother, don't be going off after any more doctors," says one of her daughters. "You know you have tried ever so many and they only made you worse." But she turns a deaf ear to them. A new hope has sprung up in her heart, and she wants to be cured.

But there is one difficulty she has not thought of—the crowd. There is an immense crowd round the Master, and she has hard work to get at him at all. Strong men elbow her back, and people say to her, "Don't crowd so. Don't you think other people want to be near him as well as you?"

But she doesn't seem to hear them. Maybe they think she is deaf. She pushes on till she is within reach of the Savior's garment, and then out comes that thin hand from under that shawl, and—O joy! Joy! She is healed.

There was more medicine in the hem of Christ's garment than in all the apothecary shops in Jerusalem.

56 Worldly Wise Man

Luke 12:13–21

Mr. Moody, having been requested by some members of the Board of Trade of Chicago to preach a sermon to the businessmen, took for his subject the life and death of the rich man mentioned by the Savior in the twelfth chapter of Luke. In spite of a severe storm with the thermometer four degrees below zero, an audience of about four thousand people assembled at the Tabernacle, in which the businessmen of Chicago were very largely represented. After reading the Scripture lesson from Luke 12:13–21, Mr. Moody proceeded.

I want to call your attention for a few minutes this evening to the man we have been reading about. You will see that he was what we would call a successful businessman; one whom worldly fathers and mothers might hold up to their sons as a model. He seems also to have been a moral man. I don't think he was a drunkard. There is nothing in the story that leads us to suppose he was dishonest. He didn't make his money by charging twenty or thirty percent interest. He didn't go into bankruptcy and compromise with his creditors by paying them fifty cents on the dollar; but, so far as we learn, he got his money honestly.

There is nothing whatever in the Bible against his business character. I don't suppose he rented buildings for brothels, or took advantage of anybody in trade. He made his money by farming, and that is about the most honest way of doing it. People called him a shrewd, long-headed man. I have no doubt his neighbors held him in high esteem, and perhaps they were thinking of sending him to Congress.

If you had spoken to this man about his soul he would have told you he was overwhelmed with business, and had no time to think of such things. Maybe he would have quoted Scripture to you and said, "not slothful in business," but probably he would have left out the rest of that verse, as people so often do, namely, "fervent in spirit, serving the Lord" (Rom. 12:11).

A man came out here once from the East, and one of our Chicago ministers asked him to preach in his pulpit, which he did, from this text, "Not slothful in business." But he went no further. After he had gotten through with his sermon, the minister said to him, "Chicago doesn't need any of that kind of preaching; we have all got that doctrine deep down in our souls: what we need is to be taught how we may become 'fervent in spirit, serving the Lord.'"

Undoubtedly this man moved in the best society. He had the best farm in all that section of country, and the best horses and cattle. If he had lived in Illinois he would have had all the fine Short-horn and Alderney stock, and all the best kinds of farming machinery. No doubt he lived in a very good house, and had large and convenient barns and other out-buildings: so that, altogether, he would be regarded as a very successful man.

It may be there were revival meetings in his neighborhood, but he was always too busy to go. One of the greatest revivals that ever took place occurred in those days under John the Baptist, and, perhaps, this great revivalist preached not far from his farm, but he couldn't leave his business to attend. He saw the crowds of people going by, on their way to the banks of the Jordan to hear this great preacher; but perhaps he thought they were fanatics.

Religious but Lost

No doubt he belonged to the synagogue, and believed in the doctrines of his sect; but he didn't believe in innovations. He had no faith in any of these irregular means of grace, and didn't care anything about hearing that wilderness preacher. It is quite possible that he heard about the Galilean prophet healing the sick, raising the dead, and casting out devils; just as he is doing now for these poor drunkards in Chicago; but I can seem to hear him say, like a great many of our businessmen here, "Oh, it is only a nine days' wonder; only an excitement; it will all be over pretty soon."

There is no doubt he lived in fine style, had the best wines on his table, used to send down to Egypt for the clothes for himself and his family, drove a fine set of horses, and was pointed out as a most popular and prosperous gentleman.

If anyone owed him a debt he looked sharp after him and made him pay it up; but all the while, though he thought himself so sharp, the devil was cheating him out of his soul.

If a friend came to see him he would take him around his farm, show him his land, his barns, and his storehouses; point out this one and that one which he was going to pull down and make larger; tell him how he was once a poor boy, and how his father died, and how the creditors came and took everything, and how he commenced life with nothing, and had worked his own way up to this respectable position; and his friend would go away almost envying him, and saying he was a most remarkable man.

Unprepared for Death

But the trouble with him was he was only living for this world. Life with him reached only just from the cradle to the grave. He didn't take death and eternity into his plans.

There is a proverb which says, "In every man's garden there is a sepulcher," but he didn't remember death or judgment. All his schemes and plans were for this side the grave; the future was a mystery to him, and so he lived for the present.

I can see him there in the parlor of his elegant mansion. It is midnight; the architect has been there, and he has been discussing plans for his new barns. He is going to have the finest barns in all Palestine. But while he is looking over the plans, all alone, his family all gone to bed, and the doors all locked, a stranger puts his hand on the latch. In spite of the double locks, and bolts, and bars, he enters, walks up to the man, lays his hand on him, and says, "Come, I must take you away."

"Who are you? What is your name?" asks the rich man, in great terror.

"Death."

Ah, Death ought not to have been a stranger to him. He had seen funerals enough; perhaps he had acted as pall-bearer, and had heard many funeral sermons. He is fifty years old, and he ought to have known and been prepared to meet death by that time.

The man tries to bribe Death to let him stay a little longer. He wants to carry out his plans; he wants at least to arrange his will. But no. Death cannot be bribed. You may bribe politicians and officers of the law, but you can't bribe Death.

The next morning he is found dead in his chair. Then there is great surprise and sorrow. Two days after there is a fine, imposing funeral; and some minister, like some of the ministers in these days, comes and pronounces a eulogy over him, and hopes he has gone to a better world. Oh, these lying funeral sermons! How men try to make out that a godless life can be followed by a death in the Lord, and a free admittance into the kingdom of heaven!

His friends and relatives try to make out that he has been a wise and successful man, but just see what the Son of God says about him: "Thou fool!"

That was his true epitaph, and it has been handed down to us for a warning. I can imagine some of you saying, "If I had known that Moody would have talked about death tonight I wouldn't have come out to hear him. Why doesn't he talk about life, about happiness? Why doesn't he tell us how to get on in business? How to get through with the battle of life?"

Death Comes Unexpectedly

I will tell you why I talk about death. It is because nine out of every ten die unexpectedly. We are all of us pretty well acquainted with Death. He comes into all our homes, and yet when he comes again we are always unprepared for him. I am speaking here tonight to some who may be in eternity tomorrow. I come to tell you to be prepared for death. Is it not downright folly to spend your lives in piling up wealth, and then to die as this man died, and have this same epitaph written against you?

Let me call your attention to the fact that the sin of this man was simply neglect. There is no evidence that his business was wrong, but he neglected his soul for the sake of his business. Some of you may say to yourselves, "Am I not kind to the poor? Am I not honorable in all my transactions? Don't I always pay a hundred cents on the dollar?" Yes, but you are dishonest to your own soul. You fold your arms and depend upon your own good deeds and don't come to Jesus Christ for salvation.

Steps to Perdition

My friends, there are only three steps down the hill to perdition. They are: first, to neglect; second, to refuse; third, to despise. All of you who are out of Christ in this audience are standing on one of these three steps of the ladder. You can see that if a man neglects his business, and leaves it to itself, he will soon become bankrupt. If a man neglects his health, he will become an invalid. It is just as true that if a man neglects his soul he will be lost.

A sailor was telling a man that his father, and his grandfather, and his great grandfather, were all drowned at sea.

"Why don't you prepare to die, then?" was the answer. "You may be drowned, too, any day."

"Where did your father die?" inquired the sailor.

"He died on the land."

"And your grandfather?"

"On the land."

"And your great grandfather?"

"On the land, too."

"And are you prepared to die?" asked the sailor.

"Well, no. I cannot say I am."

"Then why don't you get prepared?" asked the sailor. "It seems that people die on land just as well as on the sea."

I can imagine some of you saying, "I have got time enough. I don't propose to settle this question just yet. I have a good many years before me."

My friend, let us imagine that we go to the cemetery in Graceland here in Chicago and summon up the dead; or let us bring them into this hall in the midst of this audience, with their ghastly winding sheets. You would find that most of them died young. Whole generations, whole populations, are swept into eternity before they reach the allotted age of man. Instead of threescore years and ten, the average age for death today is only about thirty years.

Dear friends, you may not hear my voice again. I may be speaking to you for the last time. You may never come into the Tabernacle again, and I beg of you, as a friend and a brother, don't go out without salvation. May God wake up every soul here tonight, and when death comes to summon you, may you go to triumph over the grave, and so enter into a glorious immortality!

57 Zaccheus

Luke 19:1–10

Zaccheus Seeks Christ

Zaccheus was looking for the Savior, and the Savior was looking for him, and what a delightful time it was when they met! This man was small of stature and had a poor chance in a crowd. I can imagine the little man trying to get one glimpse at Jesus, and you can see him standing on tiptoe, but he can't see Jesus, the crowd is so great. Then he runs on ahead and climbs a sycamore tree, where he thinks he can hide, for he doesn't like to be seen looking after Christ. A great many rich men do not like to be seen coming to Jesus. By and by the crowd came along. They thought Christ would sometime be crowned king, and so he had a great many followers.

If men are going to get some high office they usually have a great many admirers; but when it is Gethsemane, humiliation, and a cross, oh, how few want to follow him then! I can see he looks at one man and says, "That is not Jesus." The crowd comes in sight. He looks at John. "That is not he." He looks at Peter. "No, that is not he." Then he sees one who is fairer than the sons of men. "That is he!" And Zaccheus, just peeping out from among the branches, looks down upon that wonderful—yes, that mighty—God-man in amazement.

At last the crowd comes to the tree, and it looks as if Christ is going by. I can see the Son of God come to the place and stop. Every eye was centered upon him; someone was going to be blessed. He looks up into the tree. There is one of Adam's degenerate sons up there.

Then he calls, "Zaccheus!"

I can imagine the first thing that flashed through his mind was, "Who told him my name? He knows all about me." Yes, sinner, God knows all about you: your name, the street you live on, in fact, he has the very hairs of your head numbered.

"Zacchaeus, make haste, and come down; for today I must abide at thy house. This is the last time I shall pass this way, Zacchaeus." That is the way he speaks to sinners. "This may be the last time I shall pass this way. This may be your last chance of eternity."

It was a strange scene. Zacchaeus was the chief publican of Jericho; the Jews wouldn't recognize him, wouldn't speak to him, and now Christ is going to be his guest!

Then we read, "He made haste, and came down, and received him joyfully." That is a good sign of conversion when a man receives Christ joyfully.

Zacchaeus's Sudden Conversion

We have a good many people who write and talk against sudden conversions. But how long did it take to convert Zacchaeus? When he went up the tree, nobody in Jericho would have told you he was a converted man; and yet he was a converted man when he came down, for he received the Lord joyfully. He must have been converted somewhere between the limb and the ground. You don't believe in these sudden conversions. You say they are not genuine. I wish we had a few more Zacchaeuses in Boston.

What did he do? He said, "I give half of my goods to feed the poor." The poor in Jericho believed in Zacchaeus's conversion.

But he did better than that, "If I have taken anything from any man by false accusation, I restore to him fourfold."

Zacchaeus gave half his goods to the poor. What would be said if some of the rich men of London did that? He gave half his goods all at once, and he said, "If I have taken anything from any man falsely, I restore him fourfold." I think that is the other half.

But to get Christ is worth more than all his wealth. I imagine, the next morning, one of the servants of Zacchaeus going with a check for one hundred dollars, and saying, "My master a few years ago took from you wrongfully about twenty-five dollars, and this is restitution money." There is restitution. I do hope we shall get back to those days when men make restitution, for when men begin to make restitution, the world will have confidence in the religion we preach. I can see him go back to Jericho into his office, and saying to his chief clerk, "I wish you would make out that man's account, I want to find out how much I have taxed him."

He looks over the account, and says, "We have taxed him four hundred dollars too much."

Zacchaeus replies, "Make out a check for sixteen hundred dollars and send it to him."

Don't you believe all Jericho had confidence in conversion as these checks went flying around? That was the most powerful way to prove it. If you have taken that which doesn't belong to you, don't think that God is going to hear your prayer. You needn't come to these meetings, and sing and pray, and think you are going to cover it up. God's eyes look down and see it. If you want the blessing of God to come upon you and your family, do all in your power to make restitution; then Christ will come into your home as he did into the home of Zacchaeus. He not only blessed Zacchaeus himself, but also his wife, Mrs. Zacchaeus, and all the little Zacchaeuses too.

While Christ was a guest with Zacchaeus, the Pharisees were grumbling and finding fault that he had gone to be a guest of a publican, and it was on this memorable occasion Christ uttered the text I have read tonight, "The Son of man is come to seek and to save that which was lost" (Luke 19:10).

Sources

Daniels, W. M., ed. *Moody: His Words, Work, and Workers*. New York: Nelson & Phillips, 1877.

Moody, D. L. *Bible Characters*. Chicago: Thomas W. Jackson Publishing Co., 1902.

Moody, D. L. *Men of the Bible*. Chicago: The Bible Institute Colportage Association, 1880.

Rhodes, Richard S., ed. *Bible Characters*. Chicago: Rhodes and McClure Publishing Co., 1905.

The extended bibliograpy for Mr. Moody's sermons may be found in:

John W. Reed, ed. *1100 Illustrations from the Writings of D. L. Moody*. Grand Rapids: Baker, 1996.

Subject Index

275

Scripture Index